D1292603

OHIO'S HERITAGE

James L. Burke and Kenneth E. Davison

➜P

Gibbs M. Smith, Inc.
Peregrine Smith Books
Salt Lake City
1984

For
Robert
and
Richard
K.E.D. , *Heidelberg College*

For
Betsy,
Bill,
and
Mike
J.L.B., *Capital University*

Consultant
Fred N. Schuld
Social Studies Coordinator
Independence High School

95 94 93 92 91 90 89 88 87 86

Manufactured in the United States of America.

Library of Congress Cataloging in Publication Data

Burke, James L., 1935-
   Ohio's heritage.

   Includes index.
   Summary: A junior-high-level textbook presenting
Ohio's history, with suggested activities and projects,
and information on ethnic composition, state govern-
ment, and life in Ohio today.
   1. Ohio—Juvenile literature. [1. Ohio] I. Davison,
Kenneth E. II. Title.
F491.3.B86 1984   977.1   83-20091

ISBN 0-87905-109-4

TABLE OF CONTENTS

MAPS AND CHARTS

Ohio's is the only state flag in the shape of a pennant.

INTRODUCTION

MAIN POINTS

1. History is an interpretation of events.
2. Ohio is a mirror of America.
3. Ohio symbols are keys to understanding the heritage of the state.
4. The people of Ohio come from many backgrounds and provide talent and leadership for the state and the nation.

1. History is an interpretation of events.

Suppose all the students in your class were to go to a ball game, but the seats were not all together. Some have box seats; others are spread out in the bleacher seats. The next day in class, you are assigned to write a report on the game. Will all the reports be exactly the same? How and why will they differ?

> Join a class discussion group to talk over your answers. Here are some key words to get you started: eyewitness, interpretation, perspective, story, value.

The history of Ohio is the story of events that have already happened. It is also the story of people. Each person who writes about Ohio tells the story a little differently. Your job, as you study history, is to evaluate the story. You can do this by comparing different accounts of a single event. You can make judgments about history according to your own system of values. You can decide whether you think a certain event was fair or right or wrong.

Another way to evaluate history is to see where we are now and find out how past events have affected our current position. Is Ohio getting better in every way? Are there improvements still to be made? If so, what can you do? Have there been some mistakes? Are these same problems likely to occur again?

You will have a chance to interpret Ohio's history by comparing and contrasting it to other states. There will be some similarities and some differences.

2. Ohio is a mirror of America.

The history of Ohio is the history of America. It is like a small mirror which reflects a larger scene. When the census of 1980 was taken, it was found that of all the 50 states, Ohio was the most normal. This means that the statistics for our state came closest to matching the national figures in most categories.

Ohio is a cross-section of the bigger nation. It is both urban and rural. It is a typical two-party state in politics. It is a state with a large number of colleges, both public and private. It is a state concerned about the same issues which trouble the larger nation—inflation and unemployment, energy costs, and the environment, to name a few.

Ohio has furnished leadership in war and in peace, in government and in business. Most of America's ethnic groups are represented here. Ohio mirrors the moods and concerns of the nation.

3. Ohio symbols are keys to understanding the heritage of the state.

Ohio's symbols remind us of the state's varied and rich heritage. The state gemstone is flint. Flint was used by the first people of Ohio to make weapons and tools. Today, a visit to Flint Ridge near Newark can help us imagine what it was like to live during earlier times in the Ohio forest.

The Great Seal of Ohio pictures a scene in the lovely Scioto River Valley of south central Ohio. It shows a rising sun behind Mount Logan. In the foreground, a sheaf of wheat points out the role of agriculture in Ohio history. A sheaf of 17 arrows tells us that Ohio joined the Union as the 17th state. The rising sun over a mountain in the background reminds us that Ohio was the first state created west of the Alleghenies in the Old Northwest Territory.

The state song, "Beautiful Ohio," is about the Ohio River. The first permanent settlements in Ohio were made along its banks. Steamboats later moved up and down the river with Cincinnati as a major stop. The Ohio River Valley made up the first American "West" and played a key part in the nation's development.

The scarlet carnation, Ohio's state flower.

A family of cardinals.

The state motto says, "With God all things are possible." This shows the religious heritage of Ohio. The motto was adopted in 1959 and was suggested by a 12-year-old boy, James Mastronardo of Cincinnati.

The state flower—scarlet carnation—was a favorite of William McKinley. He wore it as a symbol of good luck in his political campaigns. The scarlet carnation was adopted in 1904 as Ohio's official flower in memory of President McKinley, who was one of eight presidents to come from Ohio.

The state flag, or pennant, was designed by John Eisenmann to be shown at the Ohio Building at the Pan-American Exposition in Buffalo, New York, in 1901. It is the only state flag in the shape of a pennant. Its two white stripes and three red stripes represent the waterways and roads of Ohio.

The state tree is the buckeye, a native to the state. From the tree Ohio got the nickname "Buckeye State." Early settlers in the state used the wood of the buckeye tree for building. Indians called the buckeye "hetuck" (eye of the buck) because the seed of the tree looked like the eye of a buck.

The state bird is the cardinal, a further emblem of Ohio's natural heritage.

4. The people of Ohio come from many backgrounds and provide talent and leadership for the state and the nation.

People are another key factor in Ohio's heritage. From a beginning of mainly Germans and Scotch-Irish, Ohio people are now descended from many different nationalities. Nearly every ethnic and racial group may be found in Cleveland and other parts of Ohio today. About 10% of the state's total population is of black ancestry.

Ohio people have many talents. They have enriched the fields of art, music, literature, and popular entertainment. They have added to science and technology. They make up one of the more highly skilled labor forces in the nation.

Today Ohio is linked to major cities in the nation and the world. This did not happen overnight. It was a gradual process that began centuries ago. Let's find out how Ohio got its start by learning about the land on which we live.

Ohio's people come from many backgrounds.

Fruit of the buckeye tree.

Landforms of
Ohio
by
James A. Bier
Department of Geography
University of Illinois

1:1,000,000

published by the
Ohio Division of Geological Survey

Magee Marsh is one of Ohio's natural treasures. Inset is a topographic map that shows the landforms of Ohio. Can you guess which part of the state was covered with glaciers by looking at the map? Give reasons for your opinion.

CHAPTER 1

OHIO'S NATURAL TREASURES

MAIN POINTS

1. **Ohio's geologic features have changed over millions of years.**

2. **Glaciers once covered two-thirds of Ohio.**

3. **Ohio has a variety of plant and animal life.**

4. **Ohio's climate may be described as warm in summer and cold in winter.**

5. **Natural resources in the state helped build early industries.**

6. **Ohio has a great wealth of mineral resources.**

7. **Ohioans are taking steps to preserve their natural resources.**

If you had a day off from school this week and wanted to swim at the beach, could you? What main factor would affect your choice?

Wherever people live, *geology* (the natural features of the earth) has a part in their life style. Land forms and water forms are part of geology. These physical features help determine what kinds of jobs people have and what they do for fun and exercise.

For instance, someone who lives near the mountains might work at a lumber mill and ski or hike for fun. A person who lives in a *fertile* river valley might work on a farm and go fishing to relax.

Land and water forms affect weather and climate, which in turn affect the ways in which homes are built. Some houses have steep, pointed roofs to let the snow and rain run off. Other roofs are slanted like barn roofs to let in the greatest amount of sun for solar heating and cooling. What other things about buildings in your area are affected by its geologic features?

This chapter will tell how the state's geology has changed over millions of years. Many of these changes still affect our lives today.

1. Ohio's geologic features have changed over millions of years.

How old is the earth? It may be at least four billion years old. Scientists believe it began as a huge ball of molten (liquid) rock. After millions of years, the rock cooled into a solid planet. The earth has been in constant change since it was formed. While some changes took hundreds of millions of years to happen, others took place quite fast.

Three kinds of rock. The crust of the earth (its outside layer) is made up of three kinds of rock: sedimentary, igneous, and metamorphic. Only two of these kinds are found as surface rocks in Ohio.

The bedrock types which lie under Ohio are shown in this drawing. Which type of rock underlies your area?

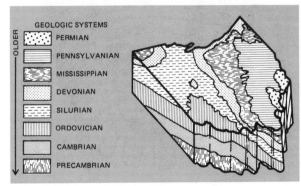

GEOLOGIC SYSTEMS

OLDER

PERMIAN
PENNSYLVANIAN
MISSISSIPPIAN
DEVONIAN
SILURIAN
ORDOVICIAN
CAMBRIAN
PRECAMBRIAN

Sedimentary rock is the type that makes up all of Ohio's exposed *bedrock*. It is made when sediment or small particles of rock settle in water or on land to form a solid mass.

Igneous rock can be found deep under the ground in Ohio.

The metamorphic type is rock that was sedimentary or igneous but has been changed by great heat or pressure. The word metamorphic means a change in form.

1. Pre-Cambrian time: the beginning. From a dim and distant 4.5 billion years ago until about 600 million years ago, there was little life on earth. This long period of time is called Pre-Cambrian.

Pre-Cambrian metamorphic rocks in Ohio are deeply buried, so they may be found only by deep drilling. Pre-Cambrian rocks were worn flat by the slow *erosion* (wearing away) of wind and water in very ancient times.

The trilobite was an early life form.

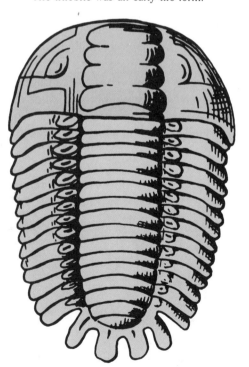

2. Cambrian period: sandstone deposits. About 600 million years ago most of North America, including Ohio, was covered by a huge sea. New sediment was left on the older, much eroded Pre-Cambrian rock. The Cambrian period in our state left sandstone and dolomite 750 feet thick. The layers, called *strata,* are deep below the surface.

Near the end of the Cambrian period, a gradual rise of the land took place. Ohio rose from beneath the sea, but not for long.

3. Ordovician period: limestone and shale. During this time (550 to 440 million years ago), the land once more began to be covered with water. Shallow seas flooded all of the state. Strata of limestone and shale were formed on top of the Cambrian sandstone and dolomite. Many *fossils* are found in Ordovician rocks.

Trilobites lived in the seas. They were the first creatures in this region to have eyes. While they crawled on the ocean bottom, there still was no life on land.

4. Silurian period: coral reefs. The Silurian period, which lasted for the next 40 million years, brought more seas and marine plants to our region. More limestone layers were made, and coral reefs grew in the seas.

5. Devonian period: the rise of the fishes. Fish were the highest form of life in the seas of the Devonian period, from 400 to 345 million years ago. In early Devonian time, Ohio was dry land. Later, oceans covered parts of the state and left strata of fine, white limestone. This type (though not this layer) of rock has been used in recent years to make buildings in the region. The Devonian strata range in thickness from 300 feet in the northwest to more than 750 feet in the center of the state.

6. Mississippian period: natural gas and oil. The Mississippian period lasted 25 million years. It was a time of large sandy deltas and gravel deposits. These deposits were later turned into sandstone and *conglomerate* (pebbles or gravel cemented together). The gas and oil in the eastern part of the state came from these deposits. Marine life is the

Glaciers ground the earth under them, leaving grooves in solid rock.

source of natural gas and oil, while coal comes from plant life.

7. Pennsylvanian period: coal forests. It was during the next period—the Pennsylvanian—that great coal deposits were formed in Ohio. For a span of 35 to 40 million years, vast swamps full of tall fern trees and other plants grew here. As these forests died and decayed, the plant debris was compressed by layers of silt and mud. Over a long period of time, this plant matter slowly changed into coal. It is one of Ohio's most valuable mineral *resources* today.

2. Glaciers once covered two-thirds of Ohio.

The ·Pleistocene epoch, which began about 2.5 million years ago and lasted until about l0,000 years ago, is best-known for its glaciers. These great ice sheets moved forward slowly and gorged out new river and lake basins. Their melting waters then filled the basins to form the Great Lakes and changed the flow and location of rivers. The last of up to 10 glaciers to cover Ohio was the Wisconsinan glacier.

How glaciers worked. During the Ice Age, the yearly *mean* temperature of the earth dropped only 5° to 10° Fahrenheit. But this drop cooled the oceans and changed the rains and ocean currents. Snow over the land added to the coolness. Ice began to pile up in those areas with frigid climates.

The debris under the glacier served as grit, grinding the land and rocks over which it passed. A good example may be seen today on Kelleys Island in Lake Erie. Called the "Glacial Grooves," this place shows the force of glacial movement better than any other spot in the world. The ice that moved over the land left deposits of clay and debris as it went. All of the state that was covered by glaciers has these deposits today.

The Pleistocene Epoch had many kinds of plants and animals. Fossils found in Ohio give us clues as to how it looked 10,000 years ago. Birch, aspen, fir, and spruce were the main types of trees at that

How does this mammoth's tooth seem well-suited for grinding tough grasses?

time. The animals in the state were elk, bison, beaver, peccary (a pig-like animal), taper, mastodon, and mammoth.

The largest creatures were the mastodon and the mammoth, both types of elephants. They were strictly vegetarians (ate no meat). The ground sloth and the giant beaver (eight feet long) roamed the region along with the elk, bear, and bison. Some of these large animals disappeared about 10,000 years ago. Only bear, elk, and bison remained when the first Europeans came to Ohio about 1700 A.D.

Migration of plants to Ohio. After the last glacier, the climate warmed up until it was a few degrees warmer than now, with slightly less moisture. The first plants formed cold, wet forests. Then plants that were common in other parts of the country began to grow here. Tulip poplar, magnolia, and rhododendron are now found in parts of the state. These plants *migrated* (moved) here from places in the South, their seeds carried by the wind or by birds and animals.

Five natural regions were left after the glaciers disappeared. When the last glacier melted, it left a changed landscape. One part of Ohio not affected by glaciers was the southeastern section. Called the *unglaciated* Appalachian plateau, it covers about 22 counties. This is the hilly part of our state, with deep valleys and winding streams. It is rich in mineral resources like coal and clay, but has poor, rocky soil.

The *glaciated* plateau lies to the west and north of the unglaciated part. Here the valleys are less deep and the hills more rounded because of glacial deposits.

The glaciated Till Plains make up over one-third of Ohio and are in the western part, south of Lima, Findlay and Tiffin. Great ice sheets passed over this part of the land. Glacial *till* to depths averaging 50 feet was deposited here. The land surface is either rolling or level. Glacial till soil is very rich and good for farming.

The Lake Plains are found in the northwest part of Ohio. A narrow band stretches along the shore of Lake Erie to the northeast corner of the state. All of the Lake Plains area is quite flat. The Lake Plains have the state's best farm land.

The Lexington Plain or Bluegrass region is a small wedge-shaped piece of land mainly in Adams County near the Ohio River. It was not covered by glaciers. This place has hills and forests with limestone bedrock. Unusual plant life that was not destroyed by glaciers grows on these limestone hills.

Virginia bluebells. Many plants entered Ohio by migration.

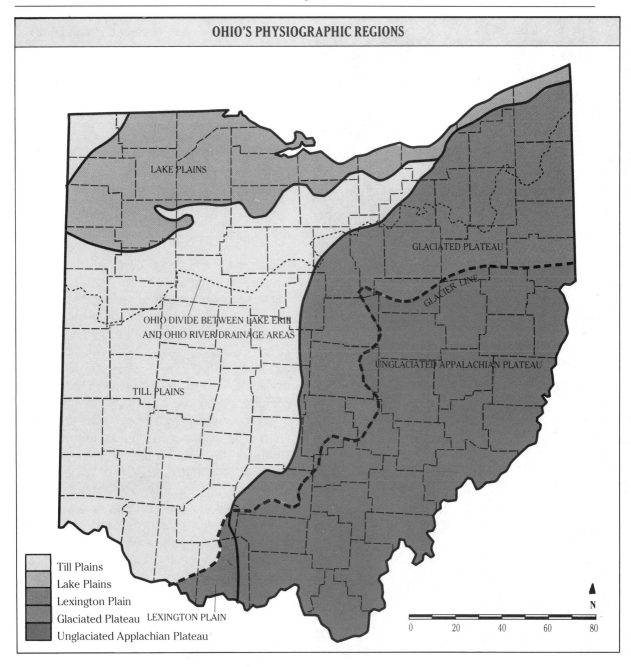

OHIO'S PHYSIOGRAPHIC REGIONS

LAKE PLAINS

GLACIATED PLATEAU

GLACIER LINE

OHIO DIVIDE BETWEEN LAKE ERIE
AND OHIO RIVER DRAINAGE AREAS

UNGLACIATED APPLACHIAN PLATEAU

TILL PLAINS

N

Till Plains
Lake Plains
Lexington Plain
Glaciated Plateau   LEXINGTON PLAIN
Unglaciated Applachian Plateau

0   20   40   60   80

The **Ohio Divide** is the ridge of land that runs east to west across the state. It separates the rivers that flow north from those that flow south. About 80% of Ohio's land area drains southward to the Ohio River. The other 20% drains into Lake Erie.

The screech owl and red fox are both common to Ohio.

3. Ohio has a variety of plant and animal life.

Mild climate and lush forests helped make early Ohio a good place for wild animals to live. Indians and Europeans sought these animals for their valuable furs. One French explorer wrote in 1687:

I cannot express what quantities of deer and turkeys are to be found in these woods. . . . At the bottom [south] of the lake [Erie] we find beeves [bison] upon the banks of two pleasant rivers. . . .

Beaver, otter, elk, and mink were also common. Because their pelts were desired for trade, the number of animals began to decline. By 1803, there were no more bison left. By the 1840s, the wolf, mountain lion, lynx, wolverine, pine marten, and beaver had been wiped out by settlement and hunting. Elk vanished from the state's list of mammals in the 1820s. Bear lived on only in the northern counties.

Today our state is a place where plants and animals from other parts of the country have met. Hemlock from the north shades southern rhododendron in the same forest. We find purple sand grass from the Atlantic Coast growing near the tall grasses of the western prairies.

The state is home for many birds, fish, and small animals. There are some 350 bird species here, with at least 180 native to the state. Woodland warblers and savannah sparrows are some of the songbirds. Game birds include ducks, geese, partridges, pheasants, quail, and ruffed grouse. Fish in local streams and lakes include bass, bluegill, catfish, muskellunge, perch, and pike. There are more than 170 different kinds.

Deer are found in the state, as well as badgers from the prairie states. Wild creatures include muskrats, opossums, rabbits, raccoons, red foxes, squirrels, skunks, and woodchucks. More than 60 species of wild animals are here at this time.

4. Ohio's climate may be described as warm in summer and cold in winter.

Our state is between 38.4° and 41.9° north latitude. Midway from the equator and the North Pole, it is a place where cold, dry polar air and warm, wet tropical air meet.

There are four well-defined seasons each year. The average temperature is 52°. January is the coldest month, with an average of 31°, while July is the warmest, at 71°. The coldest day on record was minus 39° in Perry County on February 10, 1899. The hottest day was July 21, 1934, when the temperature rose to 113° at Gallipolis.

Lake Erie modifies the effects of cold temperatures in the north. This extends the growing season for crops there to 198 days. In the central parts, the season is just 160 days, and near Cincinnati it is some 180 days.

Rainfall. Records from throughout the state show yearly rainfall of 27 inches in the north and 45 inches in the south. The statewide average is 38

XENIA TORNADO, 1974

IN the afternoon of April 3, 1974, a tornado tore through the central part of Xenia. The city of 25,000 was ripped apart as the tornado created a path of destruction nearly one mile long. Thirty people were killed and over 500 were injured.

Letters and newspapers from Xenia were scattered all over northern Ohio from the winds that went through Xenia. The Ohio National Guard kept order in Xenia as the cleanup process began. Nearly $40 million was spent to restore the city.

THE WRECK OF THE *EDMUND FITZGERALD*

BAD storms have caused the bottoms of the five Great Lakes to be strewn with sunken ships. Many of them have never been found.

Known as "the lake that does not give up its dead," Lake Superior's November gales are *notorious* among lake sailors. On November 11, 1913, 12 ships went to the bottom during a fierce storm. In 1930, on the same November date, five ships were sunk with 67 lives lost.

The best-known shipwreck of recent years was the loss of the 729-foot ore ship *Edmund Fitzgerald*. This November 1975 event was made famous by Canadian singer Gordon Lightfoot. The $7 million ship left Superior, Wisconsin, on a Sunday in early November. The *Fitzgerald*, with Ernest McSorley in command, was one of the largest ships on the lakes.

On Monday a storm hit Lake Superior, causing 30-foot waves and hurricane-force winds. The ore boat was just 15 miles from the safety of Whitefish Bay when the captain radioed the ship *Arthur M. Anderson*. He said his ship was leaking water through two broken vent covers, but was in no real danger. Suddenly, the *Anderson* lost sight of the *Fitzgerald's* running lights as it went off the radar screen.

It is not known for sure what caused the vessel to sink and take its 29 crew members to their deaths. One theory is that the ship was riding two waves at the same time, one at the bow and one at the stern. This would have left the 26,000-ton cargo without a support. The ship may have cracked in half and been driven to the bottom of the lake in seconds.

This event and Lightfoot's song remind us of the harsh storms that sometimes affect the Great Lakes.

---

inches, with spring and summer months getting the most rain.

A strange weather year was 1816. It snowed every month and pioneers called it "the year without a summer." The worst blizzard of recent times took place January 26-27, 1978. High winds blew a snowfall of more than 10 inches into drifts up to 25 feet deep.

> Do you know of any weather records set in your town or county? Where could you find records of the weather over the past 100 years?

Weather patterns. Cold waves, hot spells, and stormy periods are typical patterns in Ohio. Storms are often "hung-up," that is, they stay for a long time. In recent years there have been tornadoes here. The one which struck Xenia in 1974 was one of the worst in Ohio history.

Weather and farming. When monthly weather varies much from the normal, crops may be hurt. Rain is the most important factor for nearly all of the summer crops in the state. With the right amount of water in the soil at the critical time of growth, plants will produce a large yield.

All winter crops, such as wheat, barley, and oats, are affected most by the snowfall. Heavy snow in January is important as a cover. Too much snow in February has a bad effect. Heavy snowfall in March is very harmful. Any big change in the time of the first frost in the fall is also very important.

5. Natural resources in the state helped build early industries.

Natural resources are things in nature that can be used for our benefit. These include soil, water, timber, and plants, as well as other things.

Because this region had good resources, people who came to live in the state could start *industries* (factory businesses). They used the natural resources to make power and as *raw materials* from which to produce goods for sale.

Lumbering was one of the state's first industries. The many streams supplied water power to drive the sawmills and served as routes to carry the lumber to market. Walnut, cherry, oak, hickory, chestnut, and maple were all plentiful in the forests. Boatwrights and coopers (barrel makers) set up their yards along the lakes and rivers.

When the steamboat era came along, much Ohio lumber was used to build boats. The state's water routes were important for getting products to markets in the South and the East.

The iron industry began in the early 1800s. The state's first iron furnace was built in 1804 in the Mahoning Valley. It used *ore* from local mines. The industry grew in the "Hanging Rock Region" from Hocking County to the Ohio River. This region got its name from the undercut rock layers found there. It had the resources needed to make *malleable* iron (iron which could be hammered into shapes) and high-grade cast pieces.

Other resources were used in the iron industry. Trees were sources of timber for work sheds and charcoal for fuel. Limestone was used to help separate iron from its ore. There was plenty of water for steam engines. Sandstone was suitable to build the huge blast furnaces.

In 1850 Ohio ranked second among the states in the production of pig iron. By 1865 there were 65 furnaces in the Hanging Rock Region, but timber supplies in the southern part of the state soon ran out. In 1888 it was said that 88% of the state's forests had been used.

The most famous iron-producing area in Ohio was centered in the Hanging Rock region. This building housed an early charcoal iron furnace.

HANGING ROCK IRON REGION

The increased cost of timber and new sources of cheap, high-grade ores from Lake Superior and elsewhere helped close down the state's iron furnaces.

6. Ohio has a great wealth of mineral resources.

The large supplies of minerals found in the state have been used to support various industries.

Limestone has many uses, from roadbeds for railroad tracks to the making of concrete. Many buildings have been made from this beautiful white or blue-gray stone. Even statues and grave markers have been carved from Ohio limestone that was formed millions of years ago. Today, its main uses are in the chemical industry, in fertilizer, and in construction projects.

Gypsum is an important mineral resource that is mined near Port Clinton. It is used to make plaster and cement. This makes it valuable to the building industry. While most of the supply comes from two mines in Ottawa County, the state is one of the main sources of gypsum in the nation.

Sandstone was a common building product long before limestone was used. In 1832, the Berea sandstone (named for the town of Berea in northern Ohio) was *quarried* (mined) for building locks, dams, and bridges along the state's canals. By the 1850s, Ohio sandstone was being shipped by rail to other states.

Sand and gravel, both glacial deposits, are the state's fourth leading resource. These materials have been used as an aggregate in building roads and making concrete. Only California and Michigan mine and use more sand and gravel than does our state.

Clay has been in use in the state for more than 130 years. Clays are used in most types of industries. Our brick, sewer tile, and ceramic products have been praised world-wide for their quality, beauty, and resistance to wear. East Liverpool was, at one time, the world center for terra cotta, a hard ceramic clay used for building decoration. The Zanesville and the Roseville-Crooksville regions are well known for their fine pottery. The state ranks second in the nation in the making and use of fired clays.

Ohio's gypsum comes from the Port Clinton area in Ottawa County. Why is gypsum such an important mineral resource?

Gypsum quarries

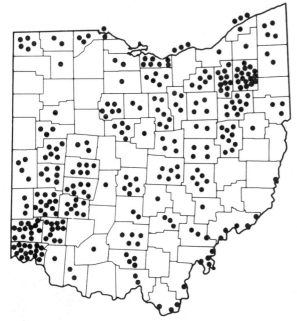

Sand and gravel operations are widespread throughout Ohio.

Salt is a thick sedimentary deposit left by the Silurian seas, and there is much of it in the state. Most of the salt comes from mines deep below Lake Erie. Their entrances are along the shore, but the mines themselves extend for miles under the lake bed. Most of the salt is used in the chemical industry and not for table salt.

Oil is another important resource. Many barrels of oil are pumped from wells in our state each year, although the amount is now less than in earlier years. Oil is used in many items produced in the state, from plastics and toys to gasoline.

Natural gas ranks as one of the state's three most important resources. It is a fuel gas. Large amounts have been taken from wells near Findlay and Lima which were first opened up in the 1880s.

Most salt mining takes place in mines deep below Lake Erie.

Ohio caverns in West Liberty is a spectacular part of our natural heritage. Which formations are stalactites and which are stalagmites?

7. Ohioans are taking steps to preserve their natural resources.

For a long time, the people of the state have known that natural resources can be used up. There is a limit to minerals and forests. Minerals will not last forever. Forests are renewable, but it takes time. Wise planning will help us *preserve* (save) our natural resources.

Our state has led the way in the movement to preserve resources. For years, groups have worked to save our natural heritage. *The Ohio Naturalist* was founded in 1900 to promote the natural history of the state. In 1915 it became *The Ohio Journal of Science.*

In 1917 a Park District Law was passed which permits buying land for forest reserves and *con-servation* of natural resources. This led to the building of many natural parks within the large cities.

In the 1920s, the Ohio Association of Garden Clubs drew attention to conservation through a crusade to "Save Outdoor Ohio."

Some of our state agencies have bought and now protect natural lands. Nature preservation means to save remnants of our original natural landscape, our natural heritage in Ohio. Cedar Bog in Champaign County is a good example. Purchased in 1942 by the Department of Public Works, it is now run by the Ohio Historical Society.

The state's Department of Natural Resources buys and cares for other state nature parks. This office also oversees lands that are owned by private persons and groups. Our nature parks aid research as they provide homes for birds, animals, and plants. At a preserve, people may learn to appreciate nature and to care for it.

> What is *your* role in saving our state's natural *environment?* Join a discussion group to share your opinions.

WORDS FOR STUDY

geology	resource	raw materials
fertile	mean	notorious
bedrock	migrate	ore
erosion	unglaciated	malleable
strata	glaciated	quarry
fossil	till	conservation
trilobite	natural resources	environment
conglomerate	industries	

QUESTIONS FOR REVIEW

1. What type of rock makes up all of Ohio's exposed bedrock?

2. Name seven geological periods.

3. During what geological period did coal deposits form in Ohio?

4. For what was the Pleistocene Epoch famous?

5. Name the five landform regions.

6. What is the Ohio Divide?

7. Name five animals that once lived in the state which are no longer found here.

8. Describe Ohio's climate.

9. What is the average yearly temperature for Ohio?

10. What is the average yearly rainfall in the Lake Erie region? What is the average for the state?

11. What are two main weather factors which affect agriculture?

12. Name four natural resources of the state that were used by early industries.

13. Name five minerals found in the state, and tell how they are used.

14. Describe two actions taken by Ohioans to help preserve the environment.

GOING FURTHER

1. What impact did the Ice Age glaciers have on Ohio's environment?

2. Why do you think many animals vanished from the region in the late 1700s and early 1800s?

3. How has Ohio clay helped the economy of the southeastern part of the state?

FOR THOUGHT AND DISCUSSION

1. Ohio's forests were important in developing the state. Do you agree? Present evidence.

2. Find another state or country that is located at the same latitude as Ohio. Do you think its climate, jobs, and agricultural products are similar to ours? Why or why not?

3. What part do you think the rich environment of the area played in attracting early people—Indians, trappers, settlers? Would you say the same is true today?

4. In the next century, will our state's natural resources keep up with the demand? Will Ohio still be an important supplier of minerals to the rest of the country? Explain.

PROJECTS AND REPORTS

1. Write to the Ohio Department of Natural Resources for information on current efforts to reclaim strip-mined land. Report to the class.

2. Research to learn about hunting wild game in the state. Note which animals may be hunted and when. Make a visual presentation of your findings.

3. Research to find out why Lake Erie has been so dangerous for shipping. Make an oral or written report.

4. Study about glaciers that once covered Ohio and present your information to the class in writing and visually.

5. Suggest and follow through on a project to preserve the natural environment.

A carved-stone pipe from the Adena culture which existed between ca. 1000 B.C.-A.D. 100

CHAPTER 2

THE FIRST OHIOANS

PREHISTORY-A.D. 1843

MAIN POINTS

1. The first people to live in Ohio can be put in two groups: prehistoric Indians and historic Indians.
2. Early prehistoric Indians were hunters and gatherers.
3. The Woodland Indians developed new methods in the areas of food, pottery, art, and earthworks.
4. Historic Indian culture was changed by contact with European goods and ideas.
5. Historic Ohio Indians can be grouped by tribe, language, or source of food.
6. Indian life style was arranged in a formal way, with strict rules and strong leadership.
7. Many reminders of our Indian heritage can be seen in Ohio today.

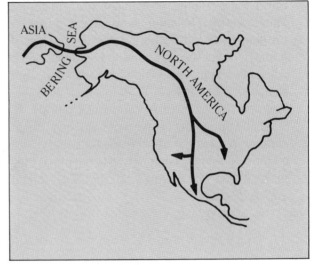

Early people likely walked across a land bridge from Asia to present-day Alaska.

Most scientists think that the first people to reach North America came about 40,000 years ago. They likely walked across a land bridge from Asia to present-day Alaska. The Bering Strait now covers that bridge. Over many years, these early people spread over the land, tracking herds of animals and gathering food.

1. The first people to live in Ohio can be put in two groups: prehistoric Indians and historic Indians.

The first people of Ohio came from the west about 16,000 years ago. Because there is no written record of them, we call these Indians *prehistoric* people. Most prehistoric Indians were gone from here by 1500 A.D.

For the next 200 years, few Indians lived in Ohio.

Then some new tribes came here in the early 1700s. By that time, Europeans were exploring the land and they began to write about the people they saw. These later groups are called *historic* Indians because there are written records about them.

Artifacts and archaeologists. What we know of prehistoric people comes from the study of their *artifacts,* or things they made. People who do this kind of work are called *archaeologists.*

Like an historian reads letters, diaries, and records, an archaeologist "reads" artifacts. Much can be learned about early people by studying the things they made and used. By digging up Indian campsites and villages, archaeologists find tools, pots, weapons, jewelry, and bits of food. These and other artifacts tell a story. How they are made, the materials used, the shapes, and the places where they are found are all clues to the past.

Artifacts show that prehistoric Indians used the environment very well. There were both flat lands and rolling hills in Ohio. The melting glaciers left lots of rivers. The area was rich with trees and plants, large and small animals. Archaeologists have found that camps were set up in the river valleys, where the river was a source of food as well as a travel route. Homes were made from materials found nearby. Trails ran along natural ridges on the land. Some Indians buried their dead in glacial *kames*. Kames are sand and gravel deposits left when glaciers melted. Ohio flint made strong and sharp weapons and tools. Pipestone from the Scioto Valley was used to carve ceremonial pipes.

All the things that people make and do is called *culture*. We may study the foods, beliefs, and customs of historic people as well as the things they make. Those who do this kind of work are called *anthropologists*.

A mound or kame left by melting glaciers.

2. Early prehistoric Indians were hunters and gatherers.

Archaeologists divide the prehistory of Ohio Indians into four time periods. Those people in the first two periods were hunters and gatherers. They hunted wild animals and gathered plants, fruits, and nuts for their food. Because the animals ranged over

CHRONOLOGY OF OHIO PREHISTORY		
PALEO-INDIAN		14,000-8000 B.C.
ARCHAIC	Archaic (Early & Middle)	8000-2500 B.C.
	Late Archaic (Glacial Kame)	2500-1000 B.C. (later in some areas)
WOODLAND	Early Woodland (Adena)	100/800 B.C.-A.D. 100
	Middle Woodland (Hopewell)	100 B.C.-A.D. 500-600
	Late Woodland	600(?)-1000 (1200-1600 in some areas)
MISSISSIPPIAN	Fort Ancient	
	Monongahela	1000-c. 1600
	Whittlesey/Sandusky	
HISTORIC (Wyandot, Shawnee, Delaware, Miami, etc.)		1654-1843

large areas and the plants were soon used up, these people often moved in search of new food supplies. On the other hand, people in the last two prehistoric periods learned how to grow crops. This meant they could stay longer in one place. They built huge mounds and *earthworks.*

Paleo-Indians (14,000-8,000 B.C.). The earliest people who came to live in the Ohio area are called Paleo-Indians, which means "ancient Indians" or "the old ones." This is what archaeologists call them. No one knows what they called themselves.

Paleo-Indians were early hunters who killed large Ice Age mammals such as mammoths, mastodons, and giant beavers. They hunted in groups of 10 to 30. To kill a large animal, they would surround it and throw sharp spears at it. Proof of this method is found in their tools—flint spear points, knives, and scrapers. In some states, spear points have been found near or among the skeletons of animals. Hunting was the main source of food, and no part of the animal was wasted. Hides were used for clothing, sinews for sewing thread, and bones for tools and jewelry. Paleo-Indians also gathered plants for food and used plant fibers to make cloth or rope.

These ancient people lived in shelters that could be easily built or moved to a new place. Some of them lived in natural shelters, such as caves. Near the end of the Paleo-Indian period, the Ohio climate and surroundings began to change. Lake Erie's size and shoreline changed several times as the glacier moved back and forth before it melted. The kinds of plants and animals in the region also changed. Spruce and fir forests slowly were replaced by maple, oak, and chestnut trees. Mastodons, mammoths, and giant beavers followed the melting glacier north. It is not known just how the Paleo-Indians reacted to those changes.

Archaic Indians (8000-1000 B.C.). The second time period of prehistoric Indians is called Archaic (early or primitive) era. The people of this age were great hunters and gatherers. Instead of mastodons, they hunted deer, elk, raccoons, wild

An Indian burial which was found in Ater Mound, Ross County.

turkeys, and waterfowl. They also fished and gathered shellfish. Many stone *mortars* (bowls) and *pestles* (pounding or grinding tools) have been dug up from Archaic sites. These tools show that Archaic people used large amounts of plant foods. Walnuts, hickory nuts, acorns, and butternuts were sources of protein. The nuts were sometimes mashed into a thick paste with the mortar and pestle.

Hunting was made easier by a new device, the *atlatl,* or spear thrower. This was a wooden stick about two feet long. One end was held in the hunter's hand while the other hooked into the end of a spear shaft. When the hunter threw his spear, the *atlatl* gave it extra speed and distance.

When hunting, the men lived in lean-tos or small huts. Homes at their base camps were more sturdy. Some people of southern Ohio lived in shelters under overhanging rocks.

About four thousand years ago, a group called the Glacial Kame people started trading with others beyond Ohio. Some things they traded for were

This effigy mound in Adams County was a work of the Woodland culture. Because it looks like a large snake, it is called the Great Serpent Mound. The mound area has been set aside as a state park.

Lake Superior copper and shells from the Atlantic Coast. Jewelry could be made from these things. These people got their name because they used kames as burial grounds.

In 1980, a Glacial Kame burial ground was found at a building site near Lima, Ohio. Since then it has been under close study by archaeologists, who hope to learn more about these people.

3. The Woodland Indians developed new methods in the areas of food, pottery, art, and earthworks.

WOODLAND INDIANS 1000 B.C.-A.D. 1600

The third and most important prehistoric Indian period in Ohio is called Woodland. These Indians lived mainly in central and southern Ohio.

Several things make the Woodland era stand out:

1. They started to raise crops. This made the food supply much more certain than in the hunting and gathering economies of the Paleo-Indian and Archaic times. People no longer had to go far away for food. Their grown crops plus game, fish, and wild plants meant they could live in one place for a longer time.

2. The Indians learned to make pottery, giving them a better way to store their crops. They made large earthen jars in which they kept foods cool and dry.

3. Their art works showed much more skill and care than in times past.

4. These Woodland people were better able to pass on knowledge. This is shown by the plans and designs of their huge earthworks, which were made by moving earth or cutting into it. The most common type of earthwork from the Woodland period is the mound, or large pile of earth. Because of these huge mounds, Indians from the Woodland era are often called *Moundbuilders*.

Adena people. One group of the early Woodland people is called the Adena. Their name comes from the place where evidence of their culture was first found. The Adena people were Ohio's first farmers and potters, which let them lead a more settled life style. They lived in round houses which measured

Hopewell Indians constructed the Octagon and Great Circle Mound in Newark. This construction is presently part of a golf course.

18 to 45 feet across the center. These houses were made of wooden posts driven into the ground. The walls were woven like baskets from sticks, bark, and hides. Thatch, bark, or skins were used to cover the roofs. Archaeologists who uncover an Adena site today can find the outlines of those homes because of where the rotted wall posts left holes in the ground.

The Adena are noted for making tube-like pipes and cutting geometric designs on flat pieces of stone. The best-known Adena pipe was found in an earth mound at Chillicothe in 1902. Carved from soft Ohio pipestone, it is in the form of a dwarf figure 8½ inches high, dressed in a loincloth. The dwarf has a bustle on its back and large spool-shaped earrings. We do not know what the pipe means or why it was used, but it is a fine piece of early Indian art.

Hopewell people. Around 100 B.C., another group of Moundbuilders called the Hopewell came into Illinois and Ohio. These people settled in the wide river valleys of central and southern Ohio, just as the Adena had done. The first artifacts of these people were found on the Hopewell farm in Ross County.

The most common Hopewell remains are earthworks in the form of walls. The walls are as high as 15 to 20 feet and as wide as 50 feet. They are grouped in geometric shapes—squares, circles, and octagons. The earthworks cover anywhere from 20 to 100 acres. The largest one that can be seen today is in Newark near the Licking River. Another type of Hopewell site is built on the top of a hill like Fort Ancient in Warren County.

The earthworks were used for large group functions such as funerals, social and political meetings, as well as the making and trading of goods. When a leader died, the body was brought to a special *charnel house.* After several days of mourning, the house might be torn down or burned and a mound built over the remains. Most of the mounds at Mound City near Chillicothe are examples of this practice.

Trading with other Indians in North America was an important activity of the Hopewell. They got

Consider the workmanship in this Adena leaf point. What does it tell you about the maker's skill and love of beauty?

mica and pottery from North Carolina, ore from Missouri, and grizzly bear teeth and claws from the West. Obsidian (volcanic glass) came from Wyoming, shells from Florida, and silver from Ontario. In exchange, the Hopewell traded Ohio flint and pipestone.

Skilled workers cut, chipped, pounded, drilled, and molded the raw materials into art objects. These were used in ceremonies or as status symbols for the owners. Copper plate and mica sheets were cut in the forms of birds and animals. Obsidian was chipped to make large, sharp spear points and knives. Bear teeth and claws were drilled and strung as necklaces. One of the best-known Hopewell art objects is the small platform *effigy* pipe. An effigy is shaped like something in nature. This might be a bird or an animal—a hawk, a raven, a bear, or a toad.

The Hopewell lived mostly in small towns of rectangular houses built along fertile river bottoms. They spent much of their time hunting, fishing, gathering wild plants, and tending to their crops.

Something happened in the region between 500 and 700 A.D. that caused the Hopewell culture to vanish. Scientists have thought of a few possible reasons. There might have been a climate change which affected crops, a loss of trade, disease, a breakdown of Hopewell social order, or even war. No one knows for sure just what happened. Only the results are clear. In southern Ohio, building of earthworks stopped, trading for resources slowed down, and the skilled crafts were no longer used.

Mississippian period (1000-1600 A.D.). The fourth age of Indian prehistory is called Mississippian. This is due to some major culture changes which took place in the central Mississippi Valley. From 800 to 900 A.D., new art and pottery were brought from Mexico. Also came new types of corn, beans, and squash. Larger crops helped towns grow in size from hundreds to thousands of people. The mounds began to look like those of Mexico—pyramid-shaped with flat tops. By 1100 A.D., huge cities lined the Mississippi Valley from Alabama to Wisconsin. Similar towns rose along the Ohio River and other places.

Fort Ancient people. Changed by the new ways from Mexico, Fort Ancient people made a new culture in southern Ohio. Hunting was improved by use of the bow and arrow, but more effort was spent on food they could grow. This increased the size and population of their towns.

Fort Ancient sites have been found in large river valleys such as the Miami, Scioto, and Muskingum. In those places gardens could be planted in the rich

An Indian village protected by a high stockade.

river-bottom soil. Their rectangular houses were built on terraced land above the rivers. Often houses were protected by a wooden stockade. Few Ohio towns had large pyramid mounds like those of Mexico, but most had an open courtyard in the center where large groups could gather. When the fertile soil was overused and firewood became scarce, these people moved and started new towns.

Whittlesey and Sandusky people. Near Cleveland, a culture called Whittlesey began around 1000 A.D. A similar group developed in the Sandusky Bay-Maumee drainage region about the same time. They were called Sandusky. At first, these people moved when the seasons changed. In early spring, they fished along the lakes and rivers. Next, they moved inland to small towns where they grew crops during the summer. In fall, they made use of deer and nuts in inland areas, as well as fish and fowl along streams and lakes. In the winter, they split into small groups and hunted game for themselves.

After 1300 A.D., the Whittlesey and Sandusky people began to depend more and more on crops they raised. They stayed longer in their towns, but fished and hunted birds from fall to early spring. Finally, they lived year-round in long apartment-like homes called "long houses." Their villages were surrounded by earthen walls or stockades.

Monongahela people. In eastern Ohio, a third culture called Monongahela lived in small round houses arranged in a circle around a central plaza. Wooden stockades were built around the whole village. The people lived by farming, hunting, and gathering. Not much is known about them because archaeologists have not been able to fully excavate one of their town sites. Many of the sites have been destroyed by modern strip mining for coal.

End of the prehistoric Indian cultures. By the 1500s, most tribes had left the region. Some may have died of disease, starved to death, or been killed in wars. Others might have moved to seek new land or to escape their enemies. Many of those left were forced from Ohio in the mid-1600s by the Iroquois tribes of New York. The Iroquois wanted to gain new hunting grounds in the state.

The prehistoric age of Indian culture ended in 1654 A.D. At that time explorers and Catholic missionaries began to write about the early people of the region.

4. Historic Indian culture was changed by contact with European goods and ideas.

For a time in the 1600s, no groups of people lived in Ohio except for the Iroquois who hunted there. In the early 1700s, Indians slowly began to return. They came from different places and had been affected by contact with the Europeans.

What changes would you imagine the new European religions might bring to an Indian's way of life?

TERRITORIES OF MAJOR TRIBES AT BEGINNING OF EUROPEAN SETTLEMENT

A boy of the Miami tribe.

The historic tribes of the state did not live a pure Indian way of life. Their customs had been changed by European goods and beliefs. For instance, they grew to rely on white man's weapons and tools. Some partly adopted European cooking and eating utensils. A few liked the new kinds of clothing. Others were converted to Christian ways by Jesuit or Moravian missionaries, which brought even more change. Such changes made the historic Indians quite different from the early ones.

5. Historic Ohio Indians can be grouped by tribe, language, or source of food.

Tribes. The Miami tribe is the only Ohio historic group of Indians of any great size to come from the west. They arrived from the south and west shores of Lake Michigan to settle the western part of the state. Miamis first entered the Maumee Valley as hunters between 1701 and 1730. Some later moved farther south to the Miami Valley. One of their major centers was Pickawillany, near present Piqua. Another was Kekionga, near Fort Wayne, Indiana.

The Wyandots came to Ohio in the 1730s from near Detroit and southern Ontario. Several of their key towns were found near Sandusky Bay. Their last large village was near present-day Upper Sandusky. The Wyandots were the last of the historic tribes to leave the state in 1843.

Parts of the Ottawa tribe settled in Ohio about 1730. They built towns on the lower Maumee River and along the west shore of Lake Erie. One of their great chiefs was Pontiac. The Wyandots and the

Ottawas were friends who hunted together in the Maumee Valley.

From the east, the Shawnees and Delawares migrated into Ohio to make new homes, not just to hunt. The Shawnees came to central and southern Ohio from the south. They set up towns in the Scioto and Miami valleys. One of their main centers was Chillicothe, the home of Tecumseh, who would become their greatest leader. Some historians think the Shawnees may have been descendants of the Fort Ancient people.

The Delawares moved to Ohio from Delaware and Pennsylvania. They settled the southeastern parts of the state near the Tuscarawas Valley. In 1772, the Wyandots gave the Delawares a large tract of land in eastern Ohio. This opened the eastern part of the Sandusky Basin to Delawares who came later. Some of the Delawares became Christians in the 1770s.

Another tribe in Ohio was the Mingos, or Senecas. They first settled the upper Ohio Valley. Later they moved to the Mohican, Scioto, and Sandusky valleys. Their great chief was called Logan.

Language groups. Ohio's historic tribes belonged to either the Algonquin or the Iroquoian language groups. The Miami, Delaware, Ottawa, and Shawnee tribes spoke Algonquin, while the Wyandots and Senecas were Iroquoian. Many had great skill at speaking, and some spoke French and English as well as other tribal languages.

In Algonquin tribes, children took the name of their father's *clan* (family) and lived by that clan's rules. In the Iroquoian tribes, the mother's clan ruled the children. After marriage, the Iroquois lived with the woman's relatives while the Algonquins lived with the man's. Iroquoian chiefs were chosen through the mother's clan; the Algonquin selected their leaders through the father's clan.

Sources of food. A third way to group historic Indians is by their most common sources of food. Most Ohio tribes lived in the woodlands and got their food by farming, gathering, hunting, and fishing. A few small groups lived on the prairies

Chief Tarhe the Crane, a famous leader of the Wyandot tribe.

and got their food from long hunts, crops they raised, and the collection of nuts, berries, and wild grains.

Ohio's historic Indians lived in three kinds of places. The permanent village had Iroquois-type longhouses (shaped like loaves of bread) or Algonquin wigwams (shaped like upside-down bowls).

The hunting camp was often a long way from home. Shelters in this kind of camp could be quickly packed up and moved. Very seldom did the women join the men on those long hunts. Each tribe had its own hunting ground.

The gathering camp or "out village" had simple sheds or shacks for shelter. Such places might be as much as 100 miles away from the permanent village.

Gathering wild rice, an important Indian food.

6. Indian life style was arranged in a formal way, with strict rules and strong leadership.

Indian society. Fear of the whites brought the tribes closer to each other for their safety. Often several languages were spoken in one town where tribes were mixed. All Ohio Indians practiced the same *extended family* life style in which many relatives lived together. This type of family differs from the *nuclear family* of just parents and their children. Each tribe or group honored the rights of others.

Where tribes were mixed in one town, the first ones there or the largest tribes set the rules for the others. Thus the Ottawas and the Delawares practiced the Wyandot life style if that was the main group in a mixed village. Delawares and Ottawas kept their own way of life in places where they had more numbers than other people or where they lived alone.

Each town was ruled by a *council.* The council members assigned farming tracts. Other jobs of the council were to set times for hunts, feasts, and raids or wars. They also chose when and where visits with other groups could take place.

A main difference between Indian and non-Indian cultures was that Indians owned only what they made. Land was not viewed as private property. It was owned by all. But each person had the right to share and use things the group owned.

In Indian society there was more than one leader. One chief headed the village. Another was the war chief. The shaman, or medicine man, cast out evil spirits from a sick person. The shaman was a religious leader as well. Most groups also had a series of women chiefs who governed various women's affairs. Women chiefs had power to stop the formation of war parties and to decide the fate of prisoners.

Shamans or medicine men were religious leaders as well as healers.

This dress was worn by a Seneca child. The moccasins and purse are made of leather; the rest is cotton or wool. From where did the cloth likely come?

Law. Indians believed strongly in the rights of each person. The village had a duty to protect personal rights. Conflicts were settled by the councils. One punishment for severe crime was to be sent away from the tribe. Treason, murder, or betrayal meant the death penalty.

Religion. Indian religions were much alike, sharing a belief in one powerful creator. There were spirits in all things. If a person stayed in favor with the spirits, life would be good and there would be rewards.

Clothing. Clothing among Indian groups varied. Some were influenced more than others by the white culture. In early times, Indians put grease on their bodies to keep warm in cool weather. Animal skin clothing was used in the winter. Leggings and blankets also helped protect them from the cold.

Headdresses were usually of three types: feathers, turbans, or skull caps. Another type for use in ceremonies was an animal skull cut to fit over the person's head.

Moccasins were the most popular footwear. Winter moccasins went high up on the leg while summer shoes were cut lower.

Indians liked to decorate their clothing. Some used a sash or a comb while others used beads made of bone, shell, or stone. Faces and bodies were often painted, especially for ceremonies, and tattoos were common.

End of the historic Indian period. When Europeans came to Ohio, the Indian way of life was destroyed. There were several factors. First, white ways and tools changed the Indian life style. Second, by wars and treaties, much land was taken away for white use. The Indians did not like losing their sacred burial places and their hunting grounds. Third, all those who survived these events were forced to move from their Ohio homes by

The Indian Mill in Upper Sandusky was built by the federal government for the Wyandot Indians.

1843. The United States government sent them to reservations farther west.

7. Many reminders of our Indian heritage can be seen in Ohio today.

Much of the state's early Indian history is with us today. Most southern Ohio cities are built on sites where the Hopewell once lived. Some large mounds remain as examples of early building skills. They are Fort Ancient near Lebanon, Seip Mound at Bainbridge, and Serpent Mound in Adams County. Historic sites like the town at Piqua or the Indian Mill and Mission at Upper Sandusky urge visitors to learn more about these first Ohioans.

Many places and rivers in the state have Indian names. Sandusky, Chillicothe, Wyandot, Seneca, Ottawa, Erie, Cuyahoga, Tuscarawas, and Muskingum are just a few.

The state's most popular outdoor historical dramas deal with Indian history. They are *Tecumseh* at Chillicothe, *Trumpet in the Land* at New Philadelphia, and *Blue Jacket* at Xenia.

Many foods we eat today were first grown by the Indians. Corn, beans, squash, and pumpkins are most common.

After many years away from the state, Indians are returning to live in large cities like Cleveland. Some come from reservations in the West and others from Canada. Cleveland's American Indian Center prints a newsletter and holds many social and cultural events. This helps preserve their customs and helps people of other cultures to learn of our Indian heritage.

There is a great pride growing among Indians in Ohio and all over the country. They are now called by a new name—*Native Americans.* They are proud that their forefathers were the first Americans. The Native Americans have given a great deal to our way of life.

WORDS FOR STUDY

prehistoric	atlatl
historic	*Moundbuilders*
artifact	*charnel house*
archaeologist	*effigy*
kame	*clan*
culture	*extended family*
anthropologist	*nuclear family*
earthworks	*council*
mortar	*Native Americans*
pestle	

REVIEWING WHAT YOU HAVE READ

1. Explain when and from where the first Ohioans came.

2. What is the distinction between prehistoric Indians and historic Indians?

3. Name the four time periods of Ohio prehistoric Indians and list some features of each period.

4. Describe the meaning of "hunters and gatherers."

5. What basic changes in life style were made by Woodland Indians?

6. Why are early Indians called Moundbuilders?

7. What products did the Hopewell people use for trade? What did they get in exchange?

8. Tell about the crafts and art skills of the Adena and Hopewell people.

9. The culture of what country influenced the Mississippian Period? What was the most common object that resulted from this influence?

10. Why did the prehistoric people vanish from the Ohio area?

11. In what three ways can historic Indians be grouped?

12. List all the historic tribes that lived in Ohio.

13. What were the two Indian language groups and which tribes in Ohio belonged to each?

14. Describe at least two types of Indian homes.

15. Describe the leadership and organization of an Indian village. How did the organization change if more than one tribe lived in a village?

16. What was Indian clothing like and of what was it made?

17. How are we reminded today of our Indian heritage?

GOING FURTHER

1. How do we know Glacial Kame Indians traded with Indian cultures from other areas?

2. How did farming help improve the life of the Woodland Indians?

3. Why did Indian cultures locate in river valleys?

4. In your opinion, what factor was most important in causing the decline of historic Ohio Indian tribes?

FOR THOUGHT AND DISCUSSION

1. Classify reasons why historic Indian tribes moved into Ohio.

2. What is the role of an archaeologist in learning about history? What do you think an archaeologist 200 years from now could learn about our modern society? What artifacts would provide the most accurate information?

3. What do you think is the most important thing we can learn from Indian cultures? Why?

4. Is it important for us to learn about our Indian heritage? Why or why not?

PROJECTS AND REPORTS

1. Build a scale model of any type of Indian technology—home, canoe, spear point, bow and arrow, pottery, or art object. Use materials from the environment.

2. Plan and construct a chart to compare and contrast the prehistoric and historic Indian cultures.

3. Learn the skills of debate and participate in a debate on this topic: Indian culture and life style was greatly weakened by contact with Europeans.

4. Study current events to find information about Indian activities today in the eastern United States. Make a bulletin board display of your findings.

5. Make a visual to show the arrangement of an Indian village. Include the outlying area where crops were grown.

6. Research and make a written or oral report on any tribe of the historic Indian period.

Marietta, established in April
1788, was the earliest settlement in Ohio. This is a view
of the Ohio River from Marietta in the early 1800s.

C H A P T E R 3

EXPLORATION AND EARLY SETTLEMENT

1615-1790

MAIN POINTS

1. The French and the British explored and fought for control of the Ohio River Valley.
2. Conflict over land ownership caused fighting between Indians and settlers.
3. Ohio played a role in the Revolutionary War.
4. The Ordinances of 1785 and 1787 outlined patterns for land settlement and government in the new Northwest Territory.
5. The first settlements in Ohio were founded by Moravian missionaries, but soon died out.
6. Most early Ohio settlements were along the Ohio River.

1. The French and the British explored and fought for control of the Ohio River Valley.

After Columbus accidentally discovered the New World in 1492, word of a *vast* wilderness spread to European countries. Columbus had been looking for a shorter trade route from Spain to India. Foreign trade was a major source of money for Europeans. One country might send fine cloth, iron products, or silk to be traded in India for spice, tea, or glass. By increasing foreign trade or owning more land, countries could gain power and wealth. So expeditions from Europe were sent to explore and claim land in New World.

The French claim to Ohio country. The first country to claim the Ohio area was France. French-man Jacques Cartier discovered and sailed up the St. Lawrence River in 1535. Though he did not go as far south as the Ohio region, he claimed all of the land which drained into the St. Lawrence on both sides. He named the area New France. By 1608, French explorer Samuel de Champlain founded the city of Quebec on a high bluff above the St. Lawrence and made it the capital of New France. From there, he felt all the land claimed by the French could be controlled.

Etienne Brulé, a French fur trader, is believed to have been the first European to enter Ohio. This was about 1615. Next came French missionaries and explorers, but they left no buildings in the area.

Discovery of the Ohio River. Robert de la Salle, another French explorer, gets credit for discovering the Ohio River. About 1670, he sold his land along the St. Lawrence River and used the profit to pay for an *expedition* into the Ohio country. With some 20 men, he reached Lake Erie and then headed south toward the Allegheny River. On this route he found and named a new river, *Belle Riviere*, or Beautiful River. (Today it is known as the Ohio River.) By right of discovery and exploration, the French claimed all of the Great Lakes area and all of the Ohio River Valley.

The British claim to Ohio country. Meanwhile, the British colonized (settled) all along the Atlantic Coast. The first colony was begun in 1607 at Jamestown, Virginia. The British pushed inland as

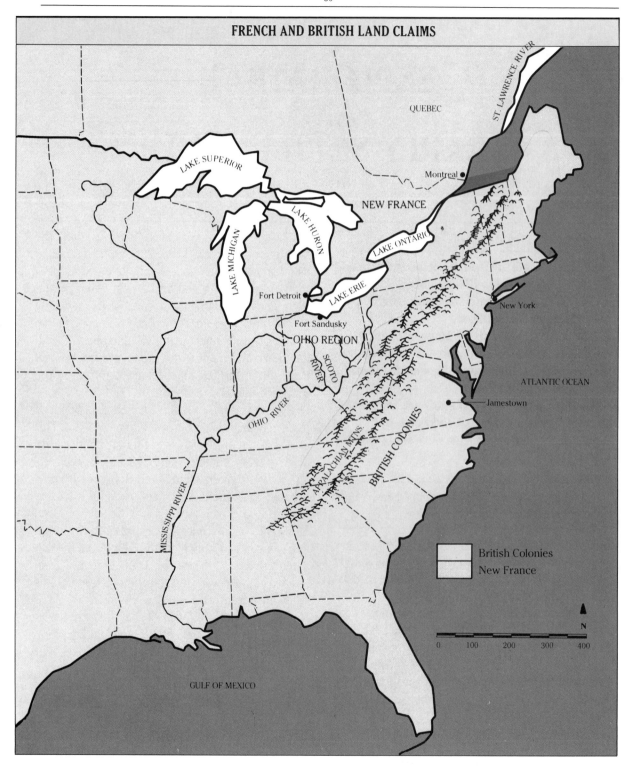

FRENCH AND BRITISH LAND CLAIMS

far as the Appalachian Mountains, but this barrier kept them out of the Ohio region until about 1740. Then they began to hear reports about the beauty of the Ohio Valley and the furs available there. A few English traders crossed the mountains. George Croghan from Pennsylvania went as far as the Cuyahoga and the Sandusky River Valleys. A few English scouting parties, sent to spy out the land, returned with valuable furs and good reports. Since the English colonies claimed that their land grants went from the Atlantic Ocean to the Mississippi River, they felt the French in the Ohio Valley were on their land.

France and England both wanted to own the land and control the Indian fur trade. Furs were very popular in Europe and there was much money to be made. The two countries were locked in a series of wars which would decide the future of America. These wars were called the Intercolonial Wars.

Intercolonial Wars, 1689-1763. By 1740, both sides were building their defenses. The British got permission from the Wyandot Indians to build Fort Sandusky near Lake Erie in 1745. A little later, a few people from Virginia started the Ohio Land Company for the purpose of founding a colony in the Ohio Valley.

In response, the French governor in Canada sent his *agent,* Celeron de Bienville, to Ohio to warn the English to leave. As he traveled down the Ohio River, Celeron buried lead plates at the mouths of several rivers, claiming the Ohio Valley for the king of France. When Celeron reached the mouth of the Miami River, he headed north to visit a Miami Indian village called Pickawillany. His effort to win support from the Indians against the English failed. Celeron returned to Canada without getting the English out of Ohio or splitting the Indians from the British.

Christopher Gist visits Ohio for the English. At this point, the Ohio Land Company sent a scout named Christopher Gist to look at the Ohio Valley and report back. During 1750-51, Gist did this with great skill. He was joined by George Croghan, a trader from Pennsylvania. Gist kept a careful record of his trip. The two men went to Hockhocking (now Lancaster), Pickaway Plains (the Circleville area), and Shawnee Town (present-day Portsmouth). They saw a pleasant land, rich in trees, full of small and large animals, with plenty of water.

Gist had friendly visits with Indians along the way. He finally reached home in Virginia in May 1751, after a successful seven-month tour of Ohio. His report urged the Ohio Land Company to start a settlement there.

French plan to hold Ohio. The French, based at Detroit, were determined to hold on to Ohio. They decided to attack Pickawillany and reduce the power of its Miami chief, Old Britain, who was friendly with the English. Before the French could act, however, a band of Ottawa Indians from northwest Ohio attacked the Miami tribe. Old Britain was killed, his body boiled and eaten, and his village destroyed by fire.

The French began to build forts between Lake Erie and the Ohio River. A young army officer named George Washington was sent from Virginia to warn the French to get out of the Ohio Valley. Washington did not do very well. The French did not heed his warning, and on the way home he fell from his raft into an icy stream and was barely rescued by his companion. A year later, Washington led an army against the French. They defeated him. During his retreat, he built a fort near present-day Pittsburgh, Pennsylvania, which he named Fort Necessity. But it was located in a low spot. The French and Indians quickly surrounded him and forced him to surrender.

British win the French and Indian War. A full-scale war now broke out between British and French forces and their Indian allies in North America. The early years of the French and Indian War (1754-63) did not go well for the British. Then suddenly, the course of the war changed when England adopted a new war strategy. William Pitt became Prime Minister in England. He chose

Chief Pontiac of the Ottawas was sometimes compared to the French emperor, Napoleon, because of his skillful military leadership.

younger and bolder leaders to head the British forces. His *ally,* Prussia, fought against France in Europe. This left the British free to fight on the high seas and in the colonies.

The new plan worked. Fort Duquesne in western Pennsylvania fell to the British and became Fort Pitt. In the greatest battle of the war, Quebec was captured by General James Wolfe's army. Montreal surrendered a few months later.

French power in North America was destroyed. The first Treaty of Paris, in 1763, officially ended the war a few years later. France gave up its claim to land in eastern North America except for two tiny islands near Newfoundland. Great Britain was now in control.

How Ohio was affected. The results of the British victory were very important for Ohio. It meant that the English language and culture would be accepted and used in Ohio instead of the French customs. Ohio government would be like England's *representative democracy,* not like the less democratic government of France. The British victory also determined the kind of education, law, and economy for Ohio and the rest of America. It had a major effect on the future of Ohio and the colonies.

2. Conflict over land ownership caused fighting between Indians and settlers.

Pontiac's Conspiracy, 1763. After the French were gone, certain Indian tribes wanted to remove the British and regain the land for the Indians. Chief Pontiac of the Ottawa tribe organized a plan among tribes living along the frontier border from Canada to the Gulf of Mexico. His idea was to attack the British forts all at once. Nine forts were soon in Indian hands.

Pontiac planned to capture the British fort at Detroit by arming his warriors with guns hidden under blankets. However, an Indian woman told Pontiac's secret to the British commander at Detroit. When Pontiac and his men arrived at the fort, they found the entire post armed and ready. Faced with sure defeat, the chief kept calm and left the fort without a fight. Pontiac kept Fort Detroit surrounded for months, but never captured it. Outlying settlements were not as lucky. Over two years, many settlers on the Pennsylvania and Virginia frontiers were killed or captured. Following is part of a speech given by Chief Pontiac in July 1763, during the watch on Detroit:

The word which my father has sent me to make peace, I have accepted. All my young men have buried their hatchets. I think you will forget the bad things which have taken place for time past. Likewise I will forget what you have done to me, in order to think of nothing but good. I, the Chippewas, and the Hurons, we are ready to speak with you when you ask us.

The Appalachian dividing line. The British government tried to avoid trouble by giving out the Proclamation of 1763. This order drew an imaginary line along the top of the Appalachian Mountains. Settlers were to stay east of this line. The territory west of it was for the Indians.

Bouquet rescues American prisoners. In 1764, General John Bradstreet and Colonel Henry Bouquet led expeditions to restore British control and to free prisoners held by the Indians. Bradstreet went to Detroit and accepted Indian promises to stop fighting. Bouquet was more forceful. He moved into central Ohio with 1,500 men to rescue the prisoners. Within 14 days, 206 prisoners—men, women, and children—were turned over to Bouquet. He and his men went safely back to Fort Pitt.

Quebec Act, 1774. The British government, anxious to keep settlers out of Ohio, passed the Quebec Act. This law moved the border of Canada as far south as the Ohio River. Colonists were very angry about the Quebec Act. Many of them thought they would receive land in Ohio as a reward for helping England defeat the French and Indians. But England seemed to ignore their wishes.

Other problems were growing between the colonists and England. England would not let the colonists be represented in Parliament. Colonists did not want to pay taxes to England without having a vote. They wanted to help make the rules. Talk of breaking away from English rule was spreading in the colonies. Each conflict between settlers and England increased tension, leading up to the American Revolution.

Chief Logan of the Mingo tribe, a peaceful man, went on the warpath to avenge the deaths of family members and friends.

Fighting between Indians and settlers began again. The Proclamation of 1763 and the Quebec Act were hard to enforce. Settlers began to spill over the Appalachian dividing line. This invasion of the Ohio Valley by white settlers caused the Indians to attack. War broke out all along the western frontier.

In April 1774, several groups of whites moved down the Ohio River and killed all the Indians they met. Especially brutal was the murder of relatives and friends of Chief Logan, head of the Mingo tribe. Logan had been neutral during most of the fighting, but now he went on the warpath. He promptly took 30 white scalps in revenge for the death of his mother, sister, and friends. Beneath a giant elm tree

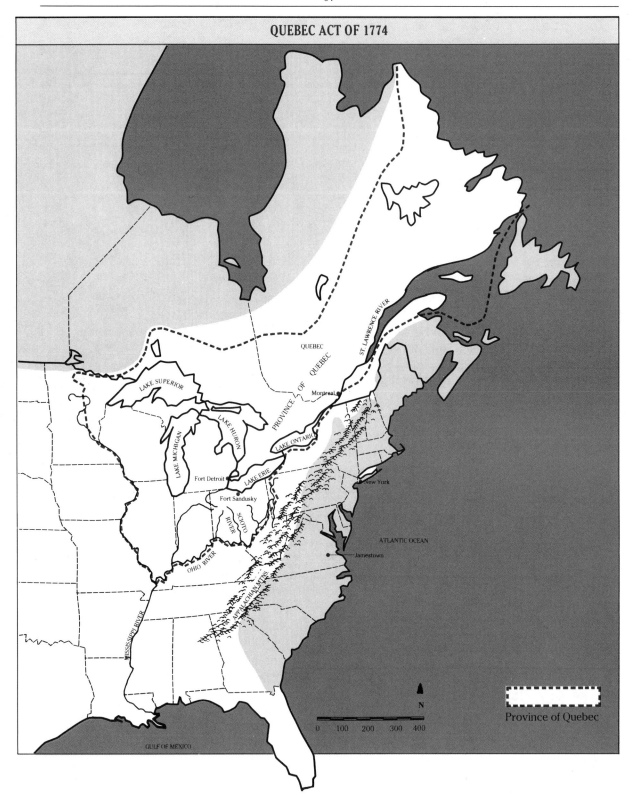

QUEBEC ACT OF 1774

near present-day Circleville, Logan gave a famous speech explaining his action:

I appeal to any white man to say if he ever entered Logan's cabin hungry and he gave him not meat; if he ever came cold and naked and he clothed him not. During the course of the last long and bloody war, Logan remained idle in his cabin, an advocate *for peace. Such was my love for the whites that my countrymen pointed as I passed and said, "Logan is a friend of the white man." I have even thought to have lived with you but for the injuries of one man. Colonel Cresap, the last spring in cold blood and unprovoked, murdered the relatives of Logan, not even sparing his wives and children. . . .This called on me for revenge. I have sought it. I have killed many. I have fully glutted my vengeance. For my country I rejoice in the beams of peace; but do not harbor a thought that mine is the joy of fear. Logan never felt fear. He will not turn on his heel to save his life. Who is there to mourne for Logan? Not one.*

3. Ohio played a role in the Revolutionary War.

Lord Dunmore's War, 1774. Lord Dunmore, the governor of Virginia, organized an army of 1,500 men to restore order in Ohio. He had a strong interest in western land and dreamed of building an *empire* for himself in the American West. Contrary to England's wish to keep settlers out of Ohio, Dunmore urged pioneers to enter the Ohio Valley. This caused more trouble, and Dunmore used it for an excuse to declare war on Ohio Indian tribes. He moved at once against the Shawnee in the Scioto Valley. The brief Lord Dunmore's War of 1774 ended with the defeat of the Shawnees. Indians were forced to accept white settlement south and east of the Ohio River.

Battle of Point Pleasant. There were two famous events in Lord Dunmore's War—the Battle of Point Pleasant and the Fort Gower Resolves. Dunmore built Fort Gower at the mouth of the Hocking River

as a supply depot. Then he traveled up the river to the area of Chillicothe and Cornstalk's Town, both Shawnee villages. Meanwhile, Colonel Andrew Lewis approached the Ohio River from the south with an army.

Chief Cornstalk of the Shawnee tribe thought his chances would be much better if he attacked the Lewis group before it joined Dunmore's main army. On the morning of October 10, about 1,000 Indians fought Lewis' men in a bloody hand-to-hand combat which neither side could win. Here is Cornstalk's decision:

What shall we do now? The Big Knife is coming on us, and we shall all be killed. Now we must fight or we are done. Then let us kill all our women and children and go fight until we die? I shall go and make peace!

The next day Cornstalk withdrew. He met with Lord Dunmore to talk peace. The Shawnees agreed to stay north of the Ohio River. New settlers now moved freely into West Virginia and Kentucky.

Fort Gower Resolves. On their way back to Virginia, Dunmore's men stopped briefly at Fort Gower. There the other major event of the war took place. At the fort they heard of problems between the colonists and the British. They learned about trouble in Boston, and of decisions made by the First Continental Congress against England. The Congress was a group of elected representatives from the colonies.

Dunmore's men decided to write and sign the Gower Resolves. This was the first time a military group had asked for freedom from Great Britain. This action was taken a full six months before the start of the American Revolution. As far as the Ohio frontier is concerned, the Fort Gower Resolves marked a major turning point in loyalty to England.

End of war in Ohio. A few more marches took place before peace returned to Ohio. In late August 1782, British officers Caldwell and McKee led a force from Detroit through western Ohio to attack

George Rogers Clark led the last campaign of the Revolutionary War in Ohio.

Bryant's Station in Kentucky. The Kentucky defenders under Daniel Boone won the battle. Then the Americans grew overconfident and careless. A short time later, they suffered defeat at Blue Licks, Kentucky.

George Rogers Clark, an American military leader, made his last *campaign* into Ohio. He destroyed the Miami Indian village of Pickawillany and burned Loramie's Post farther north. These fights were the last battles fought by Americans in the war.

The first and last shots of the American Revolution were fired in Ohio. The first one was during Lord Dunmore's War in 1774, and the last was during Clark's attack of 1782.

Peacetime problems. The second Treaty of Paris, signed in 1783, officially closed the Revolutionary War. The British gave to the new United States all land west to the Mississippi River and north to the Great Lakes, except for Spanish Florida.

Independence brought new problems. What would the new country's government be like? How would the new Americans get along with Native Americans? How would land claims be handled? Most of all, how would Ohio be settled and governed? It would take several years for all of these problems to be solved.

4. The Ordinances of 1785 and 1787 outlined patterns for land settlement and government in the new Northwest Territory.

Land settlement and government were important issues in Ohio. They were settled by the Ordinances of 1785 and 1787. They applied to all of the Old Northwest of which Ohio was a part. Today, we call this area the Great Lakes States.

The Land Ordinance of 1785. As one of the first steps in building a new nation, the United States government outlined a way to measure and identify lands for sale. The Land Ordinance encouraged orderly growth and settlement. Because land cost so much, many people had settled on land without paying for it. These people were called *squatters.* The government had no way to keep track of the squatters or the lands they were on.

First used in Ohio, the Ordinance of 1785 was later applied to the sale of land across the rest of America.

Surveying for townships. The system of land *survey* was based upon a grid pattern similar to a sheet of graph paper. Like a graph, the Ohio country (except the Virginia Military Tract) was carefully divided into square blocks called *townships.* The townships were six miles long on each side. (The one exception to this rule was in the Western Reserve counties of northeastern Ohio. This area was saved by Connecticut for its people. There,

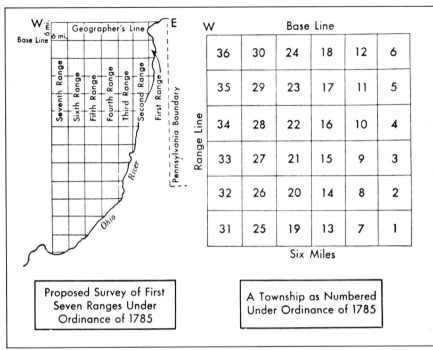

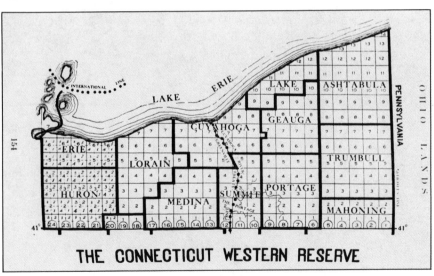

A township, as set up under the Ordinance of 1785, contained 36 sections and was six miles long on a side.

The Connecticut Western Reserve was surveyed in townships just five miles long on a side. Why do you think townships were made square rather than rectangular?

townships were just five miles long on a side.) Surveyors used rods and chains to measure the land. They gradually traced and marked nearly all Ohio lands in this *grid* fashion. The result was a series of square blocks either 36 or 25 square miles in area.

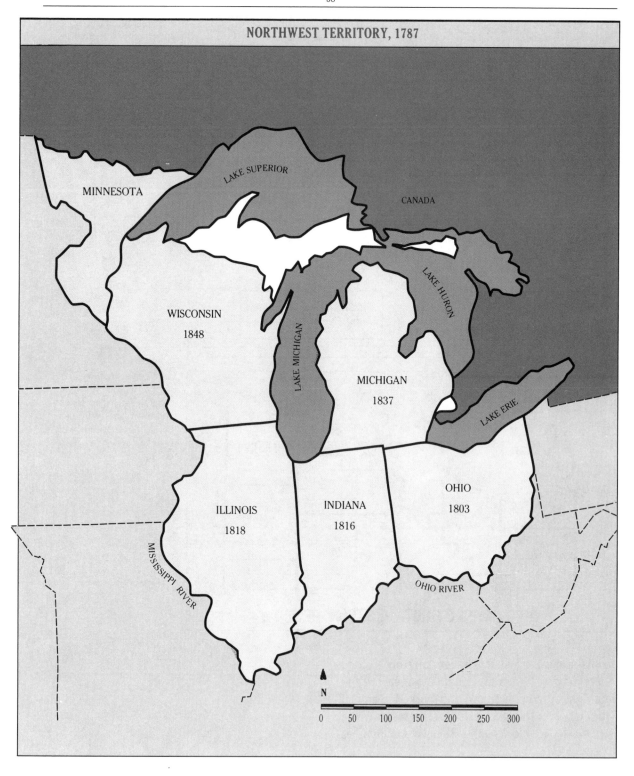

NORTHWEST TERRITORY, 1787

MINNESOTA

LAKE SUPERIOR

CANADA

WISCONSIN
1848

LAKE MICHIGAN

LAKE HURON

MICHIGAN
1837

LAKE ERIE

ILLINOIS
1818

INDIANA
1816

OHIO
1803

MISSISSIPPI RIVER

OHIO RIVER

N

0   50   100   150   200   250   300

Each township was given its own name and was also registered by number and location. The townships were further subdivided into 36 (or 25) smaller blocks called sections. Each section was one mile long on every side. A square mile section was 640 acres. Each section was numbered so it was easy to find in a township.

Cost of land. At first, the smallest amount of land anyone could buy was a section. Prices were a dollar or more per acre. Only wealthy people could afford to purchase property. Later, sections were cut into halves (320 acres) or quarters (160 acres). Eventually, *parcels* (pieces) as small as 80 or 40 acres were available. An average person could then buy a small farm, and many did.

A certain amount of land was saved in every township. The income from this portion was used to supply money to finance local schools. By this method, the public education tradition of New England was planted in Ohio. This system of supporting schools spread throughout America.

One group of people who were interested in the new land were called *speculators.* They wanted to buy land from the government and resell it to settlers at a higher price. With these and other people moving into the area, it was time to start a plan of government that would help keep order in the area.

The Northwest Territory was created. The Northwest Ordinance of 1787 was passed by Congress. It created the new Northwest Territory and outlined a system of government. Borders of the territory were the Ohio River on the south, Canada on the north, the Mississippi River on the west, and the original states on the east. The government of the territory was made up of a territorial governor, a secretary, and three judges. All of these officials were appointed by Congress.

The Northwest Ordinance set a three-stage plan for a territory to become a state. First was the stage where the territory was ruled by appointed officials. The second stage began when the population grew to have 5,000 free males. Then the people who

lived in the territory could choose representatives to help govern them. The people chosen served in the lower house of a territorial legislature. All free males over age 21 who owned some property could vote for the legislators. These elected representatives chose five more people to serve with the appointed officials in the other house of the legislature.

The third stage came when an area in the territory reached a population of 60,000 people. At that point, the territorial legislature could ask to become a new state and Congress would vote on it.

The Northwest Ordinance encouraged religion, *morality,* and public education. It outlawed slavery in the territory. Trial by jury and other civil rights were promised to people who settled there.

Arthur St. Clair was the first and only governor of the Northwest Territory. In July 1788, he arrived at Marietta to begin his term of office. Marietta was the first capital of the Northwest Territory. While St. Clair was often *overbearing* in his rule, a good system of democratic government was begun. This system was the model for all territories and states that came later on.

5. The first settlements in Ohio were founded by Moravian missionaries, but soon died out.

A pioneer group of people who came to Ohio in the early 1770s were the Moravian missionaries, led by John Heckewelder and David Zeisberger.

Founding of Schoenbrunn. In 1772, Zeisberger founded Schoenbrunn. In German this means "beautiful spring." The site he chose was near a spring in the Tuscarawas River Valley.

There, Moravian missionaries lived with about 400 Indians who were *converted* to the Christian faith. Zeisberger wanted to preserve the Indian way of life, but add to it Christian beliefs. Ohio's first church was built at Schoenbrunn.

Life at Schoenbrunn was a blending of Indian and white customs and manners. Indians learned to use plows, axes, and cooking utensils as whites

A reconstruction of the school house which was built at Schoenbrunn.

did. Indians and whites worked together and shared goods in common.

The success of the Schoenbrunn experiment led to the founding of other Moravian towns like Gnadenhutten, Lichtenau, Salem, and Goshen.

Schoenbrunn did not survive the Revolutionary War. The Moravians and the Christian Indians tried to remain neutral between the British and the Americans. But the Americans felt that the Indians were either *for* or against them. There was no middle ground possible. Also, other Indians did not like or trust the Christian Indians at Schoenbrunn.

For these reasons, a final service was held in the Schoenbrunn church in 1776. Then the members tore down their building rather than leave it to be destroyed by enemies. Then everyone left town. It was later burned to the ground.

WILLIAM CRAWFORD

COLONEL William Crawford caught the revenge of the Indians for the murders at Gnadenhutten.

He had been a strong leader during the Revolutionary War. In May 1782, Crawford led a group of 500 Pennsylvania volunteers from Mingo Bottom on the Ohio River toward the Sandusky River. He ended up near some Wyandot and Delaware Indian villages.

The Battle of the Sandusky followed. Angered by the massacre, the Indians were very strong in battle. Even so, neither side won the battle at the start. Then more Indians arrived. Trying to get away, Crawford's men sneaked out at night. But the next day, they were caught and defeated by the Indians along the Olentangy River. Colonel Crawford was captured, tied to a stake, and slowly tortured with fire until he died.

Murder of Indians at Gnadenhutten. Even sadder was the fate of Gnadenhutten. Near the end of the Revolutionary War, Colonel David Williamson led the massacre of 96 Christian Indians. This violent act by whites was a response to Indian raids on settlers in western Pennsylvania. It did not matter that the Indians at Gnadenhutten were a peaceful group. Before leaving the scene of the massacre, Williamson's men burned the village and the bodies of their victims. Years later, missionaries went back to the place and buried the remains of the victims in a *common* grave.

6. Most early Ohio settlements were along the Ohio River.

As more and more people moved into the Ohio country, permanent settlements appeared all over the area. Most were located along the Ohio River. The river became an important travel route to the Northwest Territory.

The earliest American settlements to last in Ohio were grouped in the Ohio River Valley at places like Marietta, Belpre, Gallipolis, Manchester, and Losantiville (Cincinnati). Marietta was the first, founded in April 1788 by the Ohio Company of Associates. This organization of New England men named their town after the Queen of France (Marie Antoinette) to show thanks for French help during the Revolutionary War. Remains of prehistoric earthworks in Marietta remind us of its even older Indian heritage.

Belpre, Manchester, and Cincinnati. Other towns soon sprang up. Belpre was really an offshoot of Marietta. It was begun in 1789, when some people from Marietta moved downstream and started their own place.

Manchester was founded in 1791, as the first town in the Virginia Military Tract. It was the sixth town in Ohio.

Columbia and Losantiville (1788) were built near the site of Fort Washington in the southwestern corner of Ohio. Fort Washington was the capital of the Northwest Territory for a short time. Losantiville soon changed its name to Cincinnati in honor of Revolutionary War officers who had formed a society named for Cincinnatus, the Roman soldier who left his farm to fight for his country. Columbia later merged with Cincinnati.

Cincinnati in 1802.

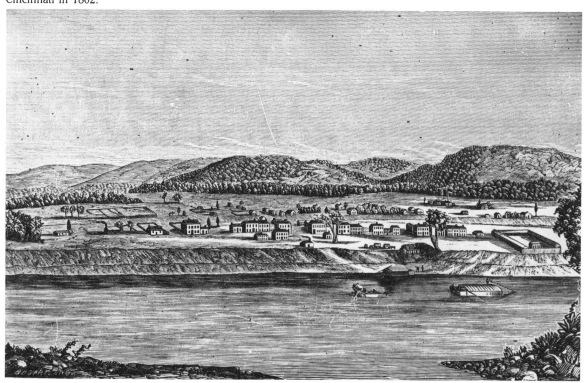

MAJOR TOWNS BEFORE 1800

LAKE ERIE

GRAND RIVER

Cleveland
1796

CUYAHOGA RIVER

Warren
1799

MAUMEE RIVER

SANDUSKY RIVER

Ravenna
1799

Youngstown
1798

MAHONING RIVER

SCIOTO RIVER

GRAND LAKE ST. MARYS

INDIAN LAKE

LICKING RIVER

TUSCARAWAS RIVER

Steubenville
1798

Franklinton
1797

BUCKEYE LAKE

Zanesville
1799

OHIO RIVER

Dayton
1795

LITTLE MIAMI RIVER

Lancaster
1800

MUSKINGUM RIVER

Marietta
1788

HOCKING RIVER

GREAT MIAMI RIVER

Hamilton
1795

Chillicothe
1795

Athens
1797

Belpre
1789

Cincinnati (Losantiville)
1788

Manchester
1791

Gallipolis
1791

OHIO RIVER

N

0   20   40   60   80

French settlers arrived at Gallipolis in 1791 expecting an established settlement with nice homes. Instead, they found a few cabins in the Ohio wilderness. What does the picture show about their readiness for life on the frontier?

Gallipolis, "City of the Gauls." Perhaps the early Ohio town with the most unusual story is Gallipolis. It was started in 1791 by about 400 Frenchmen who were tricked by advertisements that did not tell the whole truth about lands being sold by the Scioto Company. The French had bought land from the Scioto Company in good faith, only to find that the company did not own the land. In addition, the land was not as good as promised. Only a few cabins existed on the site where nice large homes were expected. The French were not farmers and did not know how to cope with the Ohio wilderness. Instead, they were craftsmen, teachers, lawyers, and doctors. But some of these French settlers learned how to survive in the wilderness. They added a colorful chapter to Ohio's cultural history.

Other towns that had early beginnings were Chillicothe, Franklinton, Dayton, Columbus, and Cleveland. All were near rivers or creeks. Why do you think people wanted to be close to the waterways? Are most towns today built near rivers? Why?

By 1790, the foundations of Ohio were established. Americans moved quickly into the Ohio country to build a new and free society. There was plenty of land with rich resources. They formed a government based on the principles of freedom and equality for the individual.

WORDS FOR STUDY

vast	*survey*
expedition	*township*
agent	*grid*
ally	*parcel*
representative democracy	*speculator*
advocate	*morality*
empire	*overbearing*
campaign	*converted*
squatter	*common*

QUESTIONS FOR REVIEW

1. Who were the first Europeans to see Ohio?
2. What was the purpose of the Ohio Land Company?
3. What effect did the Treaty of Paris, 1763, have on the Ohio country?
4. Why did Pontiac organize a conspiracy in 1763?
5. What was the purpose of the Proclamation Line of 1763?
6. What happened to the settlements of Schoenbrunn and Gnadenhutten?
7. What was the importance to Ohio of Lord Dunmore's War?
8. Explain the purpose of the Fort Gower Resolves.
9. What were the purposes of the Land Ordinance of 1785?
10. Why was the Northwest Ordinance of 1787 important?
11. What was the first permanent settlement in Ohio?
12. In what ways was the Ohio River important in Ohio's early development?

GOING FURTHER

1. Why did the English become interested in the Ohio country after 1740?
2. Why did Pontiac's resistance movement against the English fail?
3. Was the English policy of the Proclamation Line of 1763 bound to fail? Explain.
4. Why did the early settlements that were started by Moravian missionaries fail?
5. Why were the American colonists angry about the Quebec Act?

FOR THOUGHT AND DISCUSSION

1. In what ways would Ohio be different today if the French had won the French and Indian War? Give some specific examples.
2. Why do you think the English had more problems with the Indians than the French did?

3. "American colonists did not respect Ohio Indians." Do you agree or disagree with this statement? What historical evidence during this period supports your opinion?
4. Explain the importance of Ohio in the American Revolution.
5. In what ways were the ordinances of 1785 and 1787 important to the future of America? Are there examples in your community that support your opinion?

PROJECTS AND REPORTS

1. Write a speech expressing the ideas and feelings that an Indian living in Ohio might have had just prior to the American Revolutionary War.
2. Research and report on a military leader of the day. Some possibilities are: young George Washington, George Rogers Clark, William Crawford.
3. Research and report on an Indian leader of this time period. Chief Logan, Pontiac, or Old Britain are some possible choices.
4. Analyze the leadership characteristics of military leaders and Indian chiefs during this period. Compare these qualities with those needed by leaders today.
5. Make a scale model of a surveyed township.
6. Gather information and write a report on any of the first permanent settlements in Ohio. Analyze how the early patterns of settlement still affect the community today.
7. Study to learn the main reasons for the American Revolutionary War. Record your findings on a chart or other graphic display.

Since much of Ohio's land was covered with trees,
clearing land to grow crops and to build cabins was one
of the first tasks for early settlers.

CHAPTER 4

LIFE IN FRONTIER OHIO

1790-1830

MAIN POINTS

1. Life on the frontier was dangerous and very hard.

2. Frontier families liked to spend leisure time with neighbors.

3. Three major battles between the Americans and the Indians led to the opening of interior Ohio for settlement.

4. The Treaty of Greene Ville brought peace to the Ohio territory for a period of 16 years.

Have you ever thought about going to another planet to live? What would life be like on a far planet? Would it be like space movies you have seen? You might be a little bit nervous about living in a new space age frontier. Two hundred years ago, new settlers who moved into Ohio must have felt the same way. The land was still a wilderness where people faced many hard problems.

1. Life on the frontier was dangerous and very hard.

When the United States became a free nation, there were only 13 states. The area between Pennsylvania and the Wabash River, from Lake Erie to the Ohio River, was a wide *frontier* called the Ohio country.

Much of the Ohio country was a forest. In some places the trees grew so thick that the sky could not be seen. Traveling through the forest was very

hard and sometimes impossible. There were no roads, but only paths and trails that had been made by bison that lived in the area. For many years, travel was possible only on the streams and rivers.

One urgent task for new settlers was to plant some crops to be used for their own food and for farm animals. The trees had to be cut down to make room to grow crops and to build houses. Some settlements, such as Marietta, had some cabins ready for their people, but most had to build their own shelters. There was little time for anything other than work.

Two main dangers to settlers were Indians and disease. The Indians were trying to get their lands back and did not like whites coming in to settle. It was dangerous for settlers to live very far from a fort. For example, in the 1790s, about 40 people moved 30 miles up river from the forts at Marietta. At a place called Big Bottom on the Muskingum River, they built cabins. In January of 1791, Indians made a surprise attack on Big Bottom. Most of the people were killed and the cabins were destroyed.

In the early days of Ohio, diseases such as smallpox, malaria, and cholera killed most of their victims. There were few medicines to cure sick people, even in the towns. Pioneers had to use their own skills and home brews to treat illness. Cholera caused more deaths among children than any other sickness. A pioneer woman wrote about hard life on the frontier:

The thick forests made settling the Ohio country difficult.

We lived in log houses; some with two rooms, but more with only one room. In 1818, and from then to 1826, very often there was not a family but had one or more cases of ague and fever. . . . When not sick, women would spin wool for clothing and bedding. . . . Some women had looms in their houses and did their own weaving, and also wove for their neighbors. Now, what with sickness, spinning, weaving, coloring, cutting, making, and mending, (which was not a playspell), besides knitting, dipping candles, making soap, cheese and butter; without carpets or lamps, . . . no door or window screens; flies and mosquitoes plenty . . . [life was not easy for anyone on the frontier].

Purchasing land. Along the Ohio River were towns where people could buy land. The river was the main way to enter the Ohio country. The pioneers often wanted to live near friends who had come before them. People from the South generally moved to the Virginia Military District, while New Englanders often preferred the Western Reserve in the northeast part of the state.

Since the cost of land was so high, a lot of people moved in without buying the rights to the land. Time after time, these squatters were forced from their homes by the soldiers. They would pack up and move to another vacant area to start a new home.

Many people, however, paid for their land at a local land office. Others were given plots of land as payment for serving in the Revolutionary War.

In most parts of the Ohio country, claims were marked off in townships and sections as called for in the Land Ordinance of 1785. Another way was used in the Virginia Military District. Known as the "metes and bounds" survey, this plan used natural markers such as trees, rocks, and river bends to divide the land.

What do you suppose happened over the years when the natural markers changed or disappeared? Talk over with your class some problems that might come up. What method of marking the land is used in your area today?

Clearing the land was not easy in those days. The forest trees had to be cut down so that crops could be grown on the land. Sometimes the settlers would *girdle* the trees before chopping them down. This means that a ring would be cut into the bark around the tree. Over a year or two, the tree would die and be cut down for firewood. Girdling a tree took time, though, and most pioneers could not wait for a tree to dry out before they cut it down. Pulling out tree stumps was always a hard

Some people, who could not afford to buy land, settled and built cabins on land they did not own. What were they called?

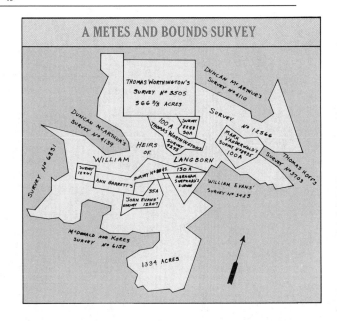

A METES AND BOUNDS SURVEY

job. Several oxen or horses might be used to pull the stumps from the ground. Or the stumps might be left to dry and then be burned out. Once enough trees were cut down and removed, a cabin could be built and the land could be used for farming.

Building a house. In the clearing, a house could be built. At first, settlers usually built temporary shelters, like the one pioneer John Cleves Symmes wrote about.

Symmes bought lands between the Miami rivers near Cincinnati. He told in letters how hard it was to build a shelter during the winter. First, he set two forks of little trees in the ground. Then he placed a pole across the forks and leaned boards from their boat against the cross pole. The front of the shelter was open to the January weather, and there Symmes built a fire to make heat for the family. The Symmes family lived in that shelter for six weeks during the winter of 1788-89. In the spring, they built a comfortable log cabin and moved into it.

Some people lived in hollowed-out trees or built lean-tos against the side of a hill. Later, they built permanent log cabins. Often the neighbors would

Most cabins had one big room. A large fireplace provided heat, light, and a place to cook meals. Other rooms were added later as people could afford them, and cabins were made more comfortable.

join in a "cabin raising." With everyone's help, the cabin could be built in just a short time.

Chopping down large trees with an axe was slow and difficult. Stripping the bark and cutting the logs into planks for the cabin was also hard. Once the cabin was built, chairs, tables, benches, and beds had to be made. The beds were often made with ropes crossed between wooden planks, and then straw or grass was used as a mattress.

The log cabins varied in size and quality. Most homes had dirt floors, but some had wooden floors made of planks. Each cabin had a big stone fireplace, often four or five feet high. The fireplace was used both for cooking and heating.

Some cabins had a loft above the ceiling. These upper rooms could be used for sleeping or to hide from wild animals. Instead of glass, windows were covered with waxed paper which let in light, but kept out the wind. Dim night light was made by the fireplace, from rags dipped in oil and set on fire, or from homemade candles.

Most cabins had only one room, but if a family did well, they might add more rooms or build a stone or a wood house.

Food for the table. Frontier families were *self-sustaining.* They provided their own food by planting and hunting. Many of them brought cows for milk and pigs for meat. There was also much wild game, such as deer, bear, wild hogs, squirrels, raccoons, and possums. When people moved in, the

This plow was pulled by a horse and guided by a person holding the two handles.

A broad ax and a buck saw were used to clear trees and build cabins. What tools would be used to do these jobs today?

game began to move out, and hunting was much more difficult. Still, fish could be caught. Muskrats and other animals were used for food and furs.

The settlers grew their own vegetables, including corn, squash, turnips, and greens. Growing wheat to make bread was a problem, since wheat crops needed a lot of land. Cleared land was in short supply. Honey was used as a sweetener and salt was in demand because it was used to help preserve meat. In fact, some settlements in the "Salt Spring Tract" of Trumbull County were built just because there were natural salt licks nearby.

Planting and harvesting crops was not easy in early Ohio. First, the ground had to be turned by shovel. Then a wooden plow was pulled by a horse, oxen, or a person.

The main crops were wheat, oats, rye, and corn. Once the crops were planted, the farmer hoped for good weather. If the crops grew well, then the hard job of harvesting was at hand. Wheat, rye, and oats were cut with a sickle or a scythe and gathered by hand. Then the grain was beaten to separate the seed from the stalk. The process of gathering and *gleaning* a 10-acre field took the whole winter.

Farmers gathered to help each other harvest the crops. These men are using cradle scythes to harvest grain in the Sinking Springs area, just as earlier farmers did.

Harvest time was made more pleasant as people joined to help each other during "thrashing time." The men and boys worked in the fields while the women and girls fixed huge amounts of food for the noon meal.

2. Frontier families liked to spend leisure time with neighbors.

Fall was a time which passed too fast for some. Life on the frontier was lonely, and harvest time was a good chance for the people to talk over events, gossip, and swap recipes. When the families returned to their homes they were tired from the work, but very happy.

Pioneer families had little time away from work. They seldom wasted time in play and often combined *leisure* with work. Hunting and fishing, house raisings, husking bees, and thrashings are examples. Husking bees were social events where teams competed to see who could peel the most husks from the corn. A big dinner would follow the contest.

Besides fixing meals for the crowd, the women also spent time quilting, spinning, and talking. Quilting bees and apple butter bees were common ways of making fun. Can you think of any events today that could be called "bees"?

Blending farm and city life. Not all of the people in frontier Ohio were farmers. Many people

At apple butter bees, people met to make apple butter, relax, and visit. This was a pleasant way to combine work and play.

lived in the towns. There were storekeepers, teachers, soldiers, blacksmiths, and doctors. Tailors, tanners, shoemakers, bakers, and gunsmiths were also part of the economy.

City dwellers relied on the farmers to bring food to town. Farmers took wagonloads of produce to town to sell. Sometimes the whole family went along for the ride. Then it was fun for everyone to look in the shops and visit with city folks.

3. Three major battles between the Americans and the Indians led to the opening of interior Ohio for settlement.

The Indian tribes of southern Ohio watched the boatloads of settlers with anger. Their Indian hunt-

ing grounds were being ruined and sacred burial grounds were sometimes disturbed.

At the end of the Revolutionary War the feelings between the Indians and the Americans were not very good. The Ohio River was to be the dividing line between Indian and American lands. When more towns were started inside Indian territory, the Shawnee and Miami tribes prepared for war. They hoped the Wyandots and the Delawares would join them, but those two tribes had signed peace treaties with Territorial Governor Arthur St. Clair.

Governor St. Clair could not convince the Indians to give up their lands north of the Ohio River. Small Indian groups had been attacking travelers on the

Josiah Harmar led 1,500 troops against the Indians in 1790. The Indians defeated his poorly-trained volunteers near present-day Ft. Wayne, Indiana.

river, and others had been stealing horses. The British, who still held forts on American soil, helped the Indians by giving them weapons.

Harmar's expedition, 1790. President George Washington decided to take action against the Indians in order to make the Ohio country safe for settlement. He chose General Josiah Harmar to lead the troops. Harmar and St. Clair hoped that their army would be big enough to scare the Indians into a surrender without a fight. But there were only 1,500 men and most of them were poorly trained volunteers. To add to the problems, many of the

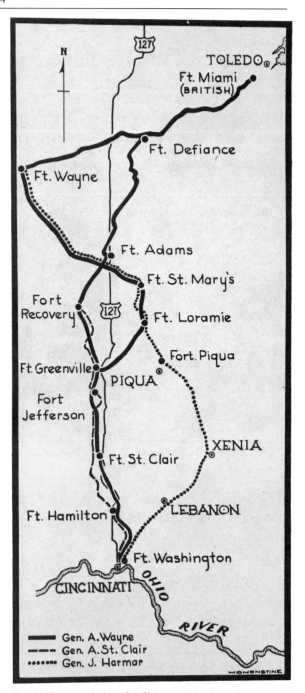

Josiah Harmar, Arthur St. Clair, and Anthony Wayne led forces against the Indians in an attempt to open the Ohio country for settlement.

volunteers had brought their wives and children along for the march!

Harmar's army left Cincinnati in September 1790, heading north. The Indians thought their best chance to win was to surprise the army. The Indians deserted their village where the St. Marys and St. Joseph rivers met. Harmar's troops destroyed the village, but they found no Indians.

After letting the army march nearly 200 miles into Indian territory, the Indians attacked. The site was near present-day Fort Wayne, Indiana. Part of Harmar's army was drawn into a trap and defeated on October 12, 1790. Had it not been for the skill of the regular army men in the group, the whole force might have been destroyed.

St. Clair's disaster, 1791. Braver from their victory, the Indians made more attacks on the frontier settlements. The U.S. Congress voted to spend $300,000 for another fight against the Indians.

Governor St. Clair personally led the new army of 3,000 men. Although he and most of his troops had little experience fighting Indians, he planned not to fall into a trap as Harmar had done. The governor decided to build a string of forts 25 miles apart from Cincinnati to Lake Erie. The army would always be close to supplies and shelter. But building the forts caused two problems. First, the work took time and winter was rapidly coming. Second, men had to be left at each fort to defend the post. As time went on, many of the soldiers deserted the army and went home. Therefore, St. Clair's army was cut in size to about 1,400 fighting troops.

The expedition left Cincinnati in September 1791. They built Fort Hamilton at the present site of Hamilton, Ohio. They built Fort Jefferson 70 miles from Cincinnati. By November, St. Clair's army was in present-day Mercer County on the east bank of the Wabash River. The Miami chief Little Turtle and the Shawnee chief Blue Jacket (who was a white man) attacked St. Clair's forces by surprise on November 4. The battle was a *rout!* Of 1,400 in the army, over 900 were killed or wounded. St.

Chief Little Turtle of the Miamis, together with the Shawnee chief Blue Jacket, destroyed most of St. Clair's army.

Clair showed great personal bravery in the battle, but it was not enough to save the day.

Wayne's victory at Fallen Timbers, 1794. After this big win, the Indians demanded that the Ohio River be the boundary between Indian and white lands. National leaders saw that the Indians were gaining ground. When it was learned that the British had taken over Fort Miami again, American demand for a final settlement of the Indian problem grew. President Washington appointed a proven military hero of the Revolutionary War to command the western army. The man was General Anthony Wayne.

Wayne gathered an army of 2,500 troops, scouts, and spies. He drilled his men and taught them how to load a rifle while running. He also taught the troops how to use a bayonet, which was a long knife

The Indians were finally defeated by General Anthony Wayne at the Battle of Fallen Timbers.

stuck on the end of a rifle. He also had *cavalry* units ride on both sides of his army to scout for Indian ambushes.

In December 1793, Wayne's army built Fort Recovery near the site of St. Clair's defeat. While his army kept on training, Wayne asked Little Turtle and Blue Jacket to talk peace. The meeting was useless. Then Wayne built his strongest fort deep in Indian territory where the Auglaize and the Maumee rivers met. He named this Fort Defiance.

On August 20, 1794, Wayne's army met about 2,000 Indians led by Blue Jacket. Little Turtle wanted peace and had refused to join in the fight. The Indians waited for Wayne on the banks of the Maumee River about one mile from Fort Miami.

Blue Jacket's braves hid in an area of fallen timbers which had been uprooted by a tornado. Wayne's forces had a big victory after a 45-minute battle. The Indians fled to the British fort, but the British refused to let them in. Wayne's forces suffered about 140 losses. The Indian losses were twice as much.

4. The Treaty of Greene Ville brought peace to the Ohio territory for a period of 16 years.

General Wayne called for a meeting of the important Indian chiefs at Fort Greene Ville (present-day Darke County) in June 1795. Over 1,000 Indians came, led by Tarhe the Crane of the Wyandots, Little Turtle of the Miamis, Blue Jacket of the Shawnees, and Buckongahelas of the Delawares.

The Treaty of Greene Ville was signed in August 1795. The *treaty* said that all prisoners from both sides would be freed. The Indians were to get $20,000 worth of goods immediately and $9,500 worth of goods each year. A treaty line was drawn from the Cuyahoga River south to Fort Laurens, then west to Fort Recovery and south to the mouth of the Kentucky River. All of the land north and west of that line was to be Indian territory forever.

Wayne's victory and the Treaty of Greene Ville were important in Ohio history for a couple of reasons. There was peace in the Northwest Territory for the next 16 years, and the interior of the Ohio country was settled by Americans. Also, the

The Treaty of Greene Ville set a line between Indian territory and lands open for settlement. The treaty document lies on the table. Little Turtle and Anthony Wayne are standing in front. Also in the painting are other notable Indian chiefs and military men.

British influence on the Indians was destroyed by the events at Fort Miami.

Peace in the Ohio country would last for only a short time. One young Shawnee warrior already had dreams of a giant Indian union. He saw the union driving the Americans back across the mountains. That young Shawnee was Tecumseh. His name would become famous on the eve of the War of 1812.

GREENE VILLE TREATY LINE, 1795

WORDS FOR STUDY

frontier
girdle
self-sustaining
glean
leisure
rout
cavalry
treaty

QUESTIONS FOR REVIEW

1. Why was it hard to travel in the Ohio country in frontier days?

2. What were three different ways early settlers got land in the Ohio country?

3. Name two urgent tasks that faced settlers.

4. Tell how the pioneers girdled a tree and the advantages of girdling.

5. How did early settlers heat and light their cabins?

6. Describe the pioneer methods of planting and harvesting.

7. Why was harvest time enjoyable for pioneer farmers?

8. After the Revolutionary War, what developments led to conflict between the Indians and the frontier people?

9. What problems did Generals Harmar and St. Clair have in forming armies to fight the Indians?

10. What military methods did General Wayne and his men use to fight the Indians?

GOING FURTHER

1. What events affected the food supply of the settlers? How?

2. How did the roles of women and men differ on the frontier?

FOR THOUGHT AND DISCUSSION

1. In what ways is your life different from the lives of early Ohio settlers? In what ways do you think it is the same?

2. Do you think the Indians got a fair deal in the Treaty of Greene Ville? Explain your answer.

3. Suppose you were a government official during frontier days. Think of some alternate solutions to the problem of land claims between Indians and settlers.

4. Do you think life today is easier, as hard, or harder than in frontier days? Why?

PROJECTS AND REPORTS

1. Research at local city and county offices to find out how land in your area is surveyed. Get (or draw) a sample of the measurement of the property on which your school is built.

2. Make a scale model of a frontier farm or cabin.

3. Plan and hold a "bee" of some sort in your neighborhood or at school.

4. Report on any of the Indian leaders who were present at Greene Ville.

5. Locate a copy of the Treaty of Greene Ville and read it through completely. Write a report on your feelings about this treaty.

6. Find a recipe for soap or dipped candles and make a sample to bring to class.

7. Construct a chart comparing and contrasting frontier life with your life today.

An early view of Cleveland.

CHAPTER 5

STATEHOOD AND DEVELOPMENT

1788-1830

MAIN POINTS

1. During the 1790s, the Ohio region prepared to become a state.

2. Ohio became a state in 1803, and its constitution outlined the form of government.

3. Self-rule brought political struggles and political parties.

4. Columbus became the permanent state capital in 1816.

5. The War of 1812 was the final battle for permanent control in Ohio.

6. Growth came to Ohio as a result of improved transportation.

7. New people brought ideas for a better system of education.

---

1. During the 1790s, the Ohio region prepared to become a state.

The white settlers and the Indians got along well after the Treaty of Greene Ville was signed. During those years of peace, more people moved into the Northwest Territory. A stronger government was built to give order to the new settlements.

The reasons any people need government are to make and enforce laws, to protect rights, and to have peace. The Northwest Territory needed law and order so people would be willing to live there.

Government in the territory. Governor St. Clair and his advisors wrote a basic set of laws. One law arranged for a court with three judges. One of the judges had to hold court in each new county at least once a year.

In January 1790, St. Clair moved the capital to Losantiville, which was near the center of the territory. He changed its name to Cincinnati after the Order of Cincinnati, a group who had served in the American Revolution.

Territorial Governor, Arthur St. Clair, the only governor of the Northwest Territory.

The territorial legislature adds more laws. The first legislature met at Cincinnati in September 1799. Many of the *delegates* had a hard time getting there. Some rode on horseback or traveled on boats. Several arrived late, after the session had started.

The lawmakers passed many *bills* (plans for law) ranging from defense to control of liquor sales to Indians. They voted down a request to allow people to bring slaves into Ohio.

Planning for statehood. As time passed, the people made it known that they wanted more say in the government. They wanted to become a state and rule themselves. Governor St. Clair did all he could to resist statehood. Perhaps he feared losing his power or thought the people were not ready for self-rule. Whatever his reasons, he made a lot of enemies.

In 1800, St. Clair proposed a split of the Northwest Territory into three districts. His plan would have stopped any one of those parts from getting the 60,000 people required for statehood. Some strong resistance to his plan was voiced by Thomas Worthington. Worthington was known as the "Father of Ohio Statehood" due to his work against St. Clair's plan, which was defeated.

One man in Congress who opposed St. Clair was William Henry Harrison. He had another plan. Congress approved Harrison's plan to split the territory in two. The east part was still called the Northwest Territory, with Chillicothe as the capital. It would later become the state of Ohio. The western half became the Indiana Territory, and Harrison was its first governor.

Chillicothe became Ohio's first state capital. This view shows the courthouse in 1801.

The Enabling Act was signed April 30, 1802, by President Thomas Jefferson. This act let Ohio take the final steps for statehood.

The voters sent delegates to a constitutional convention, where their task was to write a constitution (set of laws) for the new state. The Enabling Act also set the new state's borders as Pennsylvania on the east and the Ohio River to the south. On the west a line was drawn north from the mouth of the great Miami River. A line drawn east from the south shore of Lake Michigan to Lake Erie became the northern border.

2. Ohio became a state in 1803, and its constitution outlined the form of government.

In 1802, delegates were sent to Ohio's constitutional convention. They met at Chillicothe on November 1 of that year. Today the office of the *Chillicothe Gazette* is a replica of the building where they met—"the Cradle of Statehood."

Edward Tiffin of Chillicothe was named president of that body. When the writing began, not all agreed on the issues. Debates over the topics were so hot that some members lost their tempers. But after 25 days, a 20-page document was drafted. The U.S. Congress approved it and Ohio became the 17th state on March 1, 1803. (Or did it? Congress failed to adopt an official resolution at that time. It was not until 1953, during the *sesquicentennial*—150 years—celebration, that Congress passed a resolution for Ohio's statehood.)

The 1802 constitution was the law of the state until a new one was made in 1851. Let us look at some of its main points.

The governor had limited power. Elected by the people, he was the head of the state militia. He could grant *pardons* (releases) to those who had been jailed, and he could fill state offices when the lawmakers were not in session. He could call for special sessions of the assembly. Beyond that, the governor had little power over the legislature.

The General Assembly (legislature) had the most power in government. It was split into two parts: the house of representatives and the senate. Members of the house were chosen each year, while senators held two-year terms. They wrote laws and appointed judges and other state officers.

The court system. People of Ohio thought the court system was quite slow. A supreme court with three judges was set up. The judges were chosen by the legislature for seven-year terms. Each county had a court of common pleas, but a judge from the high court had to preside. The supreme court was to hold a session once a year in each county. Since there were 44 counties in 1803, it took a long time for the three judges to make the rounds. Later, a series of lower courts was set up to speed the legal process.

A bill of rights in the constitution outlined the rights of each person. Some of these were freedom of speech, freedom to bear arms, and freedom of worship.

One law set restrictions for voters. A voter had to be 21, male, and white. He had to pay a county or a state tax, or work on the state roads if he did not pay taxes. How are the voter laws different today?

3. Self-rule brought political struggles and political parties.

Once self-rule came to the new state, people began to take sides on the issues. Political parties sprang up. The Federalists and the Republicans were the first two groups to organize. There were more Republicans than Federalists, but they lost strength through lack of unity. Those in the south often did not agree with the northerners. Even so, the first governor and congressmen in the state were Republicans.

Edward Tiffin of Chillicothe was chosen Ohio's first governor. A native of England, he came to this land at the age of 18. His work as president of the constitutional convention earned him great respect.

Thomas Worthington (left) and Edward Tiffin were brothers-in-law from Chillicothe. Tiffin was Ohio's first governor. Worthington was one of Ohio's first two U.S. senators and later became governor.

Tiffin was re-elected in 1805 and served in that office until he was sent to the U.S. Senate in 1807. The president of the state senate, Thomas Kirker, filled Tiffin's term as governor.

Thomas Worthington of Chillicothe was one of the state's first two U.S. senators. The other U.S. senator was John Smith of Cincinnati. Smith was a minister who had been a member of the U.S. Constitutional Convention. Jeremiah Morrow of Warren County served as the only member of the U.S. House of Representatives from 1803 to 1810.

Political struggles. For a short time, the two parties worked together to write new state laws. However, by 1807, the general feeling of teamwork between the two came to a halt. Return Jonathan Meigs, Jr., was elected governor that year. He was a Federalist. The Republicans had him ousted when they learned that he had broken a rule. Meigs had not lived in Ohio for the required four years prior to the vote.

4. Columbus became the permanent state capital in 1816.

One of the biggest political battles was over the site of a permanent state capital. The constitution had said that Chillicothe was to be the location until 1808. At that time, the General Assembly was free to make a final choice. The people of Chillicothe hoped that the seat of government would be kept in their town. This would bring more business to them.

Others in the state thought Chillicothe had too much power in government.

In 1810, the capital was moved to Zanesville. Then a rule was passed that the site should be no more than 40 miles from the center of the state. Although Zanesville and Chillicothe were both just outside the 40 mile limit, after two years the honor went back to Chillicothe. Zanesville did not have enough buildings to house all the members of the assembly.

U. S. COURT HOUSE. STATE OFFICES. OLD STATE HOUSE.

In 1816, Ohio state government moved to Columbus. Shown here are the old state house and government buildings.

Several towns were viewed as the final site, but Columbus (named after Christopher Columbus) was the choice. Land agents led by Lynn Starling, James Johnson, John Kerr, and Alexander McLaughlin promised to build a new city to house the capital. The streets were to be extra wide to hold the traffic. These men gave 20 acres of land on which to build state offices and a prison.

In October 1816, the state government was moved to Columbus. Besides the office buildings and a library, there were hotels for the lawmakers. The first state house (office building) was destroyed by fire in 1852. The new capitol building was opened in 1857 and is still in use today. Stone for the new capitol came from a quarry on the Scioto River three miles north of Columbus. Both convicts and hired stonecutters worked on the building.

The move to Columbus came during a rough time in Ohio history. New settlers were moving into the state in great numbers. For the Indians, this rapid growth was alarming. They wondered if the new settlers would move into their lands north of the Greene Ville Treaty line.

5. The War of 1812 was the final battle for permanent control in Ohio.

Trouble with the Indians brewed. Between 1796 and 1811 there were few Indian raids on settlers and river travelers. But old-time frontiersmen, such as Simon Kenton, warned that the tribes were too quiet. They might be planning something big. Frontiersmen seemed very good at predicting what the Indians would do. They learned about Indians by living in the wilderness for many years.

SIMON KENTON, A FRONTIERSMAN

SIMON Kenton was the main frontiersman who helped open Ohio for settlement. He assisted early settlers with skills he had learned over many years on the frontier. Kenton was a prime example of his kind. He loved the forests and chose to live away from the settlements.

Kenton was born in Virginia in 1755. He left there at age 16, believing he had killed a man in an argument over a girl. He learned to survive in the wilderness, becoming a keen marksman and hunter. Although he admired the Indian life style, he was never friendly with them. In fact, Kenton liked to steal their horses. He was captured several times and was nearly killed when he had to run the gauntlet (between two lines of Indians with clubs). Twice he was sentenced to be burned at the stake, but managed to escape.

Though he had nine children, Kenton was not much of a family man. He was seldom home, choosing to fight Indians or stake out claims to new lands instead. Kenton never learned to read or write. After surviving 65 years in the frontier, he died a poor man in a small cabin near Zanesfield, at the age of 81.

Indians aided by British. Besides unrest over the Indians, the settlers were angered by British meddling. There were reports that they were supplying the Shawnees with guns and powder. Then too, the British were causing trouble for American ships on the seas.

Stories spread that a Shawnee chief named Tecumseh was creating a huge Indian league. His goal was to force the settlers back to the Atlantic Coast.

Battle of Tippecanoe. In 1811, Tecumseh left his home for a trip west. He hoped to convince the tribes there to join his group. Tecumseh's brother, the Prophet, was left in charge. He was a one-eyed medicine man. Tecumseh told the Prophet to avoid at all costs a fight with the whites. He feared a loss would destroy his confederation.

William Henry Harrison, the governor of the Indiana Territory, attacked the Shawnee camp on the Tippecanoe River while Tecumseh was gone. The Prophet chose to fight rather than hide in the woods, but Harrison's forces won.

The Prophet led the Shawnees into the Battle of Tippecanoe, against Tecumseh's warning.

THE PROPHET

TECUMSEH, A VALIANT INDIAN CHIEF

THE Shawnee chief Tecumseh was one of the truly noble people of his time. He was a great leader who loved his people dearly. Tecumseh was born around 1768, near the present site of Piqua. He showed signs of great leadership skills at a young age.

Tecumseh disliked what the settlers were doing to his people and hoped to keep the land from their control. He wanted the Ohio River as the boundary between whites and Indians. When he was chosen as the Shawnee chief, he urged other tribes to join him in a *confederation* (union). Tecumseh thought that by uniting, the Indians could drive the whites back to the eastern seaboard. He made friends with the British in hopes they would give aid to his people.

In 1811, Tecumseh warned of the fate the Indians would suffer unless they joined to resist the white men:

. . . But what need is there to speak of the past? It speaks for itself and asks, Where today is the Pequod? Where . . . the Mohawks . . . and many other once powerful tribes of our race? They have vanished before the . . . white men, as snow before a summer sun. . . . Look abroad over their once beautiful country, and what see you now? Naught but the ravages of the pale face destroyers meet our eyes. So it will be with you. . . . Soon your mighty forest trees . . . will be cut down to fence in the land which the white intruders dare to call their own. Soon their broad roads will pass over the grave of your fathers, and the place of their rest will be blotted out forever. The annihilation of our race is at hand unless we unite in one common cause against the common foe. . . .

Even though the confederation was never firm, Tecumseh's braves fought hard in the Battle of Tippecanoe and in the War of 1812. In fact, the British made him a general. He died from battle wounds in Canada near Detroit in 1813. Tecumseh lived bravely and tried to do the best he could for his people.

The Battle of Tippecanoe was important for several reasons. First, the grand confederation plan was ruined. If Tecumseh's tribe could not beat a few white soldiers, then how could the Shawnees lead a great war effort? Second, General Harrison found British weapons and supplies at the Prophet's village. Harrison then knew for sure that they were pushing the tribes into war with the settlers. Many Americans thought the only way to stop British aid to the Indians was to drive them from their base in Canada.

The War of 1812 began in June, as the United States and Great Britain went to war again. Ohio was not at all prepared for war. Governor Return Jonathan Meigs, Jr., hoped to persuade the tribes not to join the British. But his mission failed. The

British made Tecumseh a brigadier general in their army. As a result, many Indians joined the war on their side.

Some Ohioans did not want war. Others feared the Indians might win, so they joined the battle. Most of the Ohio troops were untrained in military ways, but they fought hard.

Hull surrenders Detroit. The key outpost in the Northwest was Detroit. Whoever held that fort could control the west shore of Lake Erie and land routes into Canada. Governor William Hull of the Michigan Territory was in command of the forces at Detroit.

Two thousand of Hull's men marched through the Black Swamp in the northern part of the state to defend Detroit and try to take Canada, as well. However, Hull was tricked by British General Isaac Brock. Hull thought that the Indian and British troops were more numerous than they really were. Afraid he was outnumbered, Hull gave up Fort Detroit.

Harrison takes over. The British soon set the Americans free at Detroit, after making them promise not to fight again. But most of them did, under General Harrison, the hero of Tippecanoe.

Siege of Fort Meigs. Some of Harrison's men lost a battle at the River Raisin in late 1812. The rest wintered at the new Fort Meigs on the Maumee. In the spring of 1813, the British struck Fort Meigs, but they could not force Harrison to surrender. When Harrison received more troops, the attackers gave up their *siege* and left. Great Britain lost the support of many of the tribes as a result of losing this battle.

The Fort Meigs area on the Maumee River.

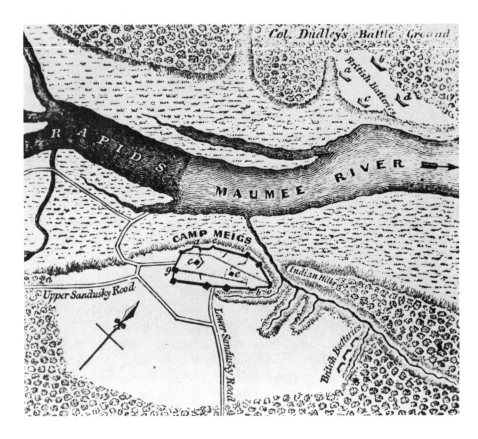

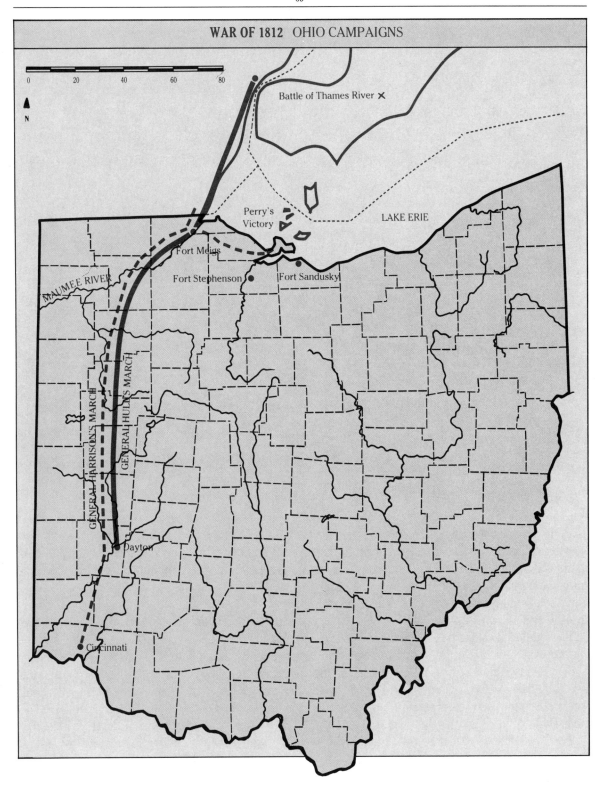

WAR OF 1812 OHIO CAMPAIGNS

Battle of Thames River ✕

Perry's
Victory

LAKE ERIE

Fort Meigs

MAUMEE RIVER

Fort Stephenson

Fort Sandusky

GENERAL HARRISON'S MARCH

GENERAL HULL'S MARCH

Dayton

Cincinnati

0   20   40   60   80

N

Oliver Hazard Perry's force defeated the British on Lake Erie in 1813. When Perry's ship, the *Lawrence*, was destroyed, he was rowed to the *Niagara* to continue the battle.

Perry's victory on Lake Erie. Harrison's next goal was to gain control of Lake Erie. By doing this, men could sail by ship to Detroit rather than make the tough march through the Black Swamp. Young Oliver Hazard Perry was put in charge of destroying the British ships on the lake.

First, a fleet of ships had to be built. This was not an easy task. Six of the ten ships were built at Erie, Pennsylvania, within four months, including two large brigs—the *Lawrence* and the *Niagara*. The other four ships were captured from the British near Buffalo.

Perry gathered an unusual crew to sail his ships. Some were Ohioans, but many were from nearby states. Most were white, while about one-fifth were black. Few of the crew had any naval fighting experience. In fact, Commodore Perry had little practice himself.

Perry decided to sail to Put-In-Bay at South Bass Island north of Sandusky. There he waited for three weeks on his flag ship, the *Lawrence*. On the morning of September 10, 1813, British commander Barclay's fleet appeared. They had run out of supplies and had come to attack Perry's crew. Perry's crew members were better trained and also had the wind at their backs to give their ship more speed and *maneuverability*.

WILLIAM HENRY HARRISON, PRESIDENT

AFTER William Henry Harrison's grand career in the military, he served in other areas of government.

In 1814 he negotiated the second treaty of Greenville which formally joined the United States and the Indians in that territory as allies.

Harrison served as an Ohio congressman from 1816-1819, and he served three years as a senator in the mid-1820s. Then, for a few years, he lived in retirement in North Bend, Ohio.

In 1835, he began to gain attention as a suitable candidate for president. In 1840, he was chosen as the Whig candidate, running against Martin Van Buren. Harrison's running mate was John Tyler. Because part of Harrison's North Bend home had been a log cabin and due to a story that he served cider at his table, not wine, Harrison's opponents called him the "log cabin and hard cider" candidate. The Whig party made use of campaign songs and slogans such as "Tippecanoe and Tyler too." These helped voters remember the names of Harrison and Tyler, and in the election, Harrison got 234 electoral votes, while only 60 were cast for Van Buren.

The inauguration took place on March 4, 1841. Unfortunately, Harrison was hit by a case of pneumonia and died April 4, 1841. He was buried in Washington, D.C., but his body was later moved to North Bend, where it now lies.

The battle was so fierce that the *Lawrence* was nearly destroyed. Perry, holding his banner that read, "Don't give up the ship," was rowed to the *Niagara.* After almost three hours of fighting, Barclay surrendered. Perry sent word to General Harrison, "We have met the enemy and they are ours." Perry was now ready to ship Harrison's troops to Detroit.

Battle of the Thames River. Perry's fleet sailed with Harrison's men to Malden, Ontario, where British General Proctor held a fort. The Americans found the fort had been deserted and burned. Harrison later met Proctor and Indian forces in the Battle of the Thames River on October 5, 1813. Tecumseh knew that this would be the last chance for the tribes to turn back the white settlers. It is likely that he had a *premonition* (feeling of warning) that he would die in the next day's fighting.

Harrison's army captured Detroit and won the Battle of the Thames River. Proctor escaped, but Tecumseh was killed. With his death, the confederation which he had planned also died. The War of 1812 continued in other parts of the country until 1815. But war in the West was over.

Effects of the war. To most Ohioans, the war was worth the effort. The state was at last made safe for settlement. Many soldiers from the East who had fought in Ohio liked the land and moved there after the war. Between 1810 and 1820, the state's population jumped from 230,000 to 581,000 as "Ohio fever" hit the East.

During the war, Ohio business boomed. Farmers grew more produce for the troops, and merchants made profits selling goods to the army. The British quit harassing U.S. ships on the seas, as well.

The war did resolve the trouble between the settlers and the Indians. But what became of the tribes? By 1843, there were no more Indians in the state. In that year, the last of the Wyandots at Upper Sandusky joined other eastern tribes on reservations west of the Mississippi.

With the end of war and outside conflicts, Ohioans turned their efforts toward making a better place to live.

6. Growth came to Ohio as a result of improved transportation.

Over the next 50 years, Ohio planned better ways to transport people and products within the state.

River travel. The rivers which brought people into Ohio were also used to ship goods. Before 1800, all types of vessels—canoes, flatboats, keelboats, rafts, barges—could be seen on the rivers. Farmers depended on the rivers to get their products to market in the East. Ohio goods, especially wheat, got a higher price there than at home because not much grain was grown in the East. For instance, a barrel of flour in Cincinnati sold for $3.50. In New York it was worth $8.00. It cost about $1.70 to ship each barrel of flour to New York. Therefore, profits in the eastern markets were greater.

An easy way to send goods to the East was to float them down the rivers to New Orleans. There the goods would be placed on large ships going to the East Coast by way of the Atlantic Ocean.

On the other hand, few goods were shipped from New York to Ohio by this route until 1820. It was hard for boats to go upstream on the rivers and fight the current. In 1807, Robert Fulton of New York built the first successful steamboat. Within 12 years, paddle wheel steamboats traveled up and down the Ohio River to New Orleans and back. The Mississippi was no longer a "one way street"!

Improved river travel was a boon for the state's river towns. They got more business and more people. But the inland towns did not have the same advantages. Roads were so poor that it was hard to take goods to the interior.

Roadways. In 1796, the first road was built through the state. Congress gave Ebenezer Zane the right to build a trail from eastern Ohio southwestward to the Ohio River. With great effort, cutting through the woods and crossing many streams, Zane's Trace was finished in 1798.

The trail from Wheeling, Virginia, ran through Cambridge, Zanesville, Lancaster, Kingston, and Chillicothe to Maysville, Kentucky. Zane's Trace was narrow—ideal for pack horses. But wagons could barely travel the road.

Flat-bottom boats such as this were used to descend the Ohio and Mississippi rivers.

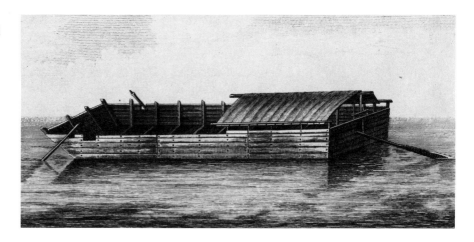

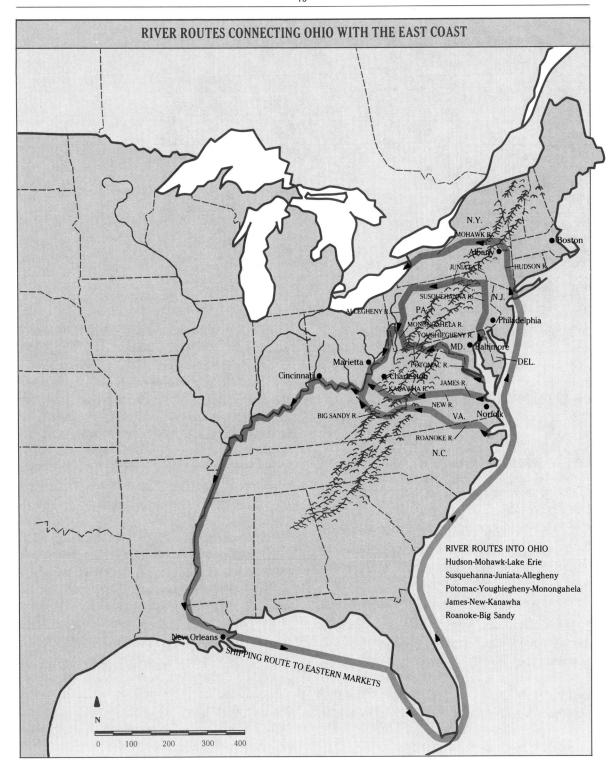

RIVER ROUTES CONNECTING OHIO WITH THE EAST COAST

N.Y.

MOHAWK R.

Boston

JUNIATA R.

Albany

HUDSON R.

SUSQUEHANNA R.

N.J.

ALLEGHENY R.

PA.

MONONGAHELA R.

Philadelphia

YOUGHIEGHENY R.

MD.

Baltimore

POTOMAC R.

DEL.

Marietta

Cincinnati

Charleston

KANAWHA R.

JAMES R.

BIG SANDY R.

NEW R.

VA.

Norfolk

ROANOKE R.

N.C.

RIVER ROUTES INTO OHIO

Hudson-Mohawk-Lake Erie

Susquehanna-Juniata-Allegheny

Potomac-Youghiegheny-Monongahela

James-New-Kanawha

Roanoke-Big Sandy

New Orleans

SHIPPING ROUTE TO EASTERN MARKETS

N

0   100   200   300   400

Fourteen-mile lock on the Ohio Canal, about 1890.

Zane's Trace was a good start, but there was a need for a road which ran east and west across the state. In 1805, Congress gave $12,000 for the Cumberland Road to be built. It was later called the Old National Road.

It was begun in Cumberland, Maryland, in 1811. The National Road went east through Washington, D.C., to Baltimore. It had a 20-foot center strip paved with stone, gravel, and sand. By 1818, the road was stretched to Wheeling, Virginia, and by 1837 it was built across Ohio. U.S. highway 40 and later Interstate 70 would closely follow this early route.

The cost of the road was hundreds of thousands of dollars, but it was well worth it. Hundreds of people had jobs building the road. Thousands of others traveled the road west to start new lives.

Many towns and stagecoach stops sprang up along the road. There seemed to be an endless train of packhorses, wagons, stagecoaches, and animal herds headed west. Farmers could ship their goods by freight wagons to eastern markets faster than before, and people in the interior could at last buy goods from the East. Women could buy fine cloth to make new dresses, for instance.

Even so, travel by road was still difficult. Harsh weather, steep hills, potholes, and sometimes bandits made the trips hard.

Canals. A better north-south route came when the Ohio Canal was built. It started as the dream of Alfred Kelley of Cleveland. Kelley found a friend in Governor Ethan Allen Brown, who thought a system of canals was the answer to the state's transportation problems. Brown was eager to see boats filled with wheat float through the canals to Lake Erie, then on to Buffalo and along the Erie Canal.

Work on the Ohio Canal was started in 1825. Tons of earth were moved by shovel. In order to raise and lower canal boats over high ground, a series of 461 locks was built. The canal was finished in 1832, at a cost of nearly $5 million.

By 1845, the Miami and Erie Canal was built from Cincinnati through Dayton, Piqua, Defiance, and Toledo. *Feeder canals* were added to the main lines at Columbus, Athens, and Marietta. In the end, the state had nearly a thousand miles of canals. Many towns like Akron, Lockbourne, Canal Winchester, Canal Fulton, Roscoe Village, and others grew up near the canals.

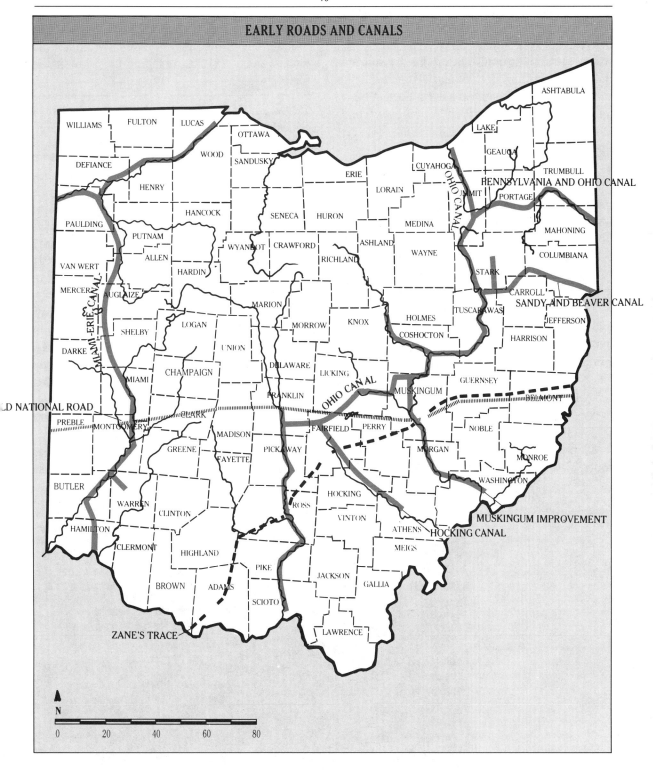

EARLY ROADS AND CANALS

ASHTABULA

WILLIAMS FULTON LUCAS

OTTAWA

DEFIANCE WOOD SANDUSKY LAKE GEAUGA

HENRY ERIE LORAIN CUYAHOGA TRUMBULL

PENNSYLVANIA AND OHIO CANAL

PAULDING HANCOCK SENECA HURON MEDINA SUMMIT PORTAGE

PUTNAM WYANDOT CRAWFORD ASHLAND MAHONING

VAN WERT ALLEN RICHLAND WAYNE COLUMBIANA

MERCER HARDIN STARK

AUGLAIZE MARION MORROW KNOX HOLMES COSHOCTON TUSCARAWAS CARROLL

SANDY AND BEAVER CANAL

SHELBY LOGAN UNION JEFFERSON

DARKE HARRISON

MIAMI CHAMPAIGN DELAWARE LICKING GUERNSEY

FRANKLIN OHIO CANAL MUSKINGUM BELMONT

LD NATIONAL ROAD CLARK

PREBLE MONTGOMERY MADISON FAIRFIELD PERRY NOBLE

GREENE FAYETTE PICKAWAY MORGAN MONROE

BUTLER WARREN HOCKING WASHINGTON

CLINTON ROSS VINTON MUSKINGUM IMPROVEMENT

HAMILTON ATHENS HOCKING CANAL

CLERMONT HIGHLAND MEIGS

PIKE JACKSON GALLIA

BROWN ADAMS SCIOTO

ZANE'S TRACE LAWRENCE

MIAMI-ERIE CANAL

N

0   20   40   60   80

Although the new waterways could carry large, heavy items that could not be taken by land, travel was very slow. At times during the dry summer months, there was not enough water to fill the canals. Lakes, such as Indian Lake in Logan County and Buckeye Lake in Licking County, were built or enlarged to store water to fill the canals. But even that was not enough.

Ohio's canal system never did make the money that Kelley and Brown had hoped for. The upkeep was costly and the state went into great debt to build the canals. After 1856, the canals lost money. With the coming of the railroad, canals were doomed.

Railroads. Trains were the fastest mode of transportation to come along. They could haul bigger loads than ships or wagons could.

The first railroad line in Ohio was the Mad River and Lake Erie Railroad in 1838. This line operated between Sandusky and Bellevue. In 1850, there were only 300 miles of railroad track in Ohio. Ten years later, there were over 3,000 miles of track.

By the late 1800s, there was a railroad line in every county in Ohio. Most Ohioans felt the impact of the railroad in one way or another.

Ohio was a middle state in the East-West trade route. This, plus its fine systems of transportation, gave the state a big economic advantage. Ohio became one of the highest populated, one of the richest, and one of the most important states in the nation.

7. New people brought ideas for a better system of education.

Public schools. In the early years, few children went to school. They were either too busy with chores, too poor, or too far from the school. Education was more common after 1821, when the General Assembly passed a bill which set up school districts in the state. An 1825 law ruled that each county could take money from the property tax to pay for education. Thus, by 1825 there was a system of free public schools in Ohio.

One *champion* of education was Samuel Lewis, who became the first state superintendent of common schools. Lewis had come from Massachusetts where there was a very good public school system. In his first year as superintendent, Lewis traveled over 1,500 miles on horseback around the state. He wanted to make certain that the students had the best type of schooling possible.

Going to school in the early days. Long after public schools appeared, the one-room schoolhouse

An early train crosses a trestle in Cleveland.

was still used in rural districts. In the cities, it was common to have two grades in one room. While the teacher worked with the students in one grade, the others were supposed to study.

The subjects were reading, writing, and arithmetic. Some years later, grammar, geography, and government were added.

Students were expected to behave in school. If a child were naughty, the teacher might rap him or her over the knuckles with a stick. The worst offenders were even paddled!

The children usually walked a long way to school, especially those who lived in the country. Classes in rural schools started early in the morning and closed early each afternoon so children could do their farm chores. The city school day was similar to that of the present time. In 1829, the law said that students had to be in school for at least three months a year. Six months of schooling was the goal of Ohio schools by 1850.

High schools. There were few high schools or secondary schools in Ohio prior to 1865, and most of those were privately owned by churches. The first public high school in the state was Elyria High School (1830) near Cleveland. High school subjects included chemistry, algebra, philosophy, botany, history, and literature.

Private schools. Even though students had to pay *tuition* to attend private schools, their families still had to pay taxes for public education. Many parents thought it was worth the extra money to see their children get good religious instruction in a parochial (church) school.

The Roman Catholics led the way in private education. The first Catholic nuns arrived in Cincinnati in 1824 to teach in the Catholic schools. Wherever there were large groups of Catholics, a church school began.

Lutherans, Episcopalians, and Presbyterians also had private schools. Some groups, such as the Amish and Mennonites, were charged with not meeting the state's school standards. Today, there are strict rules that must be followed by all the

The first free school for blacks in Ohio was built in 1831 at Harveysburg in Warren County. It was established by Elizabeth Harvey. The building is now on the National Register of Historic Places.

schools, both public and private. This allows for a nice blend of public and private schools in our state.

Education for blacks. Sadly, Ohio's public school system shut out certain children. Black students were not allowed to attend public schools until 1848. This was partly because blacks were not required to pay property taxes and did not help support the schools, but mostly because of feelings against blacks.

Almost a third of Ohio's blacks lived in Cincinnati, where some small schools were set up for them. In other places, whites would not let blacks build their own schools. A law in 1848 added blacks to property tax rolls. As a result, a school had to be provided in towns where there were 20 or more black children. In most cases where there were fewer than that, black children went to school with white children.

In 1849, the state lawmakers ruled that blacks and whites could not go to the same school. This law showed anti-black feelings present in the state.

William Holmes McGuffey (1800-1873) had a great influence on education in the United States. Together with his wife and brother, he wrote the McGuffey Readers, which taught not only reading but good moral lessons, good pronunciation, and good character. For years, school children all over the country used the McGuffey Spellers and Readers.

Segregation (separation of blacks from other students) in the public schools lasted until 1887, when the 1849 law was *repealed* (dropped).

Higher education. The plan to build colleges in the state started in early days. The Ohio Land Company arranged for money from the sale of land in two townships to be used for higher education. From this money, Ohio University was built at Athens in 1804, the first college in the state. Income from the Symmes Land Grant was used to build Miami University.

The first graduating class at Ohio University, in 1815, had only two students. Miami University at Oxford had 150 students in 1839, making it the largest college west of the Allegheny Mountains.

The first church college in the state was Kenyon College at Gambier in Knox County. Kenyon College was *chartered* in 1824, due to the efforts of Philander Chase of Worthington. Chase raised $10,000 from Episcopalians in England to be used to build the college. The two people who gave the most money were Lord Kenyon and Lord Gambier; thus the names for the college and the town. Like most Ohio colleges, Kenyon was for men only. (Since 1970, both women and men have attended there.)

There have been many other church colleges in Ohio. One of the best-known is Oberlin College (1833) which was the first *coeducational* (for both men and women) college in the nation. It was also the first college in the country to serve students of different races.

Women and education. While men could get into college quite easily, women were kept out. The belief of the day was that a woman did not need higher training to be a good wife and mother. Many women resented that type of thinking, even in the 1800s. Prior to 1830, schools for females were set up at Steubenville, Cincinnati, and Somerset. At first, music, penmanship, drawing, and needlework were taught. Later the women learned biology, chemistry, algebra, and philosophy.

There was still a need for a good women's college in the state. Bethania Crocker started one at Oxford which was as well thought of as Miami University. In 1830, Oxford Female Academy was opened. Later it became Western College and was kept as a women's school until 1974, when it was made part of Miami University. Lake Erie College for Women at Painesville is also a well-known school.

Statehood brought a wide range of changes to Ohio. It began as a wilderness whose best means of travel was by river. Within 60 years, it had become a complex region affected by eastern markets and improved means of travel. New wealth brought more people who, in turn, brought new ideas for a better state.

This growth was to be halted for a short time. The nation was on the brink of a civil war where brother would fight against brother.

WORDS FOR STUDY

delegates	siege	tuition
coeducational	maneuverability	segregation
sesquicentennial	premonition	repealed
pardon	feeder canal	chartered
confederation	champion	bill

QUESTIONS FOR REVIEW

1. What were some of the main concerns of the territory in the years of peace that followed the Treaty of Greene Ville?

2. Why was Governor St. Clair's plan to divide the Northwest Territory turned down?

3. In what year was Ohio accepted for statehood? What is unusual about the date of statehood?

4. Under the laws of the state constitution, who had the most power in government? Why was that true?

5. Which were the first two political parties in Ohio?

6. Briefly retell the struggle that was involved in making Columbus the permanent state capital.

7. What things about Simon Kenton made him a memorable frontiersman?

8. Why was the Battle of Tippecanoe important?

9. List the major battles of the War of 1812 that involved Ohioans. When did the war end in Ohio? When did it end in the rest of the country?

10. Why were the rivers important to Ohio, besides for transporting people?

11. What were the first two roadways in Ohio, and in which directions did they run?

12. What changes did canals bring to Ohio? Why did the canals eventually die out?

13. How many miles of railroad track were in Ohio in 1860? How much of the state was influenced by the railroads?

14. What role did private schools play in the growth of education?

15. What two groups of people were kept out of the schools in the beginning? Why?

16. Name two famous early colleges in Ohio and tell why they are important.

GOING FURTHER

1. What was the message of Tecumseh's speech to the Indian tribes in 1811?

2. Why did it take so long for public education to become common in the state?

3. How did changes in transportation affect the people who lived in Ohio?

FOR THOUGHT AND DISCUSSION

1. What kinds of problems might there have been in switching from territorial government to self-rule? What were the advantages and disadvantages of each?

2. What qualities did Tecumseh have that made him a good leader of his people? Do leaders today need those same traits? Why or why not?

3. How did the War of 1812 compare with other wars which had been fought on American soil? What were the advantages and the disadvantages of this war?

4. Why were better ways of transportation a major need at that time in Ohio's growth? Does transportation still have such an importance today? How?

5. How have the early school systems in our state influenced the quality of education?

PROJECTS AND REPORTS

1. Make a study of political parties in Ohio today to find out how they affect the making of new laws. Make a written report of your findings and conclude with your opinion on the matter.

2. Conduct a thorough study of the Ohio State Constitution and categorize the laws in a chart.

3. Choose any three articles from the state constitution and find current events that relate to the law. Set up a bulletin board display to share your discoveries with the class.

4. Research the development of any one mode of transportation in the state and make a graphic display to summarize its history.

5. Research and make a written report on any leader in Ohio from 1800 to 1860. Summarize the person's qualifications for leadership.

6. Research the history of education for women and present your report orally or in a graphic display.

7. Research the history of education for blacks and make a graphic display to show what steps have been taken toward equal opportunity in education.

DARLING NELLIE GRAY

Benjamin Hanby

1. There's a low green val-ley on the old Ken-tuck-y shore, Where I've
2. When the moon had clim'd the moun-tain, and the stars were shin-ing too, Then I'd
3. My eyes are get-ting blind-ed, and I can-not see my way; Hark! there's

whiled ma-ny hap-py hours a-way, A - sit-ting and a-sing-ing by the
take my dar-ling Nel-lie Gray, And we'd float down the riv-er in my
some — bod—y knock-ing at the door, O I hear the an-gels call-ing, and I

lit - tle cot-tage door Where lived my dar-ling Nel-lie Gray.
lit - tle red ca-noe, While my ban - jo sweet-ly I would play.
see my Nel-lie Gray, Fare - well to the old Ken-tuck-y shore.

1-2. O my poor Nel-lie Gray, they have tak-en you a-way, And I'll
3. O my dar-ling Nel-lie Gray, up in hea-ven there, they say, That they'll

nev-er see my dar-ling an-y more; I'm sit-ting by the riv-er and I'm
nev-er take you from me an-y more; I'm a-com-ing, com-ing, com-ing, as the

weep-ing all the day, For you've gone from the old Ken-tuck-y shore.
an - gels clear the way, Fare - well to the old Ken-tuck-y shore.

CHAPTER 6

THE CIVIL WAR PERIOD IN OHIO

1830-1868

MAIN POINTS

1. The slavery issue was a main cause of the Civil War.

2. Laws, particularly the Black Codes, made life in Ohio hard for blacks.

3. Ohioans were leaders in the abolitionist movement.

4. Many Ohioans helped runaways escape from slavery by the Underground Railroad.

5. Five events that directly led to the start of the Civil War were linked with Ohio.

6. Ohioans played an important role in the Civil War battles.

7. Except for the Copperheads, Ohioans at home gave a lot of support for the war effort.

8. Ohio furnished leadership for the nation during the Reconstruction era.

The American Civil War (1861-1865) was one of the most tragic periods in American and Ohio history. Americans fought each other and there were high casualties. Yet, the outcome was good. Slavery was banned forever in the United States.

1. The slavery issue was a main cause of the Civil War.

Slavery was a main *issue* of the war. Northerners were mostly against slavery, and most southerners were in favor of it. The laws of Ohio clearly outlawed slavery, and most Ohioans were opposed to

it. They believed it was wrong for one person to own another. Even as part of the Northwest Territory, Ohio had never legalized slavery.

On the other hand, slavery was a key part of the economics in the South. The huge cotton crops required much labor, and the cotton farmers felt they needed slaves to work the crops. Slave owners invested huge sums of money in slaves. A prime

Sojourner Truth, of Salem, was a leader in the movement to abolish slavery.

field worker cost about $1,500 in 1860. Some northerners wanted to free the slaves and let the master stand the loss. Others thought the owners should be paid for the freed slaves.

Southerners also thought of slavery as a system of education for the "uncivilized Africans."

Another issue that helped cause the war was called "state's rights." Most northerners thought the federal government should have power over the states. Southerners were of the opinion that the "state rules supreme." This meant that the state should make the final decision if the state and federal governments did not agree. The North had more people than the South, so they ruled in Congress. Southern states thought the only solution to this state's rights issue was to *secede* (withdraw) from the Union.

Three issues—slavery, economic differences, and state's rights—pulled the two sections of the nation apart. This division did not occur overnight. There were many events over a period of years which led to the Civil War.

2. Laws, particularly the Black Codes, made life in Ohio hard for blacks.

Blacks move into Ohio. In 1800 the black population of Ohio was about 350. By 1810 it had grown to 1,900. By 1820 Ohio ranked 12th in the nation with approximately 4,800 blacks.

Most blacks were poor and lived in the countryside. Yet few had enough money to buy a farm. Most worked as farm laborers or were *tenant farmers.* Tenant farmers lived on someone else's farm and worked for the owner. Some blacks were lucky enough to be given land. For instance, 37 ex-slaves from Virginia settled in Lawrence County in 1849. Their former master provided enough money to buy land and homes and to pay their expenses for one year. However, this example did not occur very often.

City blacks often could not find good jobs, even if they were skilled. White workers did not want to compete with blacks for jobs. One young black cabinetmaker finally found a job in Cincinnati. When he went to work, the white workers threw down their tools and refused to work alongside him. As a result, the owner dismissed the black man, and the others returned to work.

Henry Bibb was a runaway slave who found freedom in Canada. He published a newspaper called *Voice of the Fugitive.* In an 1851 edition of his paper, a song was printed which was sung by blacks on their journey to Canada. One verse of the song tells how disappointed they were in Ohio. It was sung to the tune of Stephen Foster's *Oh Susannah:*

Ohio's not the place for me;
For I was much surprised
So many of her sons to see
In garments of disquise.
Her name has gone throughout the world,
Free Labour, Soil and Men-
But slaves had better far be hurled
Into the Lion's Den.

Farewell Ohio!
I'm not safe in thee;
I'll travel on to Canada,
Where colored men are free.

The song might also have been prompted by the slave catchers that came into Ohio. They would kidnap blacks and sell them as slaves in the South.

Black Codes. Prompted to action by the large number of blacks entering the state, Ohio passed a series of laws between 1804 and 1807. These Black Codes were to limit the rights of blacks. For example, a black could not testify in court against a white. Blacks could not join the *militia.* Another law required blacks to register with a judge the name of each of their children. This listing cost 12-1/2 cents per child. An 1807 law required that free blacks post a *bond* (deposit) of $500 against becoming a public *charge* (responsibility), if they wanted to stay in the state.

This painting is entitled *Kept In*. What do you suppose this little girl might be thinking about?

Although blacks did not like those restrictions, many thought it was better than living in the South. Blacks kept coming to Ohio because it was the shortest route to freedom in Canada. Meanwhile, they hoped the Black Codes would be done away with soon.

As a result of the strict laws and the anti-black feelings of some Ohioans, racial problems increased.

The slavery issue got hotter in the 1850s when the U.S. Congress passed a new law to help southerners get back their runaway slaves. The law said that blacks accused of being runaways could be returned to slavery on the word of a man who claimed to be their owner. A dishonest slave catcher could say that any blacks were runaways and claim them as slaves!

The Ohio General Assembly of 1856-57 passed a series of laws which overruled the Fugitive Slave Laws. These Personal Liberty Laws said that Ohio jails could not be used to hold fugitive slaves. In other words, Ohio officials did not have to help return runaways. This was in direct opposition to federal law.

John Rankin lived on the banks of the Ohio River near Ripley. A light was always on in the house to act as a guide to runaway slaves crossing the river. The Rankin house was one of many stations on the Underground Railroad.

3. Ohioans were leaders in the abolitionist movement.

Regardless of the anti-black feelings in the state, Ohioans were some of the leading *abolitionists* in the nation.

The first abolitionist groups appeared in Ohio as early as 1815. Benjamin Lundy founded such a group at St. Clairsville in Belmont County. The purpose of Lundy's group was to draw attention to the plight of slaves and invite people to put an end to slavery. The members wrote letters to politicians and gave speeches on the evils of slavery.

Two Ohioans spread the word through published articles. In 1817 at Mount Pleasant, the Quaker Charles Osborn published the *Philanthropist*. This was the first American newspaper to promote the abolition of slavery. John Rankin put together a group of his anti-slavery letters in a book in 1826.

The Lane Seminary debates pointed out both sides of the issue. Many of the students at the Lane Seminary did volunteer work among the blacks in Cincinnati. They went to the homes and taught the children to read and write. Seminary students were in favor of *abolition.* Classes were cancelled at the seminary for 18 days as students debated the issue of slavery. The debates centered on whether men who owned slaves should free them at once and whether they should be paid for the loss.

As a result of the debates, 53 students and one professor left Lane Seminary. They went to Oberlin College, where their professor, Asa Mahan, became president. He invited blacks to enroll as students there.

After the debates, Ohio was more active in the abolitionist cause.

Other Ohioans speak out. Senator Thomas Morris is known as the first abolitionist senator in the United States. He spoke out against the use of slaves in the nation's capital.

Two more men active in the cause in the early years were Theodore Dwight Weld and James G. Birney. Weld got many people involved in the anti-slavery campaign, including Birney. Birney had owned slaves before he came to live in Cincinnati. In the 1840s he ran for president under the Liberty Party. That party wanted liberty for all, including blacks.

Birney started another abolitionist newspaper also called *The Philanthropist.* His paper was very critical of slavery. Fearing the loss of southern trade, leading businessmen in Cincinnati put pressure on Birney to stop his attacks. But he refused to budge.

In 1837 Birney was arrested and tried for hiding a fugitive slave. When he was convicted he was fined only $50 plus court costs. After the Birney trial, tensions grew stronger.

Runaway slaves on the Underground Railroad. What does this painting tell about the hardships they faced?

4. Many Ohioans helped runaways escape from slavery by the Underground Railroad.

There were many more people besides James G. Birney who helped slaves escape to freedom.

The *Underground Railroad* was a system to transport slaves out of the South and hide them from the law. Many of the slaves finally ended up in Canada.

The runaways were moved at night to avoid capture. Since Ohio was between the slave state of Kentucky and free Canada, it was a very important part of the escape route. Both whites and free blacks helped in the Underground Railroad. It began working as early as 1815. The price of an average slave was $1,500 at the peak of the movement. Around 50,000 to 75,000 slaves passed through Ohio. This meant that slave owners lost nearly $100 million in Ohio alone. Southerners were very angry.

One of the most active in the Underground Railroad was Levi Coffin. Coffin wrote that he first helped a slave escape when he was 15. Coffin had lived in the South, then in Indiana. He moved to Cincinnati in the 1840s where he became active in the movement.

Working on the Underground Railroad was dangerous. Coffin told of one narrow escape from slave hunters. There was a runaway living in Cincinnati near Sixth Street and Broadway. Coffin heard that slave hunters were in the area. A carriage was sent to the house and the runaway was moved to another station, or stop, on the Underground Railroad. Coffin wrote that 10 minutes after the runaway was moved, a posse of men entered the house where the runaway had been living!

Levi Coffin was called the "President of the Underground Railroad." According to his own

SOME UNDERGROUND RAILROAD ROUTES

Levi Coffin was called the "president of the Underground Railroad." What tasks would he have performed to help the escaping slaves?

Uncle Tom's Cabin. The strongest attack by the abolitionists was in a book printed in 1852. This book was Harriet Beecher Stowe's *Uncle Tom's Cabin.*

Harriet Beecher had lived in Cincinnati with her father, Lyman Beecher. She had visited among the blacks there and had been to Kentucky a few times to view slave life on *plantations.* In addition, she talked to some runaway slaves. From these experiences, Harriet Beecher Stowe wrote *Uncle Tom's Cabin* after she and her husband moved to Maine in 1850.

The book was a powerful novel which attacked the slave system. It said that slavery was totally bad for all slaves. The story told of beatings that were given to the saintly Uncle Tom, and of the daring escape made by Eliza Harris across the Ohio River.

figures, Coffin helped more than 3,000 slaves escape to freedom during his 20 years of activity.

John Rankin's place was a stop on the escape route. His home overlooked the Ohio River at Ripley and always had a light shining in the window. The light served as a guide for runaways to direct them across the river.

The story of another runaway slave became the background for a popular song of the late 1800s. The song is *Darling Nellie Gray.* It tells how a black man—Joe Shelby—felt when his darling Nellie Gray was snatched away and sold to a Georgia slave trader. The song was written by Benjamin Hanby. As a young boy, Hanby had given food to Shelby as he hid in the Hanby barn.

5. Five events that directly led to the start of the Civil War were linked with Ohio.

Over a period of 35 years, people took sides on the slavery issue. Five things happened between 1850 and 1860 that led to the start of a war.

Harriet Beecher Stowe. How did her book, *Uncle Tom's Cabin,* help lead to civil war?

Thousands of copies were sold, and many plays were based on the book. On the occasion when Abraham Lincoln met Harriet Beecher Stowe, his supposed greeting to her was, "So you're the little woman who wrote the book that made this great war!" People in the South were furious with the picture of plantation life as shown in *Uncle Tom's Cabin.*

The new Republican party is born. In 1854 Congress passed the Kansas-Nebraska Bill. This said that slaves could be taken into western areas where slavery had previously been outlawed. The Republican party was formed as a direct result of the passage of this bill. The Republican party was made up of people from different political backgrounds. The one idea which they all held in common was to stop the spread of slavery into the new territories.

The Republican party in Ohio was first organized on July 13, 1855, at a meeting in the Town Street Methodist Church in Columbus. Those at the meeting chose Salmon Chase of Cincinnati as their candidate for governor in the 1855 election. In a very good showing for the party's first effort, Chase won the election by more than 16,000 votes to become the first Republican governor in the nation.

There were some important results of this election. First, the Republican party showed that it was going to stay together. Second, the Republican candidate revealed that most Ohioans were against the spread of slavery. Third, Chase was a well-known abolitionist from one of the largest states in the West. His win showed that slavery had become the number one political issue in the nation.

John Brown was an abolitionist who led a raid on Harper's Ferry, Virginia, to try to free some slaves. He was forced to surrender and was later sentenced to hang. He became a hero for the abolitionist cause.

JOHN BROWN
1800 – 1859

The Oberlin-Wellington rescue case. A major incident over a runaway slave occurred in the communities of Oberlin and Wellington in 1858. A group of Oberlin citizens rescued an escaped slave from federal marshals at the nearby Wellington train station. In response, a federal jury charged 37 Oberlin and Wellington citizens with breaking the Fugitive Slave Law. Simon Bushnell and Charles Langston were the first two men tried in 1859. They were found guilty.

Abolitionists were upset by this case. A huge rally of 10,000 people met in Cleveland to protest the decision. The Ohio Supreme Court agreed with the federal jury and ruled that the Fugitive Slave Law was *constitutional.* This seemed to make the Personal Liberty Laws illegal. But most Ohioans kept on helping the runaways.

John Brown's raid sparks anger. John Brown's family moved to Ohio when he was five. He lived in Hudson and Akron for nearly 40 years before moving to Kansas (where he killed some pro-slavery leaders) and then to New England.

John Brown said that God had told him it was his duty to free the slaves. On the night of October 16, 1859, John Brown and 18 of his friends attacked a federal *arsenal* (a place where weapons are stored) at Harper's Ferry, Virginia. They were caught and Brown was tried. He was found guilty and was hanged in December.

Many northern abolitionists looked on John Brown as a hero for their cause. They began to write songs and poems about his great deeds. They seemed to forget that what he had done was against the law. Southerners thought there might be more people like John Brown just waiting to invade the South. They began to gather their weapons for a possible war between the North and the South.

The 1860 election led to secession. In November 1860, Abraham Lincoln was elected president of the United States. He carried Ohio by over 44,000 votes. Because Lincoln was anti-slavery, southern states made the decision to secede (withdraw) from the Union. South Carolina was the first to take action.

Ten other states soon followed. Together they formed the Confederate States of America.

The American Civil War was about to begin.

6. Ohioans played an important role in the Civil War battles.

By 1861, most Ohioans had come to believe that slavery was wrong. Even so, many did not want the war to start. People in the southern part of Ohio had close economic and personal ties with the southerners. Cincinnati businesses traded with the South. They worried about how a war might affect their profits.

Johnny Clem, the "Little Drummer Boy of Chickamauga," was the youngest person to serve in the Civil War. He was nine years old. Johnny later became a major-general in the army.

There were even some in Ohio who did not think that keeping the South in the Union was worth a war. One such peron was the editor of the *Ohio State Journal.* Following is part of an essay he wrote for the paper on November 13, 1860:

The object of the American Union is to provide for the common defence, general welfare, &c. It is so stated in the preamble to the Constitution. . . . Now, if any State or States wish to renounce the benefits of this general protection, how can they be compelled to continue the recipients of such advantages? . . .

The Civil War began April 12, 1861, when the South fired on the federal troops at Fort Sumter, South Carolina. President Lincoln called for 13,000 volunteers from Ohio and 30,000 people answered the call. By the end of the war Ohio had contributed 346,326 soldiers. A total of 11,237 died in battle, while 13,354 died from disease. Another 30,000 were permanently handicapped.

The soldiers wrote letters home, where their families waited for news of their safety. Joe Briggs of the Cleveland post office started the home

delivery service in 1862, to speed letters from the soldiers to their kin.

Preparation for war. Governor William Dennison, Jr., had a hard task to prepare so many men for war. There were training camps set up in Columbus and Cincinnati. Both were key places on transportation routes. It was important to set up protection there to be sure that troops and supplies could be moved along the rivers, roads, and railroads.

The Ohio General Assembly voted to spend one million dollars for the war. Governor Dennison sent an agent to New York to buy weapons. There were few guns, but the agent found a good buy on tent poles. He sent huge numbers of tent poles to Columbus!

Once the war was on, soldiers faced many problems other than fighting. One member of the Second Ohio Volunteer Infantry wrote that he had been issued a wool uniform in June. In his gear were a musket, a knapsack, canteens, ammunition, and a change of underclothing. He also had a dresscoat, an overcoat, an army blanket, a rubber blanket,

Camp Chase in Columbus was used primarily as a prison for Confederate soldiers.

and sewing material. Imagine how hard it was to carry all that on a long march!

Food was sometimes good and sometimes bad. One soldier going to training camp said that the rations were of the best kind. He got coffee, sugar, beans, molasses, potatoes, hominy, bread, sowbelly, and shoulders. On the other hand, an army nurse said, "I grew sick of the mould, which rose like dust when boxes were opened, and seeing fat worms drop out of broken biscuits."

Many soldiers also got sick. In dirty conditions of the camps and battlefields, disease spread quickly.

George B. McClellan, commander. At the start of the war, George Brinton McClellan was appointed to lead the Ohio Militia. McClellan was a graduate of West Point military academy. Under his command, Ohio troops defeated Confederates at the Battle of Philippi, near Wheeling, Virginia, in 1861. The troops also won several other skirmishes near there. These wins saved that territory for the Union. West

Virginia became a Union state two years later.

The hard year, 1862. In the second year, it became apparent that the war would be a long one. While the North had more people and money, the South showed better military skill.

One of the bloodiest battles of the Civil War was fought in April 1862. Ulysses S. Grant, a graduate of West Point military academy, led Union troops in the Battle of Shiloh, at Pittsburg Landing, Tennessee. Over 2,000 soldiers from Ohio alone were killed or wounded. However, Grant won the battle.

There was another military event for Ohioans in 1862. A Confederate army of 12,000 under General Kirby Smith invaded Kentucky and threatened Cincinnati. The new Ohio governor, David Tod, called for 50,000 volunteers to defend the city. Farmers packed up their squirrel-shooting guns and left their fields to meet at Cincinnati. They joined troops under the command of General Lew Wallace. The "Squirrel Hunters" never saw any action. General Smith turned back to Tennessee.

The "Squirrel Hunters" from Cincinnati were issued this certificate when they were dismissed from duty.

Ambrose E. Burnside (left) arrested Clement Vallandigham for criticizing the U.S. government's role in the Civil War.

The crucial year, 1863. The most *crucial* year of the Civil War was 1863. The war was not going well for the North. Confederates had won some big victories in the East. The length of the war caused more people to side with the anti-war *critics.* More and more men became *deserters.* The most serious anti-war activity involved Clement L. Vallandigham.

Vallandigham was a former U.S. congressman from Dayton. As publisher of the *Dayton Empire,* he was a vocal critic of the war from the very first. He told men not to enlist.

General Ambrose E. Burnside, Ohio commander, was angered by Vallandigham. Burnside issued General Order No. 38 in reaction to Vallandigham's work. This military law made it illegal for anyone to show sympathy for the South or to speak out against the U.S. government.

In May 1863, Vallandigham gave a very harsh speech against the government. In the audience at Mt. Vernon were several of Burnside's officers who took notes on the speech. Burnside ordered the arrest of Vallandigham.

A military court in Cincinnati found him guilty of treason for violating Order No. 38. He was sentenced to prison for the rest of the war. Vallandigham claimed that a military court had no right to try him since he was not under military rule. President Lincoln realized the danger of this decision. He changed the sentence and *banished* Vallandigham into the Confederacy.

This action did not remove him from the Ohio political scene. Vallandigham escaped to Canada. From there, he ran for governor of Ohio in the election of 1863. John Brough of Cleveland was the Union party candidate. (The Union party was formed in 1861 when the Democrats who favored war joined with the Republicans.) Although many people liked Vallandigham, Ohio soldiers voted against him. They did not like his anti-war activities.

If Vallandigham had won in Ohio, other states might have been persuaded to quit the war without a Union victory. In a mood of great happiness, President Lincoln sent a telegraph to governor-elect Brough claiming, "Glory be to God on highest; Ohio has saved the Union!"

Morgan's raid. Ohioans at home had their first taste of military action in July 1863. It was then that Confederate cavalry officer General John Hunt

Confederate General John Hunt Morgan made a quick raid into Ohio in July 1863.

Morgan led 2,400 men across the Ohio River into Indiana and Ohio. Morgan's raid lasted from July 9 until July 12. His motive was to draw Union troops from the battles in other places.

Morgan's men crossed into Ohio north of Cincinnati. They rode across southern Ohio searching for a place to recross the Ohio River and go back to the South. People in the path of Morgan's raid fled their homes. The state militia and federal forces followed Morgan, but did not confront him in a fight. The high waters of the swollen Ohio River made it very hard for Morgan's men to cross over to Kentucky. Some of them made it safely across the Ohio River after a small skirmish in Meigs

County. Morgan and the rest were captured near Salineville in Columbiana County. This was the northernmost advance of Confederate troops during the war.

John Morgan and a few of his officers were placed in the Ohio State Penitentiary. Morgan escaped by digging out in November 1863. He rode a train to Cincinnati and returned to the South. In terms of battles, Morgan's raid was of little value. Yet, it did cost Ohio over one million dollars to put troops in the field to chase the raiders out.

The Civil War ended in 1865. During its last two years, little of importance happened in Ohio. It was a challenge to get enough men to fill Ohio's *quota*

The "Fighting McCooks" from Carroll County had 17 members in the military. All but one became officers, and 12 became generals.

for soldiers. But there were no more outbursts of anti-war violence in the state.

Ohio soldiers played an important part in bringing the war to an end. Its troops fought in almost every major battle until the end of the war. Women and men had joined the army in the fever of excitement. But they found the glory of war soon faded. As one nurse wrote:

Dead and dying lay amongst them [the soldiers in the field], and they were carried under tents and rolled together like the logs of a corduroy road. . . . Worms soon bred in the fresh wounds.

There had been a tragic loss of lives and thousands of injuries.

Several of Ohio's military leaders gained fame. General Ulysses S. Grant became commander in chief of the Union forces in 1864. It was Grant's leadership that finally caused General Robert E. Lee of the South to surrender at Appomattox Court House, Virginia, on April 12, 1865. From this event,

U.S. Grant got the nickname "Unconditional Surrender Grant."

Grant was not a popular general. During the move on Richmond, Virginia, he lost more men than Lee had lost from his whole army of Northern Virginia. He forced Lee's men to fight until they were exhausted. Lee then surrendered to Grant at Appomattox Court House. Even so, Grant stayed active in politics after the war. He was twice elected president of the United States.

Another Ohio general who gained fame during the war was William Tecumseh Sherman of Lancaster. He was a graduate of West Point. Sherman was Grant's chief aid during the western campaign. When Grant became commander of all Union forces, Sherman became the commander of the western armies. Sherman's greatest success came when he led his army on a march from Atlanta, Georgia, to the sea in 1864. Sherman's army moved deep into enemy lands. They destroyed everything of military value along a trail 60 miles wide and

260 miles long from Atlanta to Savannah, Georgia. The blow of a Union army marching unopposed through the center of "Dixie" helped bring a speedy end to the war.

General Phil Sheridan from Somerset was a graduate of West Point. As a Union cavalry commander, he did to the Shenandoah Valley in Virginia what Sherman did in Georgia.

Lincoln's death. The thrill of victory was spoiled by news of the death of President Lincoln by an assassin's bullet, April 14, 1865. Lincoln had become more popular by the end of the war. Thousands of people mourned his death.

7. Except for the Copperheads, Ohioans at home gave a lot of support for the war effort.

Copperheads opposed the war. Even while the Civil War was in progress, not everyone at home was in favor of it. Volunteers for the army began to decline in 1862. A *draft* (law to force men to sign up) was put in place to fill Ohio's share of 74,000 soldiers.

The loudest critics of the war were called "Copperheads." They were the group of Democrats who favored peace. The best-known Copperhead in the nation was Vallandigham. Many other peace Democrats were also newspaper editors. They wrote editorials that criticized the government. They urged men to resist the draft. They wanted an immediate end to the war, even if it meant the South would become a separate nation.

Before the war was over, 11 peace Democrats were arrested. Dr. Edson Olds of Lancaster, John W. Kees of Circleville, and Archibold McGregor of Canton were three of them. Most were put into jail without a jury trial. Dr. Olds was in jail in New York City for six months before he was released. In 1863, he sued Governor Tod for kidnapping, but nothing ever came of it.

Women run the relief effort. Have you ever wondered how the families of the soldiers got along while the men were off fighting a war? At the start

Mary Ann Ball Bickerdyke was one of many women who nursed sick and wounded soldiers during the Civil War. She had a wagon loaded with herbs, medicines, and other supplies. "Old Whitey," her horse, pulled the wagon from one campsite to another.

of the Civil War there were no groups like the American Red Cross to help families in emergencies. But by the end of the war there were *civic* and church organizations to give aid. The Cleveland Soldier's Aid Society of Northern Ohio was the first of its kind in the nation.

Women were the chief workers and managers in the relief organizations. They provided food and shelter for the recruits during the first days of the war. They gathered blankets, money, and clothing to send to the soldiers in the field. The women prepared meals for soldiers who were in Ohio. They also gave food, clothing, and fuel to the soldiers' families.

Cincinnati, Columbus, and Cleveland relief agencies later became branches of the United States

Sanitary Commission. The main job of this group was to organize all of the various relief efforts in the North. The Cincinnati branch was the leader in this category because it was so close to the fighting. In 1862, the Cincinnati relief agency sent doctors and nurses, along with 32 steamboats full of hospital supplies, to the battlefields.

The United States Christian Commission had branches in Ohio. This agency helped meet the religious needs of the soldiers. The commission took Bibles and religious services to the men. Ministers, rabbis, and priests became chaplains. They went out into the battlefields to take care of the soldiers' religious needs.

All of the various state agencies and volunteer groups helped ease the suffering caused by the Civil War.

Agriculture helped in the war effort. A good variety of crops was produced in Union states. The South's crops were mostly cotton, and soldiers couldn't eat cotton! This gave the North a big advantage over the South.

In the 1850s, Ohio took the lead in the production of corn and wool. Only one other state produced more wheat. Ohio's 1860 crop was the largest ever up to that time. Ohio farmers were called on to produce even more products when the war started.

LOTTIE MOON CLARK, SPY

THERE were many spies for both the North and the South during the Civil War. One of the best was Charlotte Moon Clark from Hamilton, Ohio. As a spy for the Confederate States, she was so good at her job that the U.S. Secretary of War offered a $10,000 reward for her, dead or alive. How did Lottie Moon become a spy?

Lottie grew up in Oxford in the 1830s and 1840s, across the street from Miami University. She was quite popular—pretty and charming. She met Ambrose E. Burnside, who was a recent graduate of the military academy at West Point. Apparently, they fell in love and planned to marry. But at their wedding, Lottie changed her mind and refused to go through with it.

In 1840, she married James Clark of Hamilton. He was a lawyer and a Copperhead. Clark was asked to deliver a message to Confederate agents in Kentucky. Lottie offered to do the deed, for she thought a woman was less likely to be thought a spy than a man was. That trip began her career.

She made many trips into the South. One time, however, she was caught on her return trip and was taken to Cincinnati. She went before the commanding officer of the region to be sentenced and must have expected the worst possible punishment—death. To her surprise, the commander was none other than General Ambrose E. Burnside! Though he remembered being jilted on their wedding day, he still had affection for Lottie. He released her to return home if she promised not to spy again. Evidently, that episode ended her career.

Lottie Moon Clark died in 1895.

Blacks fought for the North during the Civil War. This group is part of the Ohio Volunteer Infantry, 126th Regiment.

The large number of cattle made Ohio third in the nation and Ohio hogs ranked sixth. In addition, Ohio cattle farmers began to experiment in breeding different types of cattle. The purpose was to start a new breed which had more meat on it. The same thing was done with hogs. As a result, "Scioto cattle" and "Poland China hogs" became nationally known for their quality of meat.

Ohio's production of wool increased. The state ranked first in that category. Much of the wool was used to make uniforms for the soldiers.

Because of these good supplies, Union troops were usually well fed and clothed. Seldom did a Union soldier go into battle on an empty stomach. The same was not true for the Confederate troops.

Ohio farmers made money during the war. Due to the increased demand, the prices of farm products rose. Wheat went up by nearly $1.50 a bushel. The cost of corn increased 50 cents a bushel and wool rose nearly 40 cents a pound. Farmers spent their money either to produce more goods or to buy other items. This spread more money around and all parts of the economy gained.

The need for more farm products led to the development of large farm machinery. Reaping machines to harvest wheat came on the scene in Ohio during the 1850s. Corn planters, steel plows, and much other labor-saving equipment helped the farmers do their work. Ohio led the nation in manufacturing agricultural equipment during this decade.

Industry grew during the war. The North had more than 90% of all industry in the United States in the mid-1800s. There were also plenty of railroad lines to move the products to market. This gave the North a stronger economy than the South.

Ohio's industries helped in the outcome of the Civil War. In the 1860s, Ohio ranked fourth in the nation in manufacturing. In response to the demands of war, factories and businesses grew.

Lack of workers was a problem during the war. The women of Ohio took jobs in the factories. However, it was hard for the women to work in the factories and care for their homes at the same time.

There were many industries. The most important products were, in order: flour and grist mill products, rolled and forged iron, men's clothing, agricultural tools, pig iron, packed meats, and lumber. Nearly 60 gunboats for the Union forces were built and equipped in Cincinnati.

Ohio's industry played an important part in the war effort.

8. Ohio furnished leadership for the nation during the Reconstruction era.

The 12 years after the Civil War are called the Reconstruction era. The South was *devastated* by the war. Farm lands were trampled. Cities had been burned down. The political structure of the South was ruined. Southern states had to be rebuilt and put back together. It took a long time because there was little money to work with. In addition, there were terms to be worked out with the government in order to bring the South back into the Union.

The issue of the black vote. The main problems Ohio faced after the war centered on treatment of blacks. The *prejudice* that people felt before the war did not disappear overnight. Many whites did not believe that blacks should be given equality in all things.

The question of whether or not blacks should get to vote became a political issue. The

Republicans supported the idea, while the Democrats were opposed to the black vote.

In 1865, the Union party won the election for governor. Their candidate, Jacob D. Cox, did not believe the two races could live together peacefully. He suggested that a territory in the southern part of the United States be set up as a place for blacks to live. Cox was elected by only 28,000 votes.

The black vote was an issue in the 1867 election. The Fourteenth Amendment to the U.S. Constitution gave certain rights to all people. But it did not include the right of blacks to vote. The amendment was passed in Ohio by the General Assembly in 1867.

In the Ohio election that year the Republican party (formerly the Union party) nominated General Rutherford B. Hayes of Cincinnati for governor. Republicans put an amendment on the ballot that would allow blacks to vote in Ohio. The amendment failed by 5,000 votes, but Hayes won by 3,000. This showed that prejudices did not die easily.

The Fifteenth Amendment gives blacks the vote. One of the good things to come about during President Grant's term was the Fifteenth Amendment to the U.S. Constitution. The Ohio General Assembly approved it in 1869. This law stated that no person could be denied the right to vote because of race, creed, or previous condition of servitude. The state senate approved the amendment by only two votes, and the house passed it by only one. This margin was not as close as it seems. Amendments must be approved by a three-fourths vote, rather than by a simple majority.

Also during Grant's term, all but three of the southern states filled the requirements to come back into the Union.

The rest of the century for Ohio would be spent in building its economy. The population of the state had grown from several directions. These new people added strength to the work force. Business and industry got the benefits. A period of growth was ahead.

U.S. GRANT, PRESIDENT

ULYSSES S. Grant was born in Point Pleasant, Ohio, in 1822. He gained fame during the Civil War as commander in chief of the Union armies.

The Republicans chose Grant as their candidate for president in 1868. (Grant had never been very *outspoken* on political matters. In fact, the Democrats had considered him as a possible candidate for *their* party.) Grant won the election that year.

President Grant proved to be a much better soldier than a president. He lacked both the political wisdom and leadership skills needed to pull the nation back together after the Civil War.

Grant liked to associate with men of wealth. His personal honesty was never in doubt, but his choice of less-than-honest people for office was questioned. Apparently, Grant did not know that some of his aides were involved in crooked deals. There was an attempt by some Republicans to get Grant out of office in the 1872 election. However, he won that year by more than one million votes.

During President Grant's second term in office, many dishonest acts began to show up. One of the scandals involved his private secretary, Orville Babcock. Babcock was accused of cheating the government out of liquor taxes by making false reports. This affair became known as the Whiskey Ring Scandal. The president tried

to defend Babcock. He lost popularity as a result. There were other *corrupt* events on the national level. The public blamed Grant since he was the president.

In 1880, Grant tried for a third term. No person had ever been elected as president more than two terms, at this time. However, the Republicans did not nominate him as their candidate. Out of a job, Grant wrote and sold his memoirs to keep the family from poverty. President Grant and his wife lived their later years in Illinois and then New York, where he died in 1885.

RUTHERFORD B. HAYES, PRESIDENT

RUTHERFORD B. Hayes was born in Delaware, Ohio, in 1822. He graduated from Kenyon College and the Harvard Law School. He served as a major-general in the Civil War. He was three times governor of Ohio.

Hayes was a champion of civil service *reform*. Civil servants are those people who are hired or appointed to work for the government. They are not elected officials. Civil service reformers wanted civil servants to be chosen because of *what* they knew, rather than *whom* they knew. Before this time, people were often given civil service jobs due to their friendships with government officials. This was called the spoils system. Often, the people hired to work for the government were not qualified employees. Hayes wanted to change this system.

Hayes was chosen as the Republican candidate for president in 1876. The Democrats chose Samuel J. Tilden of New York. The election that year was one of the most unusual in American history. Tilden seemed to be the winner in the public voting. But when the *electoral college* voted, there were 20 votes in *dispute*. The electoral college actually chooses the president. Each state gets electoral votes equal to its number of U.S. senators and congressmen. The party that wins the *popular* vote in the state gets all of the electoral votes.

Tilden had 184 electoral votes and Hayes had 165. There were 20 votes in dispute. Tilden needed only one of the 20 to be elected president. Hayes needed all 20 votes to win. An electoral commission was set up to decide who should have how many of the 20 votes. After a great debate, the commission decided that all 20 of the votes should go to Hayes. Rutherford B. Hayes became the president of the United States by the margin of one electoral vote!

As president, Hayes did bring trust and honesty back into government. He did not fully succeed in getting civil service reforms. But in the process of trying, he made many enemies among Republican leaders.

In 1877, President Hayes withdrew the federal troops from the last three states in the South. This resulted in a charge by the Democrats that Hayes had made a deal with those states. Democrats called it the "Corrupt Bargain of 1876." Reconstruction was almost over.

Hayes was known for banning the use of liquor at White House functions to avoid losing temperance votes. His wife, Lucy, was unfairly nicknamed "Lemonade Lucy." Even so, the White House was a gracious place to visit. Mrs. Hayes was a very fine hostess as first lady of the United Sates.

Hayes wanted to serve only one term as president. He did not seek re-election in 1880. He and Mrs. Hayes retired to private life at their home in Fremont, Ohio. Mrs. Hayes died in 1889 and President Hayes died in 1893.

WORDS FOR STUDY

issue	plantation	civic
secede	constitutional	devastated
tenant farmer	arsenal	prejudice
militia	crucial	outspoken
bond	critics	corrupt
charge	deserter	reform
abolitionist	banished	electoral college
abolition	quota	dispute
Underground	draft	popular
Railroad		

QUESTIONS FOR REVIEW

1. What were the three issues of the Civil War?

2. What were the Black Codes?

3. What was life like for blacks in pre-Civil War Ohio?

4. How did abolitionists work to abolish slavery?

5. Why were the Lane Seminary debates important?

6. Why did the Underground Railroad operate at night?

7. Name three Ohioans who were active in the Underground Railroad.

8. What five events between 1850 and 1860 directly led to war?

9. How did *Uncle Tom's Cabin* affect the slavery issue?

10. What action led to the birth of the Republican party?

11. What were conditions like for soldiers and nurses in the war?

12. Why was 1862 a hard year?

13. Why was Vallandigham arrested? What was the final outcome of the event?

14. What was the effect of Morgan's raid?

15. Name three Ohio military leaders who gained fame during the war.

16. What group of people at home opposed the war?

17. What role did women play in supporting the war effort?

18. How did agriculture and industry help win the war?

19. What law gave blacks the right to vote and when did it pass?

GOING FURTHER

1. How did the Ohio Personal Liberty Laws affect the Fugitive Slave Law?

2. Why was Ulysses S. Grant considered to be a better soldier than a president?

3. What role did newspapers play in spreading opinions about slavery and war?

4. How would you describe the feelings of Ohioans toward blacks prior to the Civil War? after the war?

FOR THOUGHT AND DISCUSSION

1. Ohioans and people from other states broke the laws of the land to help in the Underground Railroad. Do you think their disobedience was justified? Can you think of an instance today when it would be morally right to disobey a law?

2. Compare and contrast the treatment of blacks in Ohio between 1865 and 1867 with the actions taken against Indians in earlier days.

3. What is equality? Can equality be guaranteed by law?

PROJECTS AND REPORTS

1. Read and research the Fourteenth Amendment to the U.S. Constitution. What specific civil rights were granted by the law?

2. Study the Civil War history of your own community. Make a written or oral report to the class to relate your findings.

3. Locate and read excerpts from a diary written between 1850 and 1880. Retell at least two events from the diary to other members of the class.

4. Research and make a written report on any leader from your community or the state who was active between 1830 and 1880. Summarize the person's accomplishments.

5. Construct a map showing the major battles and campaigns of the Civil War. Compare your map to topographic maps of the various states to find out what role geography played in the Civil War strategies. Summarize your findings in an oral report to the class.

Slum areas developed in the industrial cities because the poor of the cities had little money. They lived in buildings called tenements.

CHAPTER 7

INDUSTRY COMES TO OHIO

1868-1900

MAIN POINTS

1. By 1900, cities in Ohio had become manufacturing centers.

2. Problems between labor and management appeared as Ohio became an industrial state.

3. Rapid growth during the industrial period caused many problems for cities.

4. European immigrants seeking a better life swelled Ohio's population in the late 1800s.

5. Wealthy businessmen used their influence to win political offices.

6. A surplus of farm products and manufactured goods helped cause a depression in 1893.

Ohio's industries grew quickly in the late 1800s. The state had many raw materials which were shipped by train to factories. There they were made into goods and sold throughout the country. The state's location gave it a key role in meeting the needs of a growing nation.

1. By 1900, cities in Ohio had become manufacturing centers.

Cincinnati was the state's largest factory town at the time. About 297,000 people lived there and plenty of jobs were to be had. One firm (business) in Cincinnati was Proctor and Gamble, which started out as a maker of candles, but switched to making soap. Other plants in the "Queen City" made beer, playing cards, and farm machines.

Cleveland took the lead from Cincinnati as the state's center of manufacturing after 1890, with

There were many pork-packing plants like this one in Cincinnati. That is why Cincinnati was called "Porkopolis" for many years.

Ohio had one of the biggest oil refinery businesses in the nation. This is part of John D. Rockefeller's Standard Oil Refinery in Cleveland, about 1889.

nearly 261,000 people. A main advantage that the city had was good transportation. At the mouth of the Cuyahoga River was a fine port for boats. Trains carried steel from the Mahoning Valley to plants and mills in the cities. From there, steel and goods were shipped to other states all over the nation.

Cleveland was made a refining site when John D. Rockefeller built the Standard Oil Company. Drugs, chemicals, electrical supplies, cigars, tools, copper and brass, engines, and sheet iron were made there, too.

Columbus was the third largest city by 1890 with more than 88,000 people. It had more than 300 factories which made books, wagons and carriages, tinware, gas engines and pumps, and electric motors. This was a change for a place where mostly farm goods had been sold.

Toledo was one of the last cities to be settled. It was called the Black Swamp area due to water which covered the region in early times. In the mid-1800s, Toledo began to prosper as a port city and factory town. Its industries made sewing machines, shoes, doors, safety pins, and glass.

Dayton shops and plants produced farm tools and iron and brass goods. The National Cash Register Company there was the largest of its kind in the world.

There were other cities which became factory centers by 1900. By the 1920s, Ohio ranked as one of the top five industrial states in the country. What were some of the major industries in your area prior to 1900?

As business grew, many problems came up which needed to be solved.

2. Problems between labor and management appeared as Ohio became an industrial state.

One tough problem to come to the new factory towns involved *labor* (workers) and *management* (owners). The issue was a simple one. Labor wanted as much pay as it could get, along with good working conditions. Management sought to pay wages as low as they could so profits would be high.

Some firms hired women and children when they could, because they would work for less pay than men.

Poor working conditions. Wages for factory labor after the Civil War were quite low. Skilled workers at that time earned about $7.00 a week. In the 1880s, pay rose to $13.50 a week. But by 1900, there had been only a small wage increase and owners were making bigger profits.

Work conditions were often quite poor. Factories did not have much fresh air nor were they well lighted. There were also safety risks. It was common for women's long hair to get caught in the machines with which they worked.

Workers who griped or asked for better conditions were often fired. Sometimes they were threatened with force or were roughed up.

Labor unions come on the scene. Workers learned that they would have more power if they joined together. The owners would not dare fire *all* of them if they went as a group to the boss with a complaint. As a result, *labor unions* were started in Ohio and other states.

Labor wanted the right of *collective bargaining*. This meant that workers and management could meet to discuss their problems and try to find a *com-*

William Green from Coshocton became a labor leader. He succeeded Samuel Gompers as the president of the A.F. of L.

promise solution. As a last resort, the unions wanted the right to *strike* (stop work) in order to get their needs met. How does a strike put pressure on the owners?

There had been a few unions prior to the Civil War, but they were not very strong. A main goal of labor now (1880s) was to form national unions. They felt that a group with a lot of members from all over the country would have more bargaining power than a small, local one.

The first national union that survived was the American Federation of Labor (A.F. of L.). The A.F. of L. came to Columbus in 1886. Its members were from skilled labor unions throughout the nation. Other unions, such as the United Mine Workers, were organized in Ohio in the late 1800s.

Here is a short outline of the rights of workers and of owners:

Worker Rights	Owner Rights
Fair pay	*Get fair work for fair pay*
Safety on the job	*Run own business*
Reasonable length of work day	*Make profit*

Issues between labor and management over the years have been based on these rights.

Strikes cause damage. The state's worst strikes took place in the coal mining industry. Mine work was a job filled with much danger. Workers faced the risk of cave-ins, fires, explosions, and poisonous gas. In spite of these dangers, pay for mine workers was quite low.

Coal mine operators often forced their employees to live in company towns where they had to pay high rent to the owners. Because they had to buy their food from the company store where prices were high, miners often went in debt to their bosses.

Miners were angered by these and other problems with their jobs. At times they went on strike to try to get better working conditions. One of the worst mine strikes occurred in the Hocking Valley district in 1884. A number of workers were laid off and a strike was called. Mine shafts, tunnels, and bridges were set afire. Mine owners brought in workers from other places to break the strike. In the end, the Ohio National Guard was sent to restore order and put an end to the trouble.

The coal mines burned with great heat for such a long time that farmers in the area were able to dig baked potatoes from the ground! Attempts to cut the source of air to the mines have failed. Some Perry County and Hocking County mines are still burning today.

Reform movements in the 1900s would help solve some of the labor-management problems. Meanwhile, industries kept on growing and more people got jobs as factory workers.

The late 1800s had many labor disputes. A coal mine strike in the Hocking Valley became violent. Smoke can be seen rising from the underground fires at New Straitsville.

JAMES A. GARFIELD, PRESIDENT

IN 1880, James A. Garfield was the fourth man from Ohio to be made president of the United States. He was born (1831) in a Cuyahoga County log cabin. His father died two years later and the family had a struggle to make ends meet. As a youth, Garfield worked as a tow boy on the Ohio Canal near his home. Tow boys led mule teams which pulled the boats along the canals.

He was sent to the state senate in the late 1850s, where he served until the Civil War broke out. Garfield became a major-general during the war. In 1863, he was elected to the U.S. House of Representatives, where he served for 18 years.

He went to the Republican National Convention in 1880 as the campaign manager for a friend from Ohio. When they failed to choose any of the favored candidates, Garfield was asked to run. He was well-known in Congress and was a solid Republican.

Garfield won the election, but served as president for only 6½ months. He was shot by a man who was angry about not getting a job in the federal government. Garfield hung onto life for 2½ months, then died September 19, 1881. His tomb is in Cleveland.

3. Rapid growth during the industrial period caused many problems for cities.

The new factories created many new jobs in the state. Because there were no cars or busses in which to ride, most of the workers walked to their jobs. As a result of having to live close to the factories, cities grew rapidly during the late 1800s. Hundreds of people from the farms, from the East, and from Europe moved here to find jobs.

The city governments were not ready to care for all the new people. It was hard to meet the needs of such a fast-growing population. As an example, in 1870 Cleveland had a hard time finding a supply of clean water. Their main source was a pipe which brought water from Lake Erie. The line stretched 300 feet out into the lake and was 12 inches below the lake's surface. This supply of water might have been adequate, but for one fact: the city's garbage boats dumped city wastes into the lake. The garbage was often returned to the city through the water pipes!

These people suffered the effects of unemployment and crowding around the turn of the century as they waited in line for food handouts.

public schools, colleges, and health care clinics. There were theaters, libraries, art galleries, museums, and other cultural places.

Four main problems for the cities had to be solved to make them good places in which to live and work. First, they needed to have enough money on which to operate. This goal was made hard to reach by rules of the state government. There was a limit on their right to tax and to borrow funds.

The second problem was to get rid of state meddling in city affairs. This would later be called the issue of *home rule.*

The third major need was to reduce the control of "city bosses." A city boss was a person who had much power in city government. While some of the city bosses served with the best interests of the city in mind, others gave out jobs to favored members of their own political parties. This would help them get more votes in the next election.

The fourth major problem cities needed to solve was public *apathy.* Many people did not care to help make the city a better place in which to live. As long as they did not vote or get involved in civic affairs, the bosses continued to rule.

> Can you see evidence of any of these four problems in your community today? If so, what do you think would be a way to solve the problem?

4. European immigrants seeking a better life swelled Ohio's population in the late 1800s.

All through the 1800s, people *immigrated* (moved) from Europe to the United States hoping to find a better way of life. America had land for farming, jobs in the cities, and freedom for people of all countries.

Most of the immigrants came first to New York City, where many of them stayed. But quite a few moved west to start new lives. Since the main routes of travel ran through Ohio in the late 1800s, many of the people liked what they saw and chose to stay.

Slums arose in the cities because there were too few clean places to live. A lot of people were crowded into *tenement* houses, which were often not well kept. Those who lived there sometimes tossed their trash into the streets and alleys. In the 1870s, the Over-the-Rhine area helped Cincinnati gain the "honor" of having more people per square mile than any other city in the nation. Some of Cleveland's residents lived in tar paper shanties and shacks. Disease spread quickly in such poor living conditions.

There were also some good things about city life. There were plenty of jobs. The cities had good

The Over-the-Rhine region of Cincinnati shows the difference between the city rich and the city poor. There were beautiful homes and there were slum areas.

In 1880, foreign-born persons made up about 12% of the state's total. More than 90% of the people spoke either English or German. A large part of those who spoke English had come from Ireland.

Irish-Americans had a great impact in the state. By 1870, there were over 82,000 Irish, most of whom lived in the large cities, but some of whom were very good farmers. Others worked on the Ohio Canal and helped build and lay railroad tracks. Cleveland had the largest group of Irish, and one part of the city was called Irish Town. Average wages for the Irish in the 1840s were 30 cents a day, which forced many to live in Cleveland tenements and the shack towns of Akron.

Most of the Irish were *devout* Roman Catholics. On St. Patrick's Day they came out in great numbers to honor the patron saint of their homeland. The old Irish songs were sung and there was much drinking of beer and dancing.

In politics most of the Irish voted for the Democratic party. Since they were the third largest group in the state, those seeking office made a special effort to gain their votes.

German-Americans made up the largest non-English speaking group in Ohio. By 1870, 182,000 Germans had settled all over the state. There were large German neighborhoods in Cincinnati, Akron, Dayton, Cleveland, and Columbus. Columbus's German Village today reminds us of the successful German community which grew up there. The Over-the-Rhine section was the center of Cincinnati's German culture. There were many tenements, but there were also neat and clean homes, beer gardens, and concert halls.

The Germans gained respect in the state for their hard work, *efficiency,* and *thrift.* They became lawyers, doctors, bakers, merchants, *brewers,* tailors, and tanners. Cincinnati soon became known as the brewery center of the nation.

Cincinnati became known as the brewery center of the nation. This business was just one of the industries which made Cincinnati the industrial center of the state until about 1890.

They built Lutheran and Catholic churches in their neighborhoods. They often set up newspapers in their own language and schools in which German was spoken. There were so many of them in the state that the General Assembly said the state constitution could be printed in German.

This group gave much to the culture of the state with their singing groups and their part in developing the theater. In politics, most of the Germans voted for Republicans.

By the 1900s, people had come to Ohio from most countries of Europe and some Asian nations. They added a great deal to the state's growth. Their effects were felt in the work force and in the culture of the state.

BENJAMIN HARRISON, PRESIDENT

BENJAMIN Harrison was born at North Bend, near Cincinnati, in 1833. He was the grandson of President William Henry Harrison, the first president from the state. He went to college at Miami University, then moved west to practice law. A general in the Civil War, his career in politics began in Indiana, where he lost the race for governor. He went on to serve in the U.S. Senate.

He was named by the Republicans to run against President Grover Cleveland in 1888. He won by a close vote. During his term six new states joined the Union.

Harrison lost to former President Cleveland in 1892. The loss was likely due to some bad money troubles that happened during Harrison's term.

He went back to his law practice in Indiana where he died in 1901.

5. Wealthy businessmen used their influence to win political offices.

Throughout the history of our state, most people have sought office in order to serve others. But in the late 1800s, rich men began to seek public office for their own interests. They wanted to make laws that would help them and their friends get richer. On the other hand, there were candidates who wanted to spread the wealth to many people. Those two groups clashed over many issues.

The Pendleton-Payne election. The first sign of the rich men taking control came in 1885 when the General Assembly voted to choose a U.S. senator. Those who wanted the job were Democrat George H. Pendleton and Republican Henry B. Payne. Pendleton was known as a backer of civil service reform and wanted the most able persons put in office. Henry Payne was a millionaire from Cleveland whose son, Oliver, was a leader of the Standard Oil Company.

The race was billed as a fight between civil service reform and Standard Oil. When Payne won, his rival claimed that his son had bribed the lawmakers with Standard Oil funds. There was no proof, but the public was sure that men of wealth were trying to control the government.

The Hanna-Foraker era. Some men in the 1890s seemed to have the belief that government could make the rich richer. Some of them were Joseph Benson Foraker of Cincinnati, Marcus Alonzo Hanna of Cleveland, and George B. Cox, the city boss of Cincinnati.

Foraker was named governor in 1885 and 1887. Nothing was done during the Foraker years to limit the power of big business. There were no efforts to make sure that votes were fairly counted. During Foraker's term a move was turned down which

JOHN D. ROCKEFELLER

THE story of John D. Rockefeller (1839-1937) is a typical American story of the poor boy becoming wealthy. At one time, he was the world's richest man.

The Rockefeller family moved from New York to Cleveland in 1853. At age 16, John began his financial career as a buyer and seller of grain. A few years later he formed a partnership with Samuel Andrews and Henry Flagler in the oil business.

In 1870 he and his partners formed the Standard Oil Company, worth a million dollars. Within a few years, the company controlled 90% of the oil refining industries in the nation. Rockefeller then tried to gain control of businesses which had any part in oil production. By 1882 he controlled oil wells, transportation firms, oil refineries, and others.

John D. Rockefeller made millions of dollars. Some people suffered because of his business dealings. However, many people prospered due to their association with him. Rockefeller retired from Standard Oil in 1895.

Much of the money which Rockefeller gained was returned to society through contributions.

He was one of the greatest *philanthropists* (givers of money to help others) in U.S. history. He gave away over $500 million before his death in 1937.

would have given home rule to the cities. The home rule plan was to take control of the cities away from the bosses and give it to the public.

The power of monopolies. One issue which bothered the public was the growth of business *monopolies.* This sort of thing occurs when there is only one place to buy a certain product. The business can charge any price it wants and *consumers* (people who buy) must pay it or do without. Prices charged by monopolies are often too high.

The first great monopoly was John D. Rockefeller's Standard Oil Company. They were able to buy out other firms which refined oil. When they charged buyers high prices for the oil, the public began to demand action against this and other monopolies.

Later, Congress passed the Sherman *Antitrust* Act of 1890, which outlawed monopolies. The law was not clear and proved hard to enforce. The state lawmakers passed their own Valentine Antitrust Act in 1898. This was their version of the federal law. But it was still hard to prove that someone was guilty of holding a monopoly.

In 1891, William McKinley, a young lawyer from Canton, became governor. His views found favor with a rich businessman named Marcus Hanna. Hanna knew others who felt that business should not be tampered with by the government. They wanted the rich to gain more power and money, so he raised the funds for McKinley's campaigns.

As a two-term governor of Ohio, McKinley showed attitudes that were like those of business-people. For example, Ohio Attorney General David Watson brought suit against Standard Oil in 1890. He charged that they had broken the antitrust laws. Hanna and McKinley warned Watson that his public career could be ruined by his actions, but he pushed the case anyway.

The state supreme court ruled that Standard Oil was a monopoly and that it should not stay in business as it was then set up. Standard Oil did nothing to make changes. It was the job of the governor to enforce the law, but McKinley chose not to.

This event clearly showed that money talked. People in high public office were influenced by the wealthy men of the state.

6. A surplus of farm products and manufactured goods helped cause a depression in 1893.

The factories and farms had become so efficient by 1893 that they produced more goods than consumers were able to buy. As a result of the *surplus,* prices fell. Low prices meant low profits, so business had to lay off some of the workers to cut costs. This resulted in what is called an economic *depression,* or low point. There were one million people without jobs at the peak of the 1893 depression. In other words, in this state one in five workers was unemployed.

Coxey's "army." One Ohioan was well-known in the nation for his efforts to help the jobless. He was Jacob S. Coxey of Massillon. Coxey organized a large group of unemployed people to march on Washington, D.C.

Coxey was a very rich man who had made his wealth in road construction and steel. The purpose of the march was to focus on the need for a work program for those who were out of jobs. Coxey felt that the Congress should put people to work

George B. Cox was the political boss of Cincinnati in the late 1800s. He never held an elected office, but his organization controlled the city for many years. How did political bosses keep their power?

Jacob S. Coxey from Massillon led a group of jobless people on a march to Washington, D.C., in 1894. What did Coxey hope to gain from the march?

building roads. The group of about 500 marched to Washington in 1894, but broke up when Coxey and a few of his leaders were arrested for walking on the grass in front of the Capitol building. Coxey's army achieved nothing by their march. (However, Coxey did live to see some of his ideas put to work in the 1930s.)

By 1900, the economy began to revive on its own without government help.

WILLIAM McKINLEY, PRESIDENT

IN 1896 another man from Ohio was elected president of the United States. William McKinley was born at Niles in 1843. He lived most of his life in Canton. He went to Allegheny College, but ran out of funds and never finished. He entered the Civil War as a private and was a major by its end. After the war, he went back to law school and practiced law in Canton.

McKinley served in the U.S. House of Representatives from 1876 to 1891. While there, he pushed through several bills which helped big business. His best-known bill was the McKinley Tariff of 1890. This placed a high tax on *imports* (goods coming into a country). The tax raised the price of foreign goods, so people would buy more American products.

McKinley served two terms as governor in the 1890s. He ran for president in 1896, backed by Marcus Hanna's wealthy friends. McKinley carried on his campaign from the front porch of his home in Canton, where he spoke to news reporters. Meanwhile, his rival traveled all over the states to give speeches. McKinley's "front porch" campaign worked, as he won the race.

McKinley's first term was noted for a short war with Spain. The Spanish, who owned Cuba, treated the Cubans badly. This caused the Cubans to revolt to gain their freedom. Newspapers in the East sold many copies with reports of the horrors faced by the rebels. In February of 1898, the U.S. battleship *Maine* was sunk in Havana harbor. It was assumed that the Spanish had bombed it. Many Americans called for a war with Spain and McKinley agreed.

Spain had no chance of winning a war with the United States. The war lasted only a few short months, during which the United States gained Puerto Rico, Guam, and the Philippines from Spain. Cuba won its right to be free. Although the Spanish-American War had little effect in the

state, more than 200 Ohio soldiers died in the war. More troops died from disease than from Spanish bullets and swords.

McKinley was elected to a second term. But, he was not well-liked by everyone. Rumors were spread that a group of *anarchists* (people who want no government at all) sought to kill him. The safety of the president was made more secure, but at the Pan-American Exposition in Buffalo, New York, he was shot and killed. Leon Czolgosz hid a small gun in his bandaged hand and shot the president, who died September 14, 1901. The McKinley Memorial in Canton houses his tomb.

Company F of the Second Ohio Volunteer Infantry leaves Bellefontaine in 1898 for the Spanish American War.

The century drew to a close and a new age was ready to start. Over the next 20 years, reformers would try to solve many of the problems brought on by *industrialization*.

WORDS FOR STUDY

labor	thrift
management	brewer
labor unions	monopoly
collective bargaining	consumer
compromise	philanthropist
strike	antitrust
tenement	surplus
home rule	depression
apathy	import
immigrate	anarchist
devout	industrialization
efficiency	

QUESTIONS FOR REVIEW

1. Why did industry grow in Ohio in the late 1800s?

2. Which city was the leading manufacturing center in the state in 1890? What products were made there?

3. What was the main dispute between labor and management?

4. Describe some of the poor working conditions for factory workers in the 1880s.

5. What advantage did labor unions have over the individual worker?

6. What is collective bargaining?

7. Which was the first national labor union to organize in Ohio and when did it get started?

8. What are the advantages and the disadvantages of a strike?

9. Name the three rights of workers and the three rights of owners.

10. Relate the events of the Hocking Valley coal strike.

11. Why was James A. Garfield's term in office so short?

12. Name at least five problems that grew up in the cities because of rapid population growth.

13. What were four reasons why cities had a hard time solving the problems of rapid growth?

14. What two major immigrant groups increased Ohio's population in the late 1800s? What were some specific contributions these people made to Ohio?

15. Who was the fifth Ohioan to be elected president of the United States?

16. Why was it a problem when wealthy businessmen used their power to affect government?

17. What is a business monopoly? How does it affect the public?

18. What was the major cause of the depression of 1893?

19. What was Coxey's army and why did it fail?

20. What major event happened during McKinley's first term as president?

GOING FURTHER

1. How did the company-run mining towns affect the workers?

2. What worker rights and what owner rights were involved in the coal mine strikes?

3. Why did slums develop in large cities?

4. In what ways were President McKinley's attitudes like those of businesspeople?

FOR THOUGHT AND DISCUSSION

1. What are the reasons that slums and tenements exist in some places today? Are any of the factors the same as in the late 1800s?

2. In your own city or town, what specific things have been done by the government to meet the needs of a larger population than when the city was founded?

3. How would our state be different now if Ohio had not become a leading industrial state?

4. Would you say wealth influences politics today? Give a specific example to support your opinion.

5. What surpluses of farm products exist today? Have these extra supplies affected the economic condition of our country in any way? Explain your answer with data or examples.

PROJECTS AND REPORTS

1. Make a product map that shows the industrial cities of the late 1800s and compare it with the industrial centers of Ohio today.

2. Interview someone in your community who belongs to a labor union to find out how the union works. Also interview someone who does not belong to a union and get that person's ideas. Draw your own conclusion regarding the advantages and the disadvantages of belonging to a union. Display your findings on a poster.

3. Research the life of any political leader between 1880 and 1900 and prepare a written report to tell of his or her ideas and accomplishments.

4. Study the history of business monopolies and legislation that has helped control them. Present your findings in a chart.

5. Prepare a map that shows the routes immigrants from Europe and Asia traveled to arrive in Ohio.

6. From current news sources, identify at least three examples of labor/management conflict. Analyze each example to identify the issue and the rights of both workers and owners.

Ladies pleading with a saloon keeper to close his business. This is one example of the demonstrations during the temperance movement.

CHAPTER 8

THE YEARS OF PROGRESS AND REFORM

1900-1920

MAIN POINTS

1. The progressive era was a time of change when Ohioans wanted to improve society and government.
2. Progressives wanted more popular government.
3. Religion was a major force for reform.
4. Political leaders in Ohio helped put progressive reforms into action.
5. The Constitutional Convention of 1912 resulted in the passage of many reform amendments.
6. Prohibition was adopted in the 1920s, but was later repealed.
7. Ohioans helped in the women's rights movement to gain national women's suffrage.
8. Ohioans played a role in World War I at home and in Europe.

1. The progressive era was a time of change when Ohioans wanted to improve society and government.

The time from 1900 to 1916 is called the progressive era. Those were years of great change in the United States. Many political, social, and economic reform movements took place at that time. As we learned in the last chapter, growth of industry brought many problems. *Reformers* tried to correct the faults which they saw in our society. They wanted the nation to be progressive and move forward in all ways. Those who sought reform during that era were called *progressives*.

Progressives worked to make changes that would reduce the gap between the rich and the poor. They hoped to lessen the control that wealthy people had on the government and help the common people to gain more power. A number of social reforms were also needed. Progressives worked to gain equal rights for women and some wanted to *prohibit* the use of liquor.

2. Progressives wanted more popular government.

Some political reforms. A group of writers, such as Lincoln Steffens and Ida Tarbell, wrote about some of the problems they had found. In his story "Ohio, A Tale of Two Cities," Steffens told of corruption in big city politics. He aimed to give reasons why reformers wanted more *popular government*. That meant that voters should have more power in the system. Progressives sought to make new methods part of the government process.

Initiative, or popular legislation, starts when a required portion of the voters signs a petition and gives it to the lawmakers. The petition is a call for them to act on a given problem. The issue may be taken straight to the voters as a proposed amendment to the constitution.

An example of this process in the state was a 1975 attempt to stop the use of leg-hold traps to catch wild animals. When a legislative group did not act on the issue, the initiative was used in 1977 to let the voters decide. However, they did not support the proposed amendment and it was turned down.

Referendum, or popular *veto* (rejection), means that the voters ask the lawmakers to place an issue on the ballot. Then they may vote on that issue. This process was used in 1971 when the people approved a state income tax.

Recall, or popular *impeachment,* gives voters the right to remove officials from office. Recall has never been used in Ohio at the state level, but it has been used by cities and towns. In 1982, voters in a Columbus suburb used the method to vote their mayor out of office.

Progressives worked to gain the *direct primary* election in politics. In the direct primary, voters choose members of their own party to run against candidates picked by the other parties. The direct primary makes it possible for anyone to seek a public office. The person must have a petition signed by a certain number of voters. Once that is completed, his or her name may appear on the primary ballot. Progressives wanted the direct primary as a means to take power from the political bosses. Before this time, officials were often controlled by rich men. They would vote how their "bosses" told them to or take the risk of losing their jobs.

Reformers helped to gain the direct election of U. S. senators. Prior to 1913, the constitution gave state lawmakers the power to choose the senators. Progressives believed that senators answered only to those who chose them, rather than to the will of the people.

Home rule for cities was another issue. Progressives wanted city officials to be chosen by local residents, rather than by state government. It was difficult for citizens to keep control of city affairs when they were not allowed to elect their own leaders.

Progressives worked for other reforms, such as the control of big business. They helped improve the rights of workers and some wished to give women the right to vote.

Those who opposed the reform movement were powerful and were a strong force in business and government. They did not want to lose their power. Others thought the progressives were moving too quickly with their changes. Some fought the reforms, thinking there would be more government meddling in their lives. Many men were afraid to give women the right to vote, believing that the women would likely vote for prohibition!

3. Religion was a major force for reform.

The move for reforms had actually started in the early days of statehood. As more and more people came here, many of their ideas for improving the place grew out of religious beliefs. The churches were a major influence in the social life of the communities.

From 1800 through the 1830s, *revivals* played a great role in religion. The goal of a revival was to get people enthused about religion and to gain new members for the churches. Those who led the revivals were called revivalists, and the movement was called revivalism.

Revival meetings had much loud preaching and singing. Some revivalists even let the people dance and play cards. Of course, there were always good food and drink to be had. One reason revivals were so popular was because of the social events.

It was common for thousands of people to attend these meetings over several months' time. Methodists in Chillicothe claimed that 200 people joined the church as a result of a two-month revival. While some churches joined in the revivals, others thought they were too emotional and stayed away. The Methodists and the Baptists were the most active revivalists in the state.

Methodists found another good way to get more members. They sent out *circuit riders* to preach at churches in various towns. One Sunday the rider would preach at one church and the next Sunday

Religious revivals and "camp meetings" were common during the 1800-1830s period. They got people enthused about religion and gained many new members for the churches.

he would move on to another. This went on until the whole *circuit* was covered, and then he would start again. George Callahan from Kentucky was Ohio's first circuit rider in the late 1790s. Within a few years, Methodist circuit riders were seen in all parts of the state.

Other church groups in early Ohio included Disciples of Christ, Lutherans, Moravians, Mennonites, and Roman Catholics. There were also Presbyterians, Episcopalians, Jews, Mormons, Zoarites, and Shakers. Some people did not belong to any church.

Through the 19th century and into the progressive era, church groups had much power. They took the lead in many efforts for social change and often provided food and clothing for the needy. Church socials were important events for both city and country people. While they held different views, the churches worked together to build a strong social order.

WASHINGTON GLADDEN AND THE SOCIAL GOSPEL

THERE were a lot of reforms for issues other than politics during the progressive era. There was a movement in some churches to get more involved in community life. Some clergy wanted the churches to help push reforms. One of the most respected national leaders in the "social gospel" movement was the Reverend Washington Gladden (1836-1918). He served as minister of the First Congregational Church of Columbus from 1882 to 1918.

Gladden was born in Pennsylvania and grew up in New York. For four years, he was the religious editor of *The Independent*. It was the most influential magazine of its day. Gladden was unhappy with the lack of help from society in problems such as poverty, labor conflict, immigration, religious and racial prejudice, and war.

Reverend Gladden set an example for other clergy. He refused to accept contributions for his church from people who made their money illegally. He was elected to the Columbus city council for a two-year term. As a councilman, he saw firsthand the corruption in city government.

He helped set up a home for very poor people. He also helped stop labor strikes such as the Hocking Valley miners' strike. He preached that people should tolerate other religions, and he discouraged the anti-Catholic feelings of the early 1900s.

The social gospel campaign helped open the minds of the American people to demand reforms in other areas. Washington Gladden should be remembered as a leader of the progressive era.

4. Political leaders in Ohio helped put progressive reforms into action.

Two leaders of Ohio's reform movement were Tom L. Johnson of Cleveland and Samuel "Golden Rule" Jones of Toledo. They set good examples for all progressives to follow.

Tom L. Johnson's life was a rags-to-riches story. Johnson was poor as a youth, but he was inventive. He worked hard and became rich from investments in steel works and street railroads. He became a reformer as a result of reading Henry George's book, *Progress and Poverty* (1884). Johnson was sent to Congress in 1890 and 1892.

Samuel "Golden Rule" Jones (left) got his nickname from the way he managed Toledo as its mayor. He believed in practicing the golden rule. Tom L. Johnson (right) was an outstanding reformer as mayor of Cleveland.

He served as mayor of Cleveland from 1901 to 1909.

As mayor, Johnson brought many types of improvements to aid the people of his city. He installed new street lights and a pure water system. He reduced the streetcar fare. The city's parks were cleaned up and public baths were built for the people. He made a more effective police force which helped reduce the crime rate. Johnson was a champion for home rule and other reforms in the state.

Johnson and a friend, Newton D. Baker, tried to change the tax laws of Cleveland. They found that some rich people were not paying their share of property taxes. The common people paid full taxes while the wealthy found ways to pay less and less. Lincoln Steffens called Johnson "the best mayor of the best-governed city in the country."

Samuel "Golden Rule" Jones was a reformer in Toledo. Jones became wealthy as Johnson had, making his fortune by building oil well machines. Although wealthy, he never lost sight of the problems of the poor. He was quite concerned about

the growing power of the rich and the lack of popular control on government.

Jones served as mayor of Toledo from 1897 until his death in 1904. He led many reforms, such as a minimum wage law for city workers and an eight-hour work day. Toledo also gained free public baths and playgrounds, street improvements, and a better police force.

Jones got the nickname "Golden Rule" from the way he managed the city of Toledo. He believed in "doing unto others as you would have them do unto you."

Tom Johnson and Samuel Jones helped the public see the value of being informed about their government. They showed how to bring desired change to society. Johnson and Jones helped expose corruption in government. They were models to others who would bring reforms to the state by 1916.

Reforms to 1912. Reform did not happen quickly, for there were a lot of people who opposed

Judson Harmon, a Democrat, was elected governor in 1908. He sided with many reform views.

change. But the progressive movement was sweeping the entire nation.

A major change came in 1903. Voters passed an amendment which gave the governor the power of veto. The governor could then reject acts passed by the General Assembly. But the veto could be cancelled by a two-thirds vote in each house of the assembly.

Progressives were pleased with the veto. Now all they needed was a reform governor. Tom L. Johnson lost his attempt in 1905. He was thought to be too extreme, even by progressives. But in 1908, Democrat Judson Harmon from Cincinnati

was elected to the office. While Harmon was not a true progressive, he did side with many reform views.

Harmon's election was a great win for the Democrats. It meant that support for their party was slowly building in Ohio. People began looking to them for the reforms which Republicans would not pass.

Changes under Governor Harmon. During Harmon's first term, few reform laws were passed because Republicans controlled the General Assembly. In 1910, Harmon beat out Warren G. Harding of Marion by over 100,000 votes. Then more Democrats were seated in the assembly.

More reform acts were passed during Governor Harmon's second term. A *workman's compensation* law furnished funds for workers who got hurt on the job. The state lawmakers endorsed the amendment for the direct election of U.S. senators. They approved initiative and referendum for cities, but not for state issues. Some wanted to see how these methods worked for cities before using them at the state level.

In 1910, voters called for a convention to review the state constitution. Delegates were chosen and meetings were opened in 1912. Progressives hoped that their aims would find favor with those present.

5. The Constitutional Convention of 1912 resulted in the passage of many reform amendments.

The 1912 Constitutional Convention. The state's reform movement peaked at the convention. There were four issues which were discussed most. These were tax reform, home rule for cities, court reform, and the use of initiative and referendum. When the meetings closed, 41 changes were offered. That year the voters passed 33 of them.

Among those passed were the statewide initiative and referendum. Another law caused all employers to take part in the workman's compensation program. The voters approved home rule for the cities.

WILLIAM HOWARD TAFT, PRESIDENT

THE Taft family was one of the most famous political families in the state. William Howard Taft is the only person in U.S. history to serve as both president and as chief justice of the Supreme Court. He attended Woodward High School in Cincinnati, Yale University, and Cincinnati Law School.

Taft served as Secretary of War in 1904 under President Theodore Roosevelt. Roosevelt wanted him to run for president. Although Taft preferred to be a judge, his family convinced him to run, and he defeated William Jennings Bryan in 1908.

A conservative during the liberal progressive era, he lost support when he failed to back many of the progressive reforms. Taft did have success in some areas. He broke up twice as many business monopolies in four years as Roosevelt did in eight.

In 1921, President Warren G. Harding appointed Taft as chief justice of the Supreme Court. He held that position until just before his death.

William H. Taft was one of the most unhappy men to serve as president, yet he was one of the most popular. He liked sports and was especially fond of golf and baseball. He began the custom of the president "throwing out" the first pitch of the baseball season. As a large man (six feet tall,

over 300 pounds), he had to exercise to maintain his health. Heart trouble, caused by overwork and overweight, forced him to resign as chief justice in 1930. He died a short time later and was buried in Arlington National Cemetery in the nation's capital.

One law said that private business must cease hiring prison inmates to work. Laws were passed to control working hours, conditions, and minimum wages. The voters approved many other reform measures, as well.

The progressives were quite pleased. While eight of the amendments had been turned down, years of work by the reform leaders had brought some success.

Governor James M. Cox makes progress. In 1912, Democrat James M. Cox of Dayton was

elected governor. He was a true progressive with a 56-point program for reform. Many new laws were passed. Some of these protected workers, including children. Boys under 16 and girls under 18 could no longer be hired unless they proved they had finished 10 years of school. Another law set up the merit system for *civil servants,* (non-elected state workers). This meant that civil servants would be ranked according to test scores. The Public Utilities Commission was formed to place fair rates on public services.

Governor James M. Cox, elected in 1912, was the first true progressive chosen to lead Ohio.

Eliza Jane Thompson was the leader of the temperance movement in Hillsboro. In 1873 the women of that city forced the closing of saloons. Eliza was known throughout the country as "Mother Thompson."

Cox was upset by Frank Willis of Ohio Northern University in the 1914 election. The voters must have felt that Cox had tried too many changes too soon. Cox was re-elected to the office in 1916.

In his second term, fewer reform laws were passed. But progress was made toward passage of two vital issues—temperance and women's suffrage.

6. Prohibition was adopted in the 1920s, but was later repealed.

Prohibition of alcoholic drinks (also known as *temperance*) was a prime issue to some reformers. Those who favored prohibition were called "drys."

However, the drys gained little in the temperance movement until after 1900.

In 1908, the state passed the Rose County Option Law. It gave voters in each county the choice of closing liquor outlets. By the end of 1910, 62 of Ohio's 88 counties had voted to end the sale of liquor. Nearly 2,000 saloons closed their doors.

Between 1913 and 1917, the voters turned down three issues which called for statewide prohibition. The Ohio Anti-Saloon League kept up its drive for that purpose. In 1918, the people approved a state amendment to that effect. In the same year, the Eighteenth Amendment to the U.S. Constitution was passed, creating national prohibition. Even so,

After a long struggle, women gained the right to vote in national elections in 1919. This wagon was used in caravans and demonstrations to call attention to women's demands.

many people opposed the law. Moonshiners and bootleggers made and transported illegal liquor for huge profits during those days. Crime rings controlled most of the illegal liquor business.

State law failed to say what percent of alcohol made a drink illegal. A federal law solved that problem. The Volstead Act outlawed drinks with one-half of one percent (.05%) alcohol. The state allowed a greater percentage than did the federal law. The Crabbe Act said that an alcohol content of 2.75 percent was too much.

By the 1930s, most knew that the attempt to stop the use of liquor had failed. In 1933, the Twenty-first Amendment to the Constitution repealed the Eighteenth Amendment.

The sale of liquor is now controlled through the state government. It may be bought only at the state liquor stores and other licensed outlets. Moonshiners and bootleggers still exist, but in far fewer numbers than in prohibition times.

7. Ohioans helped in the women's rights movement to gain national women's suffrage.

Women's rights. Another reform cause going on at the same time as prohibition was that of women's rights. In fact, many of the reformers were active in both issues.

Women had few legal rights until the late 1800s. Many men felt that women should not have the right to vote. They thought that women would permit their emotions to sway their judgment. It is easy to see why women of the early 1900s wanted equal rights!

Ohio women lead in the movement. Ohio was a key state in the move for women's rights. Some of the movement's leaders came from this state. Harriet Taylor Upton of Ravenna and Warren was treasurer of the National Women's Suffrage Association in 1892. In 1920, she was the first woman

Women's rights leaders, Victoria Claflin Woodhull (left) and Harriet Taylor Upton.

chosen as vice-chair of the National Republican Executive Committee.

Victoria Claflin Woodhull Blood Martin was a leader in the women's movement. In 1870, she published *Woodhull and Claflin's Weekly* which spoke for full equal rights. Rosa Segur led the Toledo women's rights efforts of the late 1800s.

As early as 1852, the Ohio Women's Rights Convention was held at Massillon. It was a meeting vital to the national effort to demand equal rights. By 1900, women had gained a few legal rights, such as the right to control their own property. Women also had the right to sue and to be sued in court. But the prime goal of the movement was to gain women's *suffrage* (right to vote). The women of Ohio organized and worked hard, but little progress was made prior to the progressive era. Delegates to the 1912 state Constitutional Convention proposed an amendment for women's suffrage. But the voters, who were all men, turned it down. However, women did gain the right to vote for local officials in some cities.

Women gain suffrage. The cause was a success when the states passed the Nineteenth Amendment to the U.S. Constitution in 1919. The law says that the right of United States citizens to vote shall not be denied because of sex.

Gaining the right to vote did not give equal rights to women in all areas. There were state laws which still *discriminated* against them. One law said that women could not work at jobs where they had to lift items of over 25 pounds. This law was passed to protect the health of women, but it did discriminate between sexes. There still exist some laws that do not deal fairly with women. Groups continue to work for reforms in women's rights today.

8. Ohioans played a role in World War I at home and in Europe.

While the progressive age was in full swing, a major war drew attention away from reforms. The war had broken out in Europe in 1914. By 1916, it was becoming hard for the United States to stay neutral.

In April 1917, our nation declared war on Germany and its allies.

World War I. Many nations wanted to be the best in the world. This is called *nationalism*. Each wished to have more wealth, stronger armies and navies *(militarism)*, and more land *(colonialism)*. Nations began to join together to defend each other in case they were attacked. The United States entered World War I on the side of Russia, England, and France.

War meant that Ohioans had to fight in Europe, but some made money from the war. Farmers had high profits from their crops which were sold in Europe. Europeans could not supply all the food needed to feed their soldiers. Demand for American farm goods grew and grew. Our state's industries also profited by making goods to meet the needs of war. Many prospered, but more than 10 million people died as a result of World War I.

Ohioans react to the war. The outbreak of war in Europe had a great impact on many who had family ties in Europe. Ohio's German-American people opposed the war. They were targets of great resentment. Some thought they might be spies. There were events in which these people were beaten. The most serious problems happened in Cincinnati, where a large German group lived.

Some people opposed the war because they did not think it concerned our country. Many liked their German neighbors and did not wish to go to war against Germany. Reverend Herbert S. Bigelow of Cincinnati was a most vocal critic of the war. A group of men who supported the war kidnapped Bigelow. They tied him to a tree and whipped him.

Some Ohioans thought killing was morally wrong. A large number of these *conscientious objectors* came from the Quaker, Amish, Mennonite, and Seventh Day Adventist groups. Conscientious objectors were often threatened with beatings.

Ohioans in the military. The state's young men were not as eager to fight as they had been in earlier wars. The peace movement and pro-German feelings were quite strong in Ohio in 1917. However,

Reverend Herbert S. Bigelow of Cincinnati was against the U.S. going to war with Germany. Do anti-war activists today receive the same treatment as Bigelow did?

150,000 Ohioans did serve in the military during the war. More than 6,500 of them died. Many more were wounded or suffered from the effects of poison gas.

Few men volunteered for the armed forces, so Congress passed the Selective Service Act of 1917. Eventually, all men between the ages of 18 and 45 had to sign up for the draft. Draftees could not hire others to take their places. But some men, such as farmers, did not have to serve. It was felt that their efforts from home were of value to the war. Conscientious objectors were not made to fight. They were asked to serve in ways other than combat.

Captain Eddie Rickenbacker from Columbus was a U.S. air ace during World War I.

Training camps. One major training camp was set up in Ohio. Camp Sherman, named for William Tecumseh Sherman, was built north of Chillicothe on the west bank of the Scioto River. Camp Sherman was huge. Seventy-five thousand troops were trained there. Mounds in the area were leveled to build barracks. (Little did the army know that it had destroyed one of the best remains of prehistoric Hopewell Indian culture in the country. Fortunately, archaeologists had found and described the mounds years before.) Mound City, now one of Ohio's two national parks, stands on the site of Camp Sherman.

Several smaller camps were built in the state. One was Camp Willis in the Columbus suburb of Upper Arlington.

Ohioans in action. The best-known of our fighting units was the Fourth Ohio Regiment of the National Guard. By the time American troops were trained and shipped to Europe, they arrived just in time to help stop the last German drive in 1918. Without the Americans, it is possible that the Germans would have won the war.

Ohioans did much for the war effort. One who gained fame was Edward Vernon Rickenbacker of Columbus. He was the American "air ace" of the war who shot down 26 planes and lookout balloons. Elsie Janis from Columbus was the first female entertainer to perform at the front lines in France. Newton D. Baker of Cleveland was an important *civilian* during World War I. As Secretary of War, he built an army of four million to fight in Europe.

The war ended on November 11, 1918. Our men and women performed well in bringing the war to a close.

The homefront. Those at home helped the war effort in many ways. Farmers increased their crop yields. Factory workers made more goods than ever before in history. Dayton became a center for the production of fighter planes. Akron plants produced great numbers of rubber items. Other Ohio cities produced many types of war goods.

Civilians helped by saving fuel and food. There were breadless, meatless, and fuelless days.

Elsie Janis, born in Columbus, entertained soldiers at the front lines during World War I. She became known as "The Sweetheart of the Doughboys."

Ohio industries aided the war effort in World War I. This Class B Liberty war truck was built in Lima.

The public gave financial aid to the war. The government asked Americans to buy war bonds. A war bond was a contract which let the government borrow the people's money. It promised to repay the buyer the amount of the bond plus interest. There were drives with rallies to inspire people to buy bonds. Ohioans bought more than $100 million worth of them.

Despite patriotism of Americans during the war, there were some events of which most Ohioans were not proud. German-Americans were beaten and their businesses destroyed. Their presses and newspapers were burned. In self-defense, many changed to English names. For example, Schmidt became Smith. In a German part of Columbus, Schiller Street was renamed Whittier Street. Sauerkraut and wieners became victory cabbage and hot dogs.

Those anti-German feelings lasted after the war. The state assembly passed the Ake Law in 1919 which stopped courses in German below the eighth grade. Some saw the teaching of German language in schools as part of Germany's effort to rule the world.

Outrage against German-Americans was a sad part of our history. They have made major contributions to progress in our state.

WORDS FOR STUDY

reformer	workman's compensation
progressives	civil servant
prohibit	temperance
popular government	suffrage
initiative	discriminate
referendum	nationalism
veto	militarism
recall	colonialism
impeachment	conscientious objector
direct primary	civilian
revival	
circuit rider	
circuit	

QUESTIONS FOR REVIEW

1. What was the progressive era? What years did it cover?

2. In what two types of reforms were progressives interested?

3. Describe five different political reforms which progressives felt would lead toward more popular government.

4. What is the difference between initiative and referendum?

5. In what way would the direct primary decrease the power of political bosses?

6. What are the advantages of home rule?

7. Name two early leaders in the state's progressive movement.

8. Describe the importance of Governor Harmon's election in 1908.

9. What was the result of the 1912 Constitutional Convention?

10. Who was elected governor in 1912 and again in 1916? What reforms were made during his term in office?

11. What was the temperance, or prohibition, issue about?

12. What rights were women trying to gain?

13. In what year was women's suffrage legally granted? Which amendment gave this right?

14. Describe the role that Ohio played in World War I.

GOING FURTHER

1. Why was the early 1900s an important time to make progressive reforms?

2. Explain the temperance issue. Why did the Eighteenth Amendment fail?

3. What rights did women gain besides suffrage?

4. What part did nationalism, militarism, and colonialism play in causing a world war?

5. Why were conscientious objectors not forced to serve in combat?

FOR THOUGHT AND DISCUSSION

1. How did the progressive era affect the American political system?

2. In what ways do reforms that were adopted between 1900 and 1920 affect your life today?

3. Would you say the progressive reform movement ended in 1920? Explain.

4. In what ways did Ohio leaders influence the reform movement?

5. Ohioans had certain anti-German feelings during World War I. Are there any similar examples from modern society? Use some news sources to support your opinion.

PROJECTS AND REPORTS

1. Write a report on any Ohio leader during the progressive era. Show how the person influenced the reform movement. One interesting person is Victoria Claflin Woodhull Blood Martin.

2. Make a study of home rule in your city or town. In what ways does state government limit home rule? Report your findings to the class.

3. Trace and analyze the progress of the women's rights movement from the 1920s to the present.

4. Make a chart showing how popular government works at the local level. Cite two examples.

5. Collect pictures or articles, and make posters to show what life in Ohio was like during the reform era. Arrange your collection in a bulletin board display.

6. Construct a map to show how countries were allied on both sides of World War I. Locate the major battles of the war. Make a map legend.

The Roaring Twenties brought prosperous times for most people. New industries grew up. There was a huge demand for automobiles, which most people could afford. But, by the late 1920s, the economy had fallen on hard times.

CHAPTER 9

PROSPERITY TO DEPRESSION AND RECOVERY

1920-1945

MAIN POINTS

1. The 1920s was a prosperous time for most Ohioans.
2. Life in the Roaring Twenties was more casual than before.
3. Prejudice against the newcomers developed among some Ohioans.
4. Economic prosperity of the 1920s ended in the worst depression in American history.
5. Government aid programs helped bring Ohio and the nation out of the depression.
6. Labor unions gained strength during the 1930s.
7. There were heavy losses in World War II, but then the nation's economy got a big boost.

There were three major trends in the years between 1920 and 1945. 1) The economy gained strength during the 1920s. 2) It hit the bottom during the Great Depression of the 1930s. 3) As the nation slowly got back on its feet, World War II started. Let's see how these events affected the people of Ohio.

1. The 1920s was a prosperous time for most Ohioans.

The 1920 national election. The twenties opened with a strange sort of political contest for the people of Ohio. Both candidates for president were Ohioans and both were newspapermen. The

Democrats offered three-time governor James M. Cox of Dayton. The Republicans ran U. S. Senator Warren G. Harding of Marion. Harding was a friendly man who had not made political enemies. His *slogan* was that the country should return to "normalcy" after World War I. Harding won the race by seven million votes, and the Republicans won control of the White House for the next 12 years.

Peacetime industry adjusts to supply and demand. For most Ohioans the twenties was a time of plenty. There were few problems as industries changed from making war goods to peacetime products. Finding jobs for the soldiers coming home was not so easy.

In general, industries changed quickly to peacetime production. The factories produced more goods and hired more people than ever before. As the population grew and people had money to spend, there was a demand for more goods.

Supply and demand is a basic rule of economics. Let's use washing machines as an example.

Suppose a plant that made washing machines had a busy year. They built 30,000 machines during the year and offered them for sale (supply). However, only 20,000 people came to look at the product and only 12,000 of those bought a washer (demand). In this case the plant had *overproduced*, and there were machines left in stock. Supply was high and the demand was low. The result might

WARREN G. HARDING, PRESIDENT

WARREN Gamaliel Harding was born in 1865 at Corsica in Morrow County, the son of a farmer and country doctor. Young Harding studied in the common schools and went to Ohio Central College at Iberia from age 14 to 17.

He worked for a year as a country school teacher. Having had some experience in a newspaper office, in 1884 he became editor and owner of the *Marion Star*. In 1891 he married Florence Kling.

In the late 1800s, Senator Joseph B. Foraker encouraged Harding to enter politics. He served in the Ohio senate from 1900-1904, and was the state's lieutenant governor from 1904-1906. In 1910 Harding lost an election for governor. Then in 1914 he ran for the U.S. Senate against his friend Foraker and won. He served in the Senate from 1915-1921. Senator Harding favored the prohibition amendment and supported women's suffrage.

In 1921, Harding became the eighth U.S. president to come from Ohio. He won the election with a front porch campaign that criticized President Wilson's administration and called for a return to normalcy after the war.

President Harding initiated the national budget system. His first budget was submitted in December 1921. He also suggested that a permanent policy on tariffs be adopted. He had no desire to increase the power of the president. Rather, he acted as a *moderator* to help gain agreements between the executive departments and the representatives. The most important move Harding made during his first year as president was to call an international conference on arms limitation.

Later in his term, Republican cabinet members were accused of being corrupt. Since Harding, himself a kindly sort of man, was still popular, he made a tour across the country to build support for the administration. On the return trip he was stricken with pneumonia in San Francisco and died on August 2, 1923.

be that the company would lay off workers. Or it could lower the price of the machines until the demand caught up with the supply.

Ohio women at work in a Westinghouse plant.

How would this affect the firm's profit? How would it affect the laid-off worker's ability to buy other products? Can you see how a bad turn of events in one industry could affect other people and businesses? Cite an example of the role of supply and demand in your own community.

On the other hand, what if more people wanted to have washers than there were washers to buy?

The demand would likely lead to a price increase. The plant owner could then hire more workers, and there would be a profit.

What would be the best condition for both *producers* (those who make the goods) and consumers (those who buy the goods)? You are right if you said both would be happy if the supply is high and the demand is high.

One of the big new industries in the 1920s was the automobile industry. Henry Ford's Model-T was in a price range that most people could afford. This

Judge Florence E. Allen, of Cleveland, was the first woman elected to the Ohio Supreme Court. In 1934, she became the first woman appointed to the U.S. Court of Appeals.

from the noise of the cities, so the building of new houses boomed during this time as *suburban* communities grew. Shaker Heights and Lakewood in Cleveland, Ottawa Hills in Toledo, and Bexley and Upper Arlington in Columbus were some of these new suburbs.

Stocks and bonds. When people could see that most industries were making a profit, they wanted to get a share. The way to do that was to buy *stock* (shares) in a company. This was one way for a firm to get *investment capital* (money used to make improvements in the business).

A *stock certificate* is a piece of paper that says the holder owns part of a company and will receive a *dividend* (share of the profit). If a lot of people have faith that a certain firm is likely to make a high profit, the value of that stock goes up. If it looks as though there will be no profit or dividends, the value of the stock will go down.

Another way a business can get extra capital is to sell *bonds.* Bonds are different from stocks in that bond holders do not own a part of the company. Rather than getting a share of the profits, they will be paid a *fixed percent* of *interest* on the loan. City governments often use the bond method for raising extra capital.

Many companies in the state and in the nation were quite active in selling stocks and bonds. A lot of people had high hopes of getting rich in the *stock market.*

Farmers overproduce. One group of Ohioans did not fare as well in the 1920s. Farmers were growing their goods at a high level to meet the needs of Europe during World War I. When the war was over, the Europeans once again produced their own farm products. As the demand for American farm goods began to fall, farmers did not cut back on the supply. They still produced huge amounts of farm goods. A surplus (excess supply) was the result, which left the farmers with too many goods and too few dollars. They could not pay off their debts. This was the first sign of the crash that would occur at the end of the decade.

helped create a huge demand for autos. Plants throughout the state made many of the parts for the new cars. While Akron made tires, and Toledo manufactured glass, the Delco shops in Dayton built electrical parts.

Housing industry. The fact that more people owned cars had an effect on the housing industry. No more did people need to live near their place of work. They sought new and bigger homes far

2. Life in the Roaring Twenties was more casual than before.

The Roaring Twenties. With money to spend and the freedoms brought by reforms, people in the twenties had a new zest for life. Social events were different from before, and clothing styles were more daring. People enjoyed life more by spending evenings out and partying. This life style was quite different from the solemn values of past years. For this reason, the decade is called the Roaring Twenties.

Many young people thought the amendment against the use of liquor was a silly one. They began to violate this law openly.

Changes for women. The twenties saw the *liberated* woman for the first time in this century. Women did not want to leave their factory jobs after the war. Single women went into fields of work that had been closed to them before. In 1922, Florence Allen of Cleveland was named to the state supreme court, where she served until 1934. In that same year, six women were elected to the General Assembly.

Women of the time shocked many people with their seeming lack of modesty. The "bobbed" hair style was in fashion. Bobbed hair was cut very short and looked much like a man's haircut. Dress styles changed as hemlines reached mid-calf. Some even crept above the knees! This was quite a change from times when dresses covered the ankles. Women wore lipstick and silk stockings and they smoked cigarettes in public. Their language was more bold.

The life style of the family changed in the twenties as well. Farm youths left the home at a younger age to seek jobs in the cities. With many women working outside the home, families were more willing to share the work of keeping house. Also, divorce became more common and was accepted by some churches.

Fun and entertainment. Going to night clubs became the most popular activity for an evening

Flapper style dresses of the late 1920s.

out on the town. Besides food and drink, night clubs had music for listening and dancing.

The new kind of music to hit the clubs was jazz. Black musicians developed this sound in the South, and it quickly spread to other states. Jazz has a fast tempo with lots of brass instruments—trumpets, trombones—and always a piano.

The "Charleston" was the favorite new dance, invented in Charleston, South Carolina. Part of the dance involved a movement where the arms were flapped against the sides. Thus another term for the twenties came into being—the "flapper era."

The movie business made great progress during the twenties. The first "talkie" film, *The Jazz Singer,* was produced in 1927. Gangster stories, westerns, and great *spectaculars* were popular film themes.

The Ku Klux Klan was an example of the intolerant attitudes of the 1920s. The Klan was opposed to anyone who was not a white, Anglo-Saxon protestant. What are the harms of practicing intolerance against other people?

3. Prejudice against the newcomers developed among some Ohioans.

Along with all the fun came problems of prejudice in the cities and towns.

The effects of mixed cultures were felt as blacks, Czechs, Poles, Italians, and others appeared in the cities. Feelings of hate and fear grew among many people in the state.

The Ku Klux Klan. The most active group that worked against blacks and immigrants was the Ku Klux Klan. The Klan was a secret club in the South that was started after the Civil War. It showed up in the North during World War I.

Klan members were opposed to anyone who was not a native white, Protestant-American. The Klan was against blacks, Catholics, Jews, and immigrants. The group used brute force and physical threats to *intimidate* those they did not like. Beatings of blacks and immigrants were reported throughout the state. There were some 400,000 Klansmen in Ohio in 1924. Some held public office. For instance, mayors in Akron and Youngstown were members of the Klan. The Klan still exists in the state at this time, although it plays a low-key role.

The unfair views of these and other persons placed a great deal of strain on the otherwise healthy social order. Even so, most of the people lived normal lives, working and playing hard. They did not dream that disaster was just ahead.

4. Economic prosperity of the 1920s ended in the worst depression in American history.

A surplus of goods was created in the late twenties in both business and farming. Prices dropped,

During depressions, people feared losing their savings in banks. There were "runs" on banks as depositors flocked to withdraw their money. This is a run on a bank in the early 1900s.

profits fell, and many jobs were lost. In spite of this condition, people were confident. They felt good about company stocks and thought that prices would go up. This is called a "bull" market. People bought stock on credit, counting on selling at a higher price to pay for it. Then in late 1929, everyone began to realize that businesses were really in trouble, and many stocks were almost worthless. This brought on a "bear" market. Stock prices fell as everyone began trying to sell at once. This was called the stock market crash.

Because of overproduction, farmers and businesses could not pay back the loans they had received from banks. Then, people got worried about the banks and flocked to withdraw their savings money. Banks had lost the money on bad loans and could not pay everyone. Many banks had to

close. One thing affected another until the entire nation was in a depression.

Effects on Ohio. In 1931, 125 of the state's banks *failed* (went out of business), and many people lost their life savings. The industrial cities were hardest hit by job losses due to the high number of people who worked in plants and mills. At the peak of the depression, nearly one out of four Ohioans was out of work. Able to work only a few hours a week, or with no jobs at all, many could not pay off their bank loans and lost their homes. This forced some to move in with family or friends and others to live in shacks or tents.

As farm income was cut in half by 1931, all groups in the state felt the depression to some degree. Bread lines and soup kitchens were formed by volunteers to give free meals to the hungry, suffering people. In Dayton alone the relief groups tried

During the Great Depression of the 1930s, many of the nation's jobless lived in shanty towns like this one in Cleveland.

to feed 3,600 families a day! Local agencies could not care for all these needs. Soon the state and federal governments stepped in to offer help.

> To learn more about life during the Great Depression, talk with a relative or neighbor who went through it. How old would a person have to be now to recall events from the thirties? Plan for the interview by writing questions you will ask. You may wish to record the interview or take written notes to be used in a class discussion later.

5. Government aid programs helped bring Ohio and the nation out of the depression.

State aid. The main problem which faced state government was where to find funds to help the cities pay for services. With so many people out of work, tax revenue dropped sharply.

Different taxes seemed to be the answer. Part of the tax on gasoline was placed in the relief fund, and part of it was used for jobs building highways. Two new taxes that were started were an inheritance tax in 1931 and a state sales tax of 3% in 1934. Taxes on tobacco and several other items were also approved.

Another boost for the cities came in the form of the School Foundation Program in 1935, which arranged for school districts to get state money based on average daily attendance. This allowed schools to stay open during the hard years. Schools even had a little money to buy shoes and clothing for needy children.

Under New Deal programs, work projects were set up to help the unemployed. These photographs show the Northwest Territory monument being constructed at Marietta, and East Main Street being repaired in Alliance.

By 1939, the state had spent almost $100 million to give aid and jobs to the poor, but that alone was not enough.

Federal aid. In 1933 Congress began to put into effect President Franklin Roosevelt's New Deal. This plan gave funds for relief, jobs, and reform acts. Congress wanted to tell the states how the money was to be spent.

State leaders did not want the money if it meant federal control of state affairs. Thus, the state did

The 1930s saw many bitter labor disputes. This is a strike at the Akron Goodyear Tire and Rubber Company in 1938.

not get as much aid as it might have. However, by 1939 Ohio had received more than $175 million in federal funds.

Ohioans worked on federal public works projects to build roads, sewers, airports, schools, and many other public projects. Farmers and home owners took out government loans to help them keep their farms and homes. State workers kept their jobs, but with a cut in pay.

6. Labor unions gained strength during the 1930s.

Labor problems. As business slowly improved, unions in this state fought to gain their share of the profits. More unions earned the right to bargain, and some industries had their own unions, such as United Steel Workers. Unskilled workers could join the unions now, where only those with job skills had been allowed to join before.

Though efforts to unionize were fruitful, many hot debates led to fighting. There were 800 strikes in the state from 1930 to 1936. Employers did not want to give up their right to control their businesses. On the other hand, labor wanted to gain the right to bargain for better conditions and wages.

The year 1937 was marked by brutal strikes in Massillon, Niles, Canton, and Youngstown. Governor Martin L. Davey had to call the National Guard to Youngstown to restore peace.

Most employers accepted labor unions by 1940. Organized labor became a strong force in the state, with labor casting most of its votes to the Democratic party. This tended to balance out Ohio's typical Republican leanings.

Over 800,000 Ohio men and women served in the armed forces during World War II.
Pictured here are some Ohioans fighting on an island in the Pacific Ocean.

7. There were heavy losses in World War II, but then the nation's economy got a big boost.

As we were still getting out of the depression, war broke out in Europe in 1939. For a while, the country stayed out of this conflict, but the war soon spread throughout the world. The nation joined on the side of England and France when Japan bombed our bases at Pearl Harbor, Hawaii, December 7, 1941. The war was ended shortly after the U.S. dropped the world's first atomic bomb on Hiroshima, Japan, August 6, 1945.

World War II was the most costly war yet fought in terms of damage and lives lost. Women and men from our state signed up in great numbers for the service, and other men were later drafted. By the time the war was over, more than 800,000 Ohioans had served in the armed forces. More than 23,000 gave their lives. All of Ohio's culture groups served. Six percent of them were black, while more than 3% were Jews.

RODGER W. YOUNG, 1918-1943

THE MacPherson Cemetery at Clyde is named for the highest ranking officer killed in the Civil War. Among the servicemen buried at Clyde is George Meek, the first sailor to die in the Spanish American War. In the northeast corner of the grounds is the grave of Rodger Wilton Young. Young received the Medal of Honor for his bravery during World War II.

Rodger Young's name was well-known during the war because of the ballad Frank Loesser wrote about him. Two of Loesser's popular songs were "Praise the Lord and Pass the Ammunition" and "What Do You Do in the Infantry?" The "Ballad of Rodger Young" became the favorite song of the *infantry* (foot troops).

Young was born and raised in Green Springs. He worked during the summer at a pickle factory or in orchards picking fruit. As a high school basketball player, Young was admired by his teachers for his hard work and quiet ways. Rodger was a small fellow (5 feet 4½ inches, 135 pounds) who joined the National Guard soon after high school. He rose to the rank of technical sergeant and was called to active duty in 1940. He was shipped overseas early in 1942. While there, Young asked that his rank be reduced because of poor hearing. He felt that his faulty hearing might place the lives of his men in danger.

On July 31, 1943, Rodger Young's outfit was pinned down by Japanese machine gun fire on three sides with a swamp to their backs. They had no food for two days and were being picked off at a rate of one a minute. As a rifleman, Young deliberately drew the fire of the Japanese so the others could retreat safely. Twice hit, Young hurled grenades into the enemy stronghold and silenced the machine guns before he died of his wounds.

Sgt. Floyd Kruse, a friend in Company B, 148th Infantry, 37th Division said, "If it wasn't for Rodger, I wouldn't be here today." Another buddy wrote of Rodger, "If it had not been for his heroism, we all would have been sunk."

Loesser wrote of Young:

Shines the name, shines the name of Rodger Young,
Fought and died for the men he marched among,
To the everlasting glory of the Infantry,
Lives the story of Private Rodger Young.

POW camps. The state saw a new side of war when prisoners of war (POWs) were brought here. Camps were set up for them at sites such as Camp Perry on Lake Erie. Some 7,000 Germans and Italians were housed there. Several thousand prisoners worked in the tomato fields and canneries at Defiance and Bowling Green. More camps were set up in Columbus, Cambridge, Celina, Wilmington, Dayton, and Marion.

Industry's role. The state's industries grew to meet the needs of a nation at war. The federal government made contracts with firms to supply iron, steel, rubber products, planes, and motor vehicles. Cleveland, Columbus, Akron, Canton, Dayton, Cincinnati, Hamilton, and Toledo had huge plants and won the contracts. By 1945, more than 5,000 firms in the state had produced some type of goods for war. Nearly 1,000 of them had made nothing but war supplies.

Labor gains. With the growth of war industries, a larger work force was needed. Wages jumped 65% during the early years of the war. More women

Ohio's industries were very important in bringing victory in World War II. Here, workers are assembling the Curtiss-Wright "Helldiver" airplane.

went to work in the factories, because they had to support themselves while the men were away at war. By 1945 nearly 40% of the workers in Columbus were women.

Another trend in labor during the war was the *migration* of blacks from the South and whites from the Appalachian Mountains. They came to the cities seeking work. The portion of blacks in the labor force rose from 3% in 1940 to more than 8% by the end of the war.

This influx of non-union workers caused problems for unions. Yet, there were few labor problems during World War II. Workers had a loyal feeling and seldom went on strike. Instead, they followed the plan set up by Michael V. DiSalle of Toledo, which used a board of citizens to *arbitrate* (referee) disputes which arose.

Agriculture responds. The demand for farm goods to feed soldiers and to sell to countries which were at war grew 200% during the war years. The need for farm labor was so great that *migrant*

Michael V. DiSalle of Toledo was the head of the Office of Price Administration during World War II. The OPA tried to prevent prices of goods from going too high. DiSalle was elected governor in 1958.

workers from Mexico and the West Indies were brought to the state to work in the fields.

The conservation effort at home. Due to Japanese victories in parts of the Pacific Ocean, some raw materials were *scarce*. Scarce means there is not enough of a thing to meet all the needs for it. Two ways were used to solve the problem of short supplies. Scientists were urged to find or invent substitutes for the scarce resources, but that would take time. For example, nylon was developed to take the place of silk. What were the uses of nylon during the 1940s?

The other method was to *conserve* (save) our resources by rationing. To ration is to limit the amount of a product which the public can buy. People received stamps which allowed them to buy a small quantity of scarce goods. The first thing to be rationed was sugar, followed by meat, gasoline, and rubber products such as tires.

Another plan to conserve was the "victory garden." Ohio and other states asked people to grow their own vegetables so most of the farmers' products could be sent overseas. Ohioans planted over two and one-half million gardens and produced more than $150 million worth of vegetables!

Victory for the U.S. and its allies came at last on September 2, 1945, when peace terms were signed. Ohioans had earned the right to be proud of their efforts at war and at home.

What problems would the people of Ohio have to face in getting back to a normal way of life?

WORDS FOR STUDY

slogan	*bonds*
moderator	*fixed percent*
overproduced	*interest*
producers	*stock market*
suburban	*liberated*
stock	*spectaculars*
investment capital	*intimidate*
stock certificate	*failed*
dividend	*infantry*

migration *scarce*
arbitrate *conserve*
migrant

QUESTIONS FOR REVIEW

1. What was Ohio's economy like in the 1920s?
2. What was the life style of the twenties like?
3. What are two ways a business can raise investment capital?
4. What are two nicknames for the decade of the 1920s?
5. How did life for women change in the 1920s?
6. What racially prejudiced group became active in Ohio in the 1920s? Who were they prejudiced against? What were their methods?
7. How were the people of Ohio affected by the depression?
8. How did the cities help take care of needy people? How did the state help? What federal plan gave relief?
9. At the peak of the depression, what percentage of Ohioans was unemployed?
10. How many labor strikes took place in Ohio between 1930 and 1936?
11. How many Ohioans served in the military during World War II?
12. What role did industry play in the war?
13. How did the farmers help support the war effort?
14. What two methods were used at home to make up for scarce goods?

GOING FURTHER

1. How does demand affect supply?
2. What were the causes of the Great Depression?
3. What did the state and federal governments do to boost the economy that cities could not do by themselves?
4. How was the labor force of the 1930s different from before the depression?

FOR THOUGHT AND DISCUSSION

1. How does Ohio's economy today compare with that of the 1920s? Explain your answer with specific examples. Is another Great Depression likely to occur soon? Why or why not?
2. How does the role of today's stock market compare with the role it played before the Great Depression? To what extent is the stock market active in your community?
3. Why do you think farmers and industries overproduced, even when they saw that demand was going down? What clues can producers watch for that will help them avoid a similar problem?
4. Why did racial prejudice become a problem in the 1930s? How do you feel about the activities of the Ku Klux Klan?

PROJECTS AND REPORTS

1. Find information on the clothing and hair styles of the Roaring Twenties. Prepare a classroom display to share your findings. You may choose to display actual clothing, photographs from a family album, pictures, or drawings.
2. Choose any of the new types of technology that came about from 1920 to 1945 and research its development. Make an oral report or poster display for the class. Examples would be: motion pictures, automobiles, atom bomb, airplanes, radios.
3. Learn a song that was popular between 1920 and 1945. Present it to the class in person or by means of a recording.
4. Write a report on any political leader from the period.
5. Draw a map to show the political alliances of World War II. Indicate the places where major battles took place.
6. Collect some newspaper articles from the 1940s that show how Ohioans felt about the war.
7. Study President Franklin D. Roosevelt's New Deal to find out what projects were built in Ohio under New Deal programs. Report your findings to the class.

In the years since World War II, the costs of constructing new buildings have soared, and new structures often lack the beautiful style and decoration of earlier times. For these reasons, many attractive older buildings are now being restored, rather than being torn down to make way for new construction. The Netherland Plaza in Cincinnati is an example of a beautifully-restored older building. The historic Art-Deco style hotel has been a favorite spot with Ohioans since 1931.

CHAPTER 10

THE RECENT YEARS

1945-present

MAIN POINTS

1. The post-war 1940s and the 1950s saw general prosperity and a move to the suburbs.
2. The Korean War led to a red scare in the early fifties.
3. The mood of the 1960s was one of protest and back-to-nature.
4. Preservation and conservation were major concerns of the 1970s.
5. The 1980s brought some tough economic challenges.

One way to look at history is through the moods of the people during certain time periods. A review of economic and political trends will help us put events in focus. In this way we may see how certain events are like things that happened before, or how events are *interrelated.* By learning about events from 1945 to the present, we can see how the moods and trends of the state and the nation affected economics.

1. The post-war 1940s and the 1950s saw general prosperity and a move to the suburbs.

A short recession, then recovery. There was a slight depression (called a recession) in the late forties as business returned to peacetime production. As veterans coming home from World War II wanted their old jobs back, many women, blacks, and Appalachian whites were laid off. They had trouble finding new jobs, so many of them went on welfare. Nearly 80% of those on welfare were women.

During World War II, the federal government controlled the prices of consumer goods. Without controls, the cost of scarce goods might have skyrocketed. After the war, when controls were lifted, prices did rise quickly. With so many people seeking jobs, employers did not need to pay high wages. Workers could not afford high priced goods, so some surpluses began to build. This overproduction in turn led to more layoffs. But within a few years, the peacetime industries grew stronger. The automobile, airplane, and construction fields were among the leaders. They hired many of the jobless. Except for a few years in the early 1950s, prosperity was quite high for most people.

Life in suburbia attracts many. As a result of a baby boom, the population of the state jumped 22% between 1950 and 1960. This brought the total to nearly 10 million people. Growth was felt in many places. As inner cities grew more and more crowded, those who could afford to moved to the suburbs. They liked the thought of having more space between houses. As shopping centers were built in the suburbs, that life style became more pleasant. The Town and Country Shopping Center on East Broad Street in Columbus was the first of its kind in the nation.

As a result of people moving to the suburbs, tax money was lost for the cities, and buildings and streets fell into disrepair.

The Town and Country Shopping Center was the first of its kind in the nation.

2. The Korean War led to a red scare in the early fifties.

In 1950, our country joined an effort to keep South Korea from being overrun by North Korean communists. President Harry Truman did not want to be too aggressive in the conflict for fear it would start another world war. After three years, the war was ended with neither side winning. Our nation lost more than 25,000 men and women in the war. Of those, 1,716 were from Ohio. Many people wondered if fighting a "no-win" war was worth the loss of lives.

The Korean War led to another communist scare in our country. President Truman ordered a search to find those in government who were not loyal to the United States.

In 1946 the Communist party claimed to have 3,500 members in our state. Five years later, Governor Frank Lausche set up the Un-American Activities Commission. By 1952, this group found that there was much communist activity in Ohio. They also found about 1,300 Communist party members, mostly in the large industrial cities. While some 700 lived near Cleveland, about 200 lived in central and southern Ohio. The rest were scattered throughout other industrial centers of the state.

Governor Frank Lausche set up the Un-American Activities Commission to investigate communism. Lausche was the only five-term governor of Ohio. He was elected to the U.S. Senate in 1956 and 1962.

Headlines like this appeared in newspapers throughout the country during the red scare of the late 1940s and early 1950s.

The communists sought to control the labor unions. However, their attempt failed. In 1951, party members in the state voted to go underground (hide from public notice). Even so, the fear of communism lasted a long while.

3. The mood of the 1960s was one of protest and back-to-nature.

The war in Vietnam (1962-1975). The nation was involved in another war to stop the spread of communism in the early 1960s. It was somewhat like the problem in Korea, but this time the country was Vietnam. At first, U.S. military leaders helped South

Vietnam turn back the communist invaders from North Vietnam. But as the war grew hotter, more U.S. troops were sent to fight. During President Lyndon Johnson's term of office, there were more than 500,000 American soldiers in Vietnam.

As the war dragged on into the late sixties, it became the least popular one our nation had ever known. Many felt that we should not be fighting to defend a country so far away.

As the number of dead began to mount higher, *protests* against the war grew louder throughout the state, as well as in the rest of the country. War critics joined forces with those who spoke out against the ills of society.

This is a view of the Kent State incident in May 1970, in which four students were shot and killed by National Guard troops. This anti-war demonstration got out of hand. Can you recall other times when people have spoken out against war? What happened to them?

The Kent State incident. In May of 1970, students at Kent State University raised a protest against the growing war in Vietnam. The protest got out of hand as buildings were burned and store windows in downtown Kent were broken. Governor James Rhodes sent the Ohio National Guard to Kent to restore order. On May 4, a large crowd of students came face to face with the guardsmen. The guardsmen, thinking their lives were in danger, fired shots into the crowd. Four students were killed and several others wounded.

The Kent State incident touched off heated *demonstrations* at other colleges all over the land. National Guard troops had to be sent to the Ohio State University campus. The protests did not calm down until the first U.S. troops were pulled out of Vietnam in the early seventies.

Consequences of the Vietnam War. Fighting ceased at last in January 1973. The war had cost the lives of more than 40,000 Americans—2,993 from Ohio. The war cost more than just lives, though. By the end of March 1973 the enemy released what they claimed to be the last of the U.S. prisoners of war (POWs). Some of them had been in prison camps for years. (There are those who believe that some POWs are still being held captive in North Vietnam today.)

Within a few years from 1975, when the last U.S. troops left South Vietnam, the Communists took control there. This loss was hard for Americans to

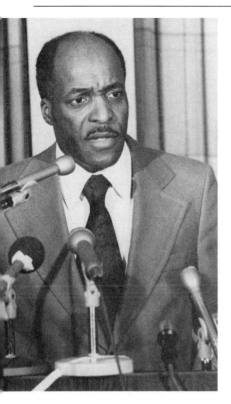 

Civil rights leaders Nathaniel R. Jones (left) and William O. Walker have worked to improve conditions for blacks.

accept. The war caused a great split between those who supported the war effort and those who were against it.

Vietnam veterans were not treated like the veterans of other wars. They were not thought of as heroes when they came home. Many vets have met painful social and economic problems. For instance, in 1982 the jobless rate among Vietnam veterans was twice that of other unemployed Americans. It is hoped that time will heal these wounds. Part of that process was started in 1982 when a Vietnam Memorial was built in Washington, D.C.

Do you know any Vietnam vets? If so, try to find out how they feel now about that war and how they have faced the problems they found at home.

The civil rights movement. The decade of the sixties was a time much like the progressive years of the early 1900s. Many people joined movements to work for reforms. The civil rights movement to improve the treatment of *minority* groups was the main effort. Blacks are the state's largest minority group. Clusters of Puerto Ricans live in Lorain and Cleveland. Some *Hispanic* people are migrant workers in the state. Minority groups have long been held back by discrimination in housing, education, and the job market. In the sixties, the civil rights movement gained strength. This led to widespread demonstrations, rallies, and new laws. Some strong leaders among minority groups led this movement in the state and the nation.

Leaders in civil rights. The National Association for the Advancement of Colored People (NAACP) took the lead in the civil rights movement. Chester

K. Gillespie of Cleveland was an NAACP leader for 50 years. He was a former chief justice of the Cleveland municipal courts. Other civil rights leaders include Carl B. Stokes of Cleveland, Nathaniel R. Jones of Youngstown, Wendell Irwin of Cleveland, Theodore Berry, Marian Spencer, and J.C. Johnson, all of Cincinnati.

Blacks in government. In recent years some big victories have been won for equal rights. In 1963 William O. Walker of Cleveland was the first black named to a governor's cabinet. Governor James A. Rhodes made him head of the Department of Industrial Relations. In 1967 Robert C. Henry of Springfield was chosen mayor by the city commission. In 1968 Robert N. Duncan was placed on the state supreme court. Bennett J. Cooper became the head of the state prisons.

Discrimination and riots in the cities. In 1960 the new Ohio Civil Rights Commission found that there was much discrimination in public life. While changes in law came about quite slowly, unfair treatment was given to people of minority races.

Minority groups, joined by some whites, began to demonstrate against those who practiced discrimination. For instance, in 1964, students from Antioch College at Yellow Springs carried picket signs at the shop of a barber who would not cut the hair of blacks. The protest got out of hand, and the police had to use force to stop it.

The tension erupted in the middle sixties as more riots broke out in major U.S. cities. In July 1966, terror, fires, and bloodshed were part of the scene in the Hough section of Cleveland. Blacks and police began shooting at each other. Governor Rhodes sent the National Guard to stop the riots, but four people were killed before the conflict ended. A few weeks later, the National Guard was called upon to quell a riot in Dayton.

Civil rights in public schools. Segregation (the separation of races) has been around for years. This practice existed either by law (*de jure*) or by action without law (*de facto,* meaning in fact).

Segregation in schools was an issue with which civil rights groups tried to deal. A 1954 Supreme Court ruling said that public schools must be *desegregated.* It was claimed that schools with mostly black children did not get the same service and quality of teachers.

Some cities in our state had trouble obeying the law. Hillsboro and Cleveland were sites of public protests. A key decision was made by the federal courts in 1976. A federal judge found the Cleveland school board guilty of practicing discrimination in the city schools. The judge ordered them to take steps at once to fully *integrate* their schools. One means has been the busing of children to schools in other neighborhoods. This is not always accepted by parents. Some think the best solution will come only when the neighborhoods have a mixture of races—black, white and Hispanic.

The turmoil of the sixties caused some changes in equal rights for minorities, both *de jure* and *de facto.* Public schools are becoming more integrated. Some all-white neighborhoods have been opened to all groups. More technical training is available for youths to give them skills to find jobs. In the eighties, black state legislators are working to gain more rights for minorities.

Find out if any bills are in process now that would improve the rights and equal treatment of blacks and other groups. Is there evidence of discrimination in your school? If so, what are some ways to solve this problem?

Back-to-nature trend. As early as the 1950s, Americans began to feel a need to get away from the crowded city life. As the protests in the sixties pointed out the ills of society, many people turned to nature for a more peaceful life. While city air was *polluted* and traffic was noisy, the forests and countrysides had clean air and the soft sounds of nature.

Camping, hiking, and backpacking gained much favor. With this movement came a new concern to save our forests. Ohio was once thickly wooded, but as trees were cleared for farms, lumber, and charcoal, much of the landscape changed. Groups

CARL B. STOKES, (1927-)

IN 1967, Carl B. Stokes of Cleveland became the first black mayor of a large U.S. city. In 1962, he had been the first black Democrat in the state legislature.

Carl Stokes was born in a poor section of Cleveland. His father died when Carl was two years old. Carl and his older brother, Louis, were raised by their mother, Louise, who worked as a cleaning woman. Mrs. Stokes taught her sons the value of a good education, but Carl quit school at age 17 to work in a *foundry* (metal casting plant). At 18 he joined the army and served in World War II. After coming home from the war, Stokes finished high school and went to college. He graduated from the Cleveland Marshall Law School and was admitted to the state bar in 1957. He was appointed as an assistant city prosecutor for Cleveland.

Stokes was active in the Cleveland chapter of the NAACP and served three consecutive terms in the Ohio legislature.

Race problems grew in Cleveland as many blacks were out of work. Stokes ran for mayor in 1965, but lost. Riots broke out the next year in the Hough section. In 1967 Stokes ran for the mayor's job once more. He was helped by a visit from Martin Luther King, Jr. (national leader in civil rights), who urged blacks to register and vote. A fine speaker, Stokes described how he rose from a poor beginning. Cleveland's two

large newspapers and most ethnic language papers backed him. Stokes also received help from businessmen and won the race for mayor.

In 1968, he was praised for the way he handled racial unrest when a group of blacks attacked members of the police force.

Stokes was re-elected in 1969, but chose not to run for a third term. He moved to New York where he worked as a broadcast newsman in radio and T.V. Stokes later returned to Cleveland, where he practiced law. His brother, Louis, served the state as a congressman from Cleveland during the seventies and eighties.

In recent years, people have turned to nature for relief from the crowding, noise, and pollution of the cities. Many groups have been formed to protect the environment.

of *environmentalists* sought to increase public appreciation for all of our country's wild lands. Due to their work and new laws to protect the environment, forests are slowly growing under good management.

Natural food movement. The return to nature brought a new interest in fresh foods. Many felt that chemical *preservatives* used to give food a longer *shelf life* were harmful to the body. The result of this concern was the appearance of *natural foods,* or foods without chemicals. This trend is still quite popular today.

The food interests also proved to be a boon for the farmers. City dwellers thought it was a treat to drive to rural spots where they could buy produce directly from the farm. They felt that fresh foods were more nutritious than canned ones.

> The back-to-nature trend kept on growing. Today there are many things in our lives that show these values. Join with a group of classmates to list 10 things that are linked to the back-to-nature movement.

4. Preservation and conservation were major concerns of the 1970s.

Energy demands. A major problem arose in the 1970s with the supply and cost of energy. The price of oil soared when rumors of an oil shortage were spread. In an effort to save oil, people were asked to cut back on buying gasoline. This led to a demand for small foreign-made cars that used less fuel. In turn, U.S. automakers were hurt because they were not prepared to make small cars. A step to conserve fuel use was taken by the federal government when it lowered the speed limit on all freeways to 55 miles per hour. Before this, cars could go 70 miles per hour, but cars at higher speeds used more fuel.

The oil shortages brought concern for other types of fuel—natural gas, electricity, and coal. The federal government stepped in again and passed a law that thermostats in public buildings must be set no higher than 68° in winter and no lower than 78° in summer. This would cut down on the use of fuels.

In an effort to save fuel, the speed limit was dropped from 70 to 55 miles per hour on the nation's highways.

Ohio is the fifth leading state in the use of energy. It uses much more than it produces. Even with large coal reserves and some oil and natural gas, there is not enough fuel to supply homes and businesses. Extra fuel must be bought outside the state. Geologists feel that there are enough coal reserves to last for over 500 years. If this estimate is right, then what is the problem about Ohio's energy demands?

One thing is that the state's coal has a high sulphur content. When the coal is burned it causes pollution. Scientists are working to find ways to "clean" the coal in order to prevent the pollution of the air. A problem with the state's natural gas

is that there is no cheap way to get the gas out of the earth. Therefore, the state has to import large amounts of gas from Texas and Louisiana. The price of gas keeps going up and up. This, in turn, raises the cost of living and doing business.

Alternative energy sources. What are some other ways to meet the state's energy demands? Nuclear power is a possible answer. There are nuclear power plants along Lake Erie, such as the Davis-Besse plant in Ottawa County, and along the Ohio River. While government rules on the building and use of nuclear plants have been strict, some people fear the chance of a nuclear accident.

Alternate energy sources promise ways to save precious fuel and cut down on pollution.

What about the use of solar power? Using the rays of the sun is another way to produce energy. Scientists say that the state has enough sunny days year round to provide solar energy. This likely source has not yet been fully developed here.

> Take a survey of your own home to find ways to conserve energy. Chart your progress over a period of two weeks.

The historic preservation trend. Another value that developed along with conservation was historic *preservation*. More and more, people saw a need to preserve (save) old things. It was felt that objects made years ago were of better quality and workmanship than the mass-produced items of today.

Grandmother's wedding gown and Uncle Joe's hand-made bench took on new historic meaning. One could learn about life in the old days from letters and diaries. Feelings for past cultures could be gained by studying things that people of long ago used and saved.

Many small towns have *restored* their old buildings as a way of ending economic and physical decay in their downtown business districts. Money to pay for this work has come from private funds, government grants, and the National Trust for Historic Preservation in Washington, D.C. The results are exciting and worthwhile. Business has improved. Second- and third-floor office space has come back into use and demand.

This wedding dress of long ago is part of a family's history and a community's history. What can we learn from it?

THE MEDINA STORY

MEDINA is a good case of the value of historic preservation. In the early 1960s the business center of the town was dying and quick action was needed to save it. At first the storefronts were covered with metal sheets. Business failed to improve, so a second plan was tried. Starting with a large bank on one corner of the town square, most of the business blocks were "face-lifted" and returned to their original nineteenth century look. Bright colors highlighted building details. New signs with special lettering were placed on storefronts. Stained-glass windows were uncovered and restored. A beautiful white bandstand was built in the center of the town square. Crowning the entire effort, the handsome Medina County Courthouse was fully restored.

The Medina project, led by a community design group, was a big success. It boosted town spirit and morale, greatly improved business, and won national praise for excellence. Medina and other towns like it have helped make Ohio a leader in historic preservation work in the Midwest. This trend spread to many other cities in the 1970s.

Fountain Center Plaza in Cincinnati, with the new Westin Hotel, built in 1981.

Urban renewal and planning. Beyond conservation and preservation, progress was made to clean up the cities. Urban sprawl, new shopping malls, and loss of inner city population meant decay for the old business districts.

Some cities tried to improve public transportation into the cities. Plans were made to renew the urban centers. Toledo restored an area that is now called the Seagate Development. Columbus, Dayton, and Cincinnati have found much success

Governor James A. Rhodes came from a coal mining family in Coalton. He was elected governor in 1962, 1966, 1974, and 1978. Governor Rhodes has been one of the best salesmen ever for the state of Ohio.

with their plans. New convention centers, hotels, and public plazas have appeared in their downtown sections.

The repair of storefronts has been matched by progress in other ways. Flowers, shade trees, cloth awnings, new street lamps, brick sidewalks, bench seats, and small parks are ways some towns have acquired a fresh look. This, in turn, draws shoppers and tourists to the central business district. Towns like Perrysburg, Sandusky, Hudson, and Chillicothe have reclaimed their pasts through historic preservation and urban renewal.

5. The 1980s brought some tough economic challenges.

The main concern of the 1980s is economics. The problem began in the seventies, but the answer must come in this decade. *Inflation* was a cause of the troubles faced by the state, as well as the nation. The jobless rate has been high, and prices are up.

In recent years, progress has been made in making the state's economy stable, but those plans have not saved us from the nation's economic decline.

The state lottery was approved during the term of Governor John J. Gilligan. How does the lottery raise money for the state? Why do some people oppose the lottery?

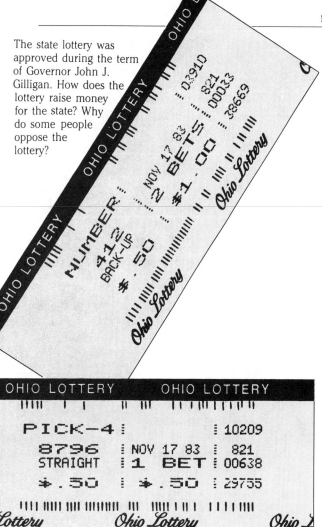

to the state and gave jobs to the people of our state.

Governor John J. Gilligan, a Democrat, increased state revenues during his term (1971-75). He had campaigned on a pledge to place a tax on income. In 1971 the first state income tax was passed. All those who earned money had to pay a tax ranging from ½% to 3½%, depending on their income.

Governor Gilligan wanted the new tax to help fund education, transportation, and human welfare. However, these monies have not done all that supporters of the tax claimed they would. Still, Ohio ranks in the lower half of the nation for the amount of income taxes paid.

A new source of revenue was approved by the voters in 1972. This was a constitutional amendment which allowed the state to run a *lottery*. A lottery is a type of gambling where people buy tickets for chances in a drawing. The lottery started in 1974 and brought the state more funds, but inflation and unemployment still cause financial problems. There are still economic issues to be dealt with by the state in the 1980s. What do you think some solutions might be?

Decades may be described by moods and trends. However, these events tend to overlap into other decades. Identifying social and economic trends makes it easier for us to focus on the main problems in each period and to trace the roots of current issues.

Republican Governor James A. Rhodes, in four terms of office, worked hard to make the economy strong. He planned to build more technical schools to train skilled laborers for the work force. Technical colleges were built in many communities. Then people could get training near their homes. All of this building cost money. The taxpayers approved new funds to pay for the programs.

In an attempt to reduce the tax load and improve the economy, Rhodes worked to find new industries for the state. He traveled to Japan, Europe, and China to open trade offices and to invite companies to build in Ohio. These new businesses paid taxes

WORDS FOR STUDY

interrelated	environmentalist
protest	preservative
demonstration	shelf life
minority	natural foods
Hispanic	preservation
foundry	restore
de jure	inflation
de facto	lottery
desegregate	
integrate	
polluted	

QUESTIONS FOR REVIEW

1. In what way does grouping events by trends help us understand history?

2. What caused the recession following World War II?

3. What drew people to the suburbs?

4. What was the reaction of people in this country to the Korean War?

5. Why did people protest the war in Vietnam?

6. What were the reasons for student protests and the shooting incident at Kent State University in 1970?

7. Why have Vietnam veterans had a difficult time getting used to life in the U.S. again?

8. What is a minority group? Give some examples.

9. What problems did minority groups face in the 1960s and before?

10. Name two members of minority groups who have served in government, and tell about their contributions.

11. Who was the first black mayor of a large city in Ohio?

12. Describe the two ways segregation may occur.

13. Give some examples of the back-to-nature trend of the sixties.

14. What steps were taken in the 1970s to conserve energy?

15. How did citizens of Medina use historic preservation to save their city from decline?

16. What is urban renewal?

17. What was the main cause of economic ills in the 1980s?

18. What programs did governors Rhodes and Gilligan set up that helped improve the state's economic outlook for the 1980s?

GOING FURTHER

1. Why was Governor James A. Rhodes elected so many times?

2. Why were the increased revenues from the income tax and lottery not enough to solve the state's financial problems?

3. Why does Ohio have energy problems with so many coal reserves in the state?

4. How was it possible to first segregate, and later desegregate, the state's public schools?

5. How have some urban centers and smaller towns improved their environments?

FOR THOUGHT AND DISCUSSION

1. Why have the economic problems of the 1980s not disappeared as quickly as those after World War II?

2. What was different about the Korean and Vietnam wars as compared with earlier wars in which Ohioans were involved?

3. Why were the protests over civil rights issues so heated? Which issues today get that much attention?

4. Who are the civil rights leaders of today—in your community? in the state?

5. Are urban renewal, back-to-nature, and historic preservation linked in any way? Explain your opinion and give evidence.

6. What is the role of government in solving the economic problems of the 1980s? What is the role of private industry and citizens?

PROJECTS AND REPORTS

1. Collect photographs and news articles from the 1940s-1950s to show what life was like then. Display your collection for the class to see.

2. Plan and carry out an experiment using an alternative energy source.

3. Study the current status of civil rights for minorities to evaluate the need for further improvements. Write a summary paper.

4. Research and report orally or in writing about any leader of the civil rights movement.

5. Research the Brown vs. Board of Education, Topeka, Kansas, case of 1954 to find out how it affected desegregation.

6. Construct a time line, and place events from this chapter in chronological order.

A pheasant farm in Urbana.

CHAPTER 11

AGRICULTURE AND RURAL LIFE

MAIN POINTS

1. As the state's largest business, farming provides a variety of products.

2. Ohio's rural counties are found in three main locations.

3. Nineteenth-century farms provided a strong foundation for agriculture in Ohio.

4. Technology and education changed farm life after 1860.

5. Twentieth-century farms are larger and more specialized.

6. Ohio's rural areas have a distinct culture and charm.

7. Farm and rural areas will decline in size to the year 2000.

Ohio is famous for its contributions in the field of agriculture. It was the first farm state to develop in the midwest and still ranks high in farm production. Crop improvements made here helped to make better farms in such states as Indiana, Illinois, and Iowa.

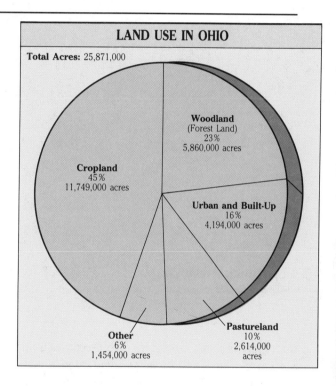

LAND USE IN OHIO

Total Acres: 25,871,000

Woodland (Forest Land) 23% 5,860,000 acres

Cropland 45% 11,749,000 acres

Urban and Built-Up 16% 4,194,000 acres

Other 6% 1,454,000 acres

Pastureland 10% 2,614,000 acres

1. As the state's largest business, farming provides a variety of products.

With two-thirds of Ohio classified as farmland, farming is the largest business in the state.

The modern term for the whole farming economy is *agribusiness*. Besides growing, it includes farm supplies, processing, transporting, and distributing of the products. Our state now has more than 90,000 farms with an average size of 150 acres. Agribusiness employs about 750,000 workers.

The worth of the state's farm products is more than $20 billion each year. These dollars generate $3 to $5 in the off-farm economy.

The state's farm products are varied. Until the mid-1950s, our farms dealt mainly in livestock. Products included milk and other dairy foods, as well as beef cattle, hogs, sheep, and poultry. This pattern has changed in recent years. At this time, more

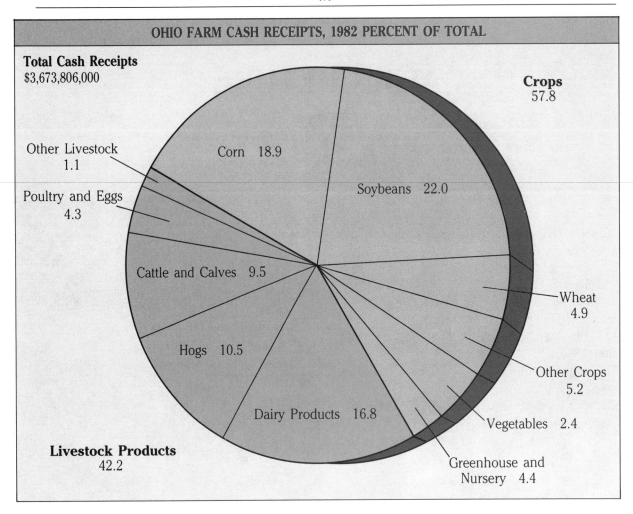

OHIO FARM CASH RECEIPTS, 1982 PERCENT OF TOTAL

Total Cash Receipts
$3,673,806,000

Crops
57.8

Corn 18.9

Soybeans 22.0

Other Livestock
1.1

Poultry and Eggs
4.3

Cattle and Calves 9.5

Wheat
4.9

Hogs 10.5

Other Crops
5.2

Dairy Products 16.8

Vegetables 2.4

Livestock Products
42.2

Greenhouse and
Nursery 4.4

than half the state's gross farm income comes from *agronomic* (field) and *horticultural* (garden) crops.

Important crops raised here are soybeans, corn, wheat, alfalfa, oats, tobacco, tomatoes, potatoes, sugar beets, and other fruit and vegetable crops.

Climate and soil are main factors which help to determine the kinds of farms that thrive in different parts of the state. The glacial limestone region in the west is prime land for corn, soybeans, wheat and tomatoes. The shale and sandstone soils found in the eastern counties are suited for dairy and beef cattle, sheep, and forest products. Fruit crops do well near Lake Erie where the growing season is longer and temperatures are mild.

As the state's oldest business, farming is still a main part of Ohio's economy and life style.

2. Ohio's rural counties are found in three main locations.

Rural people make up about 27% of the state's population, but only 3% are members of full-time farm families. More than 60,000 part-time farmers earn their main living from jobs in small towns or nearby cities.

Of the state's 88 counties, 57 today are counted by the Census Bureau as rural. They are found in three regions.

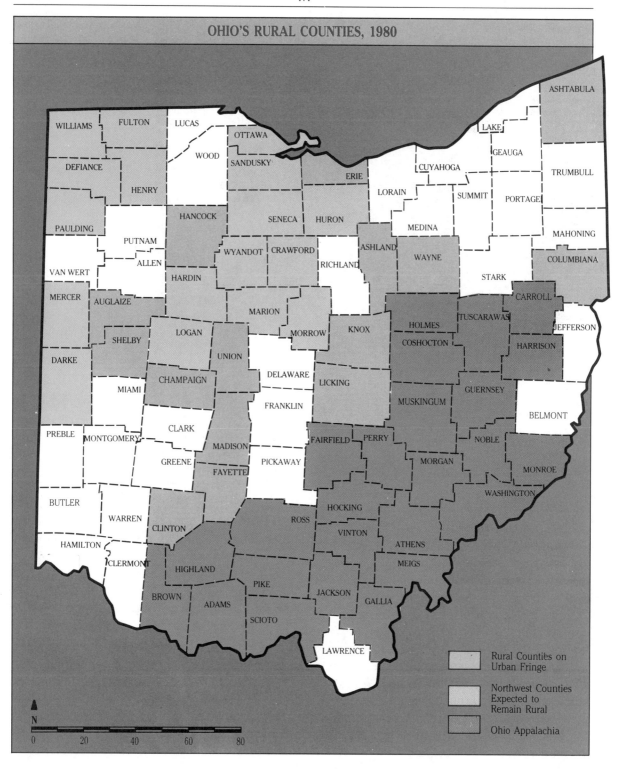

OHIO'S RURAL COUNTIES, 1980

Rural Counties on
Urban Fringe

Northwest Counties
Expected to
Remain Rural

Ohio Appalachia

A variety of activities make farming Ohio's largest business. This is the sheep judging event at the Seneca County Fair, 1983.

Ohio Appalachia. The largest rural region is made up of 25 counties in the south and southeast. This hilly and scenic region includes foothills of the Appalachian Mountains. Sometimes called "Appalachia," the area is good for forests, livestock, and minimum- or no-*tillage* crops, such as fruit orchards.

Northwest Ohio. The second group of rural counties, which includes much of the best farmland in the state, is found in the northwest. Part of this section is what used to be called the Black Swamp. The swamp was *methodically* drained during the last half of the 1800s. The farmland here is a mixture of heavy clay soils and sand ridges.

Urban fringe. The rural counties in the third group are scattered throughout the state. What these farm regions have in common is that they are on the *fringe* (edge) of cities. A number of counties in this group will lose their rural nature in the years to come as cities and suburbs expand.

3. Nineteenth-century farms provided a strong foundation for agriculture in Ohio.

Pioneer farms to 1820. You will recall that the first settlers had to clear their land of forests. Once that was done, one-third to one-half of the clearing was used to plant crops. Corn and hog raising was the basic economy. After a cleared farm was well established, the pioneer might sell his property, collect the profit, and start again at some new place in the woods.

Old cleared farms, 1820-1865. Those who stayed behind developed the early farms further. More trees were cut for farming or pasture land. Orchards and gardens were planted, and rail fences were built. Better buildings were erected—a brick house, a barn, sometimes a smokehouse for curing meat, or a *spring house* (for cooling food) over a stream.

As villages grew up, farmers were able to purchase their farm supplies and machinery from shopkeepers in town. This is Bucyrus, Ohio, in the late 1800s. Bucyrus is known for handcrafted copper kettles, bowls, and frying pans.

Meanwhile, signs of community life appeared. The building of a common school, a church, and a general store at a crossroads were sure signs of progress.

Most of the old cleared farms were used for general farming. Some land was put into pasture or meadow. The typical Ohio farmer of 1850 got cash by selling grain, livestock, wool, butter, eggs, or meat. In time, the farmers became more dependent upon others. They began to *specialize* (deal in just one or two products) and hire labor. Machinery and farm supplies were bought from shopkeepers in villages.

Products of pioneer farms. Cattle raising was one of the most important early developments. Centered first near Chillicothe and the lower Scioto Valley, cattle raising spread westward through southern Ohio to the Miami Valley. The cattle brought good prices in eastern markets. Farmers would fatten their livestock on corn during the winter and drive them east in the spring.

Settlers from Connecticut who came to the Western Reserve went into the dairy business and built cheese factories. These ventures failed until about 1860, when improved ways of making cheese made the dairies successful.

Today, festivals and fairs carry on old traditions. These people are churning butter at the Maple Sugar festival in Burton. What festivals and fairs are held in your region?

Large numbers of swine were raised in the Miami Valley. Corn for feed was plentiful there, and fattened hogs could be sold in Cincinnati. That city soon became nationally known as a pork-packing center and was often called "Porkopolis."

The sheep business in the east and southeast proved to be most profitable during the 1800s. But it had problems as the demand for wool went up and down according to U.S. tariff rates. A high tariff helped to protect wool growers from foreign competition.

By 1850, horse raising had become an important specialty. Horses were sold in the South and the East either for field work or for riding. Furthermore, the U.S. Army, as well as builders of canals,

turnpikes, and railroads, needed a lot of horses and mules. In 1860, Ohio raised more work horses than any other state.

Wheat was one of the first *cash crops* to be grown here. In the early years, surplus grain went downstream on the Ohio River to southern and eastern markets. Later, it was shipped to the East by way of the Erie Canal. Toledo and Milan (joined by a special canal with Lake Erie) were major grain ports in the 1840s.

Changes in the 1860s. Big changes took place in agriculture about 1860. One was the rise of the "middleman," who sold a variety of goods and services to the state's farmers. The general storekeeper became a key figure. He or she sold coffee, salt,

Raising horses for field work became an important specialty in Ohio agriculture.

sugar, and dry goods on credit to farm families and took farm products in trade. Other help was supplied by livestock drovers, grain dealers, horse and hog traders, wool agents, and cheese vendors.

One improvement came by way of livestock imported for breeding. Shorthorn cattle from England and several breeds of hogs came during the 1830s. Selective breeding of swine developed what came to be known as the Poland China hog. Spanish Merino sheep were sought by the state's farmers. Horses were improved with thoroughbreds, Arabians, and Percherons.

Farm organizations founded. Beginning in 1846, steps were taken to create farmer groups. One of their chief tasks was to sponsor stock shows and contests which became a part of county fairs. That year, a State Board of Agriculture was set up to make reports on farm production trends. The board sponsored the first Ohio State Fair at Cincinnati in 1850. *The Ohio Farmer* magazine first published in 1848, now has a circulation of over 100,000.

By 1850, the state was a leader in farming. New methods were helped along by iron plows and Obed Hussey's Ohio reaper, as well as good information about better ways to farm. By 1860, a fine canal system and miles of railroad took farm products to every corner of the state and to national markets. Throughout the rest of the century, the state kept its rural nature and had one large city—Cincinnati.

These farmers are stacking oats near Carey, in Wyandot County.

The nutrition barn at the Ohio Agricultural Research Center in Wooster. Here, better food for livestock is developed through experiments and research.

4. Technology and education changed farm life after 1860.

Just when Ohio had become the number one farm state, changes took place which let states farther west take the lead.

Why Ohio lost first place. The railroad was one of the factors which brought competition from the larger states of Illinois and Iowa. The more fertile prairie soils of states to the west gave them an advantage. So did the new large farm machines which could be used on their flat lands. Soil exhaustion (loss of fertility caused by planting the same crops on the same land too often) also hurt Ohio agriculture.

Certain types of farms improve. The development of farm machines such as mowers, seed drills, and cultivators caused changes in farming habits. The business grew quickly to meet the demands of more people in the cities. Hog raising expanded in western Ohio. Horse raising shifted away from light horses for carriage and riding purposes to work horses needed for heavy farm and lumbering work. City streetcars and delivery wagons were pulled by horses, which meant many of the animals were needed there. Sheep raising declined when the demand for wool dropped after the Civil War, as cotton cloth became more available.

New farm region. By the late 1800s, the northwest had grown into a rich farming region. Served by railroads and canals, it had flat, fertile land. Chemical fertilizers gained increased use after 1870, and helped to restore soils on older farms.

New farm groups. After the Civil War, farming entered a golden age. Associations for cattle, horse, hog, and sheep improvement were formed. Farmer cooperatives sold machines and insurance. The Ohio Grange was born to serve social and education needs, and by 1875 it had more than 1,100 chapters in the state.

The state gave much support to farmers. Ohio State University, founded in 1870, became a great force in farm life and production. The Agricultural

The development of farm machines, such as this Buckeye mower, caused changes in farming habits. When motor-driven machinery came into use, what big changes would have taken place?

Experiment Station was formed at Columbus in 1882 and moved to Wooster in 1892. It brought scientific farming to Ohio through research and development. In the 1880s, the State Board of Agriculture began to make regular crop reports. Farmer's institutes and agricultural extension services were started by the Ohio State University in 1902. The first county agricultural agents were hired in 1912 to help farmers learn better farming methods.

5. Twentieth-century farms are larger and more specialized.

Ohio farmers, like those elsewhere, have had many ups and downs in the twentieth century. Big machines have made it possible for farms to become larger. This made it hard for small farms to compete, and many small farmers sold out. Fewer, but bigger, farms have become the pattern in the nation.

In areas of flat land, field crops can be grown on a large scale using modern machines and harvesting methods. This view shows truck farming in the rich black soil of Huron County at Celeryville.

Changes in twentieth-century farm life. While sheep raising and wool growing have declined, dairying has enjoyed steady growth until recent years. Modern tractors have replaced farm workers and older machines. Advances by plant breeders have brought about hybrid corn, higher yielding small grains, soybeans, and alfalfa varieties. Better plant crops have helped control animal diseases. Soil and water conservation are now a part of modern farming.

Changes in communication and transportation have greatly improved farm life. New farm-to-market roads, as well as freeways, have placed farms within easy reach of the cities. Electric power allows farm families to use the same labor-saving tools and household goods that city people do. Public schools, local colleges, branches of state universities, and technical schools have made good training available to all our people.

Farm problems. The growth of cities has had some bad effects on farm business. City growth takes away more and more farmland for airports, golf courses, factories, reservoirs, and homes. The Ohio Turnpike took 7,500 acres of good land from farm use. The farmer must also compete with the city employer for seasonal labor, which raises farm costs. Heavy investments for fertilizer, machines, fuel, and power boost costs. Careful management of all resources is needed if the farmer is to survive.

Ohio farming today. Farmers now put more of their efforts into crop production. But they have changed their crop programs. Less land is devoted to fruit, wheat, oats, and hay than before. Now there is more production of corn, soybeans, and specialty crops such as tomatoes, other vegetables, and tobacco. More than 800 acres of vegetables and flowers are being grown in greenhouses in the state.

6. Ohio's rural areas have a distinct culture and charm.

A good way to learn about Ohio's rural life is by taking field trips to a few counties.

Williams County is in the northwest corner of the state. Bryan is the county seat of this very rich farm region. Williams County is typical of the large,

A farm in Darke County.

flat farm belt which covers all of northwest Ohio. At one time it was full of huge trees and wild animals. Now it is at the east end of the great American corn and hog raising region called the Midwest.

Darke County is on the Indiana border. Greenville, the county seat, is the only city (13,000 people) in a county of 50,000 persons. The land is level and the soil very fertile. Darke County usually ranks first in the state in total cash income from farm products. It is always near the top in poultry, eggs, corn, soybeans, and wheat.

Brown County is along the Ohio River at the end of the Appalachian foothills. White burley tobacco was first discovered here and is still one of the largest crops. General U.S. Grant went to school in Georgetown, the county seat. Nearby in Ripley, John Rankin operated the first Ohio station on the Underground Railroad.

Jackson County is in the rough hill country of south central Ohio. It has valuable deposits of salt, coal, limestone, iron ore, and clay. Indians once took salt from here and left behind their art work—

sandstone carvings called *petroglyphs*. Welsh people were the first white settlers in Jackson County. Beef cattle, dairy goods, and apples are the primary farm products. An apple festival is held in Jackson, the county seat, each September.

Noble County, in the southeast, was the last of the 88 counties to be formed and named. It is also the smallest one in population (about 11,000). Fruits, cattle, and sheep are the main farm enterprises. Noble County is one of the best apple growing districts in the state. It is the home, too, of the 2,000-acre Eastern Ohio Resource Development Center at Belle Valley. As the state's only Bull Testing and Ram Testing Station, it serves over 500,000 people in Appalachia.

Holmes County, in the east central region, is famous for its Amish and Mennonite farms. Ohio has the greatest number of this culture group in the nation. Several horse and buggy shops are still operating here to serve their needs. On their farms, dairy production is foremost. There are no cities in the county. Millersburg, called the "capital of Amishland," is the county seat and largest village.

White burley tobacco was first discovered in Brown County, and it is still one of the area's largest crops. This is a tobacco auction in Ripley.

Other small communities have the *quaint* names of Berlin, Killbuck, Walnut Creek, and Charm.

Wayne County, in the north central region, is the home of the Ohio Agricultural Research and Development Center (1892). It ranks as one of the best in the world. Looking like a campus, the center is connected with Ohio State University and operates its own airport and planes. Besides research on nutrition, plant life, and animal husbandry, the center offers advice on lawn care, tree planting, and home gardens. With help from the Ohio Historical Society, the first museum of Ohio agriculture will be built here during the 1980s. Wayne is the top dairy county in the state. Other

agribusinesses include general farming, food processing (canning and deep freezing), packaging, shipping, and marketing. The Amish auction on Thursdays at Kidron is a popular event.

Ashtabula County, largest in the state, is in the northeast corner and is part of the old Western Reserve. Along Lake Erie the land is level, but it becomes more rolling to the south. Dairying is the main farm activity. Ashtabula is different from the other rural counties. It has many more people and two major lake ports (Ashtabula and Conneaut), which handle iron ore and coal. Even so, the county has kept a rural and small town charm. Some farms have stayed in the same families for more than 100

A farm in southeastern Ohio around 1939.

years. Many covered bridges survive on back roads. Geneva is the home of the Grape Jamboree each September. Jefferson, the county seat, was once the home of anti-slavery leaders Joshua R. Giddings and Benjamin F. Wade. Both men are buried in the village cemetery.

Small towns hold a key role in the life of rural Ohio. By a small town, we mean one with 500 to 10,000 persons. Our state has over 400 villages of 500 to 5,000 people and 50 towns with 5,000 to 10,000 people. Quite a few of them—like Napoleon, Hillsboro, Pomeroy, and Carrollton—are county seats.

The business district in small towns is often laid out around a courthouse square. One of the roads leading from the square is the main business street. In recent years much public and private work has gone into fixing up the towns' buildings and streets. Grand Rapids, Georgetown, Jackson, Mount Pleasant, and Wellington are prime examples of restored "Main Street" communities.

Education in rural areas. Often a small town is the home of a small college. Ohio is noted for its number of small private colleges. Many are church-related and provide high quality education. Among the best known are Denison (Baptist) at Granville, Kenyon (Episcopal) at Gambier, Heidelberg (United Church of Christ) at Tiffin, and Wooster (Presbyterian) at Wooster.

Rural politics. Nearly all small towns in Ohio have *conservative* politics, and in many ways, the outlook and values of small town people reflect those of the state. They are slow to change and suspicious of quick moves. Most state leaders share this same point of view. In fact, many of these leaders have small town roots. Senator John Glenn from New Concord and former Governor James Rhodes from Coalton are examples.

Social activities in small towns. Small towns are places where rural folks go to shop and meet with friends. During the summer and early fall, parades and festivals of many types are held in the smaller

The pumpkin festival at Circleville celebrates a fine harvest.

towns. Among the more popular ones are Canal Days at Canal Fulton, Ohio Hills Folk Festival at Quaker City, Parade of the Hills at Nelsonville, and Pumpkin Show at Circleville. Milan's Melon Festival, the Honey Festival at Lebanon, Ohio Swiss Festival at Sugarcreek, and the Millersport Corn Festival draw many people.

Churches are centers for both religious and social life. Revivals, camp meetings, weddings, reunions, and suppers are just a few of the events held at country churches.

Auctions and fund-raisers for youth programs, public service, and health care groups take place in rural towns. Ox roasts, chicken barbecues, fish fries, fruit festivals, and ice cream socials are popular pastimes.

The big event of the year is the fair, which lasts up to a week. The state holds over 90 county and independent fairs annually, with several million people attending. Many of the visitors are city people who take an interest in farm activities. Livestock shows, pie baking exhibits, displays of needlework and quilting, and the junior fair (4-H and FFA) are still the most popular exhibits. These events represent and promote the culture of Ohio's rural and farm people. More than 70 of the fairs have horse races and betting. Income from the races helps pay the cost of the other events.

Fairgrounds are often used outside the fair season for big events when no other large meeting places exist. Political rallies, outdoor plays, auto races, and camporees are just a few examples. Some

Entrance to the Ohio state fairgrounds in Columbus.

farm groups have year-round offices at the fairgrounds.

County homes, once common in the state, are fading out. Run by the counties, they used to provide food and lodging for the very poor. Those who lived in such homes, called "county poor farms," often worked for their keep by helping on the farm. The few which remain today are used as nursing homes for the elderly who need constant care.

In place of the county homes, modern nursing homes now serve older patients who can help pay part of the cost. In those counties that have no county home or public nursing home, the aged and sick are placed in private nursing homes at public expense.

7. Farm and rural areas will decline in size to the year 2000.

Trends in rural Ohio. The state Department of Economic and Community Development and the Agricultural Research and Development Center keep a close watch on farm trends. They agree on these forecasts:

Decline in number of farms. The number of farms and farmers has been on the decline since 1945. But the size of the farms is getting larger. For instance, between 1945 and 1969, the number of farms fell from 221,000 to 111,000. At the same time the average size of farms rose from 99 to 154 acres. A big loss was due to the use of two million

NUMBER OF FARMS WILL DECREASE/SIZE OF FARMS WILL INCREASE

**The Number of
Farms in Ohio
Will Decrease By
More Than Half**

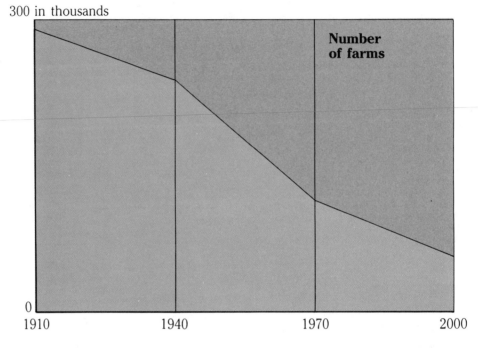

300 in thousands

**Number
of farms**

0

1910   1940   1970   2000

**And Average
Farm Size Will
Almost Double**

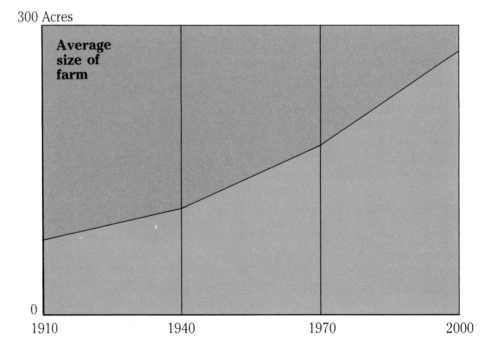

300 Acres

**Average
size of
farm**

0

1910   1940   1970   2000

acres of crop land for such things as airports, freeways, shopping malls, and urban growth.

The steep decline in the number of farms is due to *mechanization* and increased off-farm jobs. Land available for farming in the state is expected to fall some 18% by the end of the century. By then, the number of farms will be reduced from 92,000 in 1983 to about 70,000, while the average size will nearly double. Farm population, which was 853,000 in 1950, will fall to about 250,000 in the next two decades.

Decline in rural counties. Ohio's population growth by the year 2000 will be rather small. The gain in rural regions will be about 5% of the total. Just 38 of the state's counties will still be considered rural. All of these will be in either the northwest or southeast part of the state.

In the 17 northwestern counties, the price of land will rise. That will make it hard for a small family farm to compete. Large commercial farms will replace many of the small ones. The amount of land used for farming in the northwest will stay about the same, but the number of farms and farmers will be fewer.

Change will occur in the southeast, too. Seven of the counties in Appalachia will become urban. The others, which have less fertile soil and hilly land, will likely remain rural. Some abandoned farms will become forest land again. Some parts may be used for recreation and new parks. People will leave Appalachia to search for jobs in the cities or elsewhere.

State and local governments will face big problems in southern Ohio. Small towns will need help to supply public services, such as water and sewers. Schools will need state aid to stay open.

Expansion of cities into farm areas. Some rural towns, which now act as service centers for the regions around them, will change greatly. For some of the small towns this means becoming a city suburb. For others it means population growth as high as 100% to 200% per year. The lack of money, resources, and time to plan to meet such changes

OHIO'S POPULATION IS BECOMING INCREASINGLY URBAN

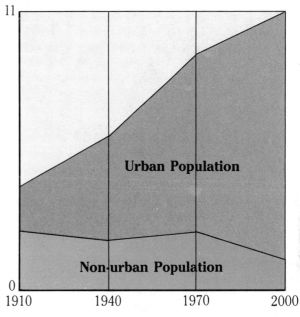

Population in millions

POPULATION OF OHIO, URBAN AND RURAL: 1800 to 1980			
	Population	**Urban Percent**	**Rural Percent**
1800	45,365	0	100
1810	230,760	1.1	98.9
1820	581,434	1.7	98.3
1830	937,903	3.9	96.1
1840	1,519,467	5.5	94.5
1850	1,980,329	12.2	87.8
1860	2,339,511	17.1	82.9
1870	2,665,260	25.6	74.4
1880	3,198,062	33.2	67.8
1890	3,672,329	41.1	58.9
1900	4,157,545	48.1	51.9
1910	4,767,121	55.9	44.1
1920	5,759,394	63.8	36.2
1930	6,646,697	67.8	32.2
1940	6,907,612	66.8	33.2
1950	7,946,627		
	Old Urban Definition	66.4	33.6
	New Urban Definition*	70.2	29.8
1960	9,707,136	73.4	26.6
1970	10,657,423	75.3	24.7
1980	10,797,630	73.3	26.7

*A change in urban definition resulted in a higher urban percentage after 1950.

will cause huge problems. Good planning and development are needed before land is put to new uses.

By the twenty-first century, most of the counties and 90% of the state's population will be urban. The pattern of rural life will be greatly changed.

WORDS FOR STUDY

agribusiness
agronomic
horticulture
tillage
methodically
fringe
spring house

specialize
cash crops
petroglyphs
quaint
conservative
mechanization

QUESTIONS FOR REVIEW

1. How much of Ohio is farm land?
2. What are five agricultural products of the state?
3. Why is agriculture called "agribusiness" today?
4. What percentage of Ohioans are full-time farmers?
5. What are the regions of Ohio's 57 rural counties?
6. Name three developments that took place in Ohio farms from 1820 to 1865.
7. What two took place in Ohio farming around 1860?
8. What four factors caused Ohio to lose its leadership in farming after 1865?
9. What two needs did the Grange fill for farmers?
10. What is the definition of a small town?

GOING FURTHER

1. Why can rural Ohio best be described as a livestock producing area?
2. Why is Ohio well suited to farming?
3. Why was wool growing a risky farm business before 1860?
4. Why was horse raising a good business before 1860?
5. In what ways did the state government help farmers in the 1800s?
6. What are some of the important activities for small towns?
7. Why will the small family farm have a difficult time surviving by the year 2000?

FOR THOUGHT AND DISCUSSION

1. Why are there fewer but bigger farms in Ohio in the twentieth century?
2. Do you think the growth of cities has improved Ohio farm life? Explain.
3. The authors conclude, "By the twenty-first century most of Ohio's counties and 90% of the state's population will be urban. The pattern of rural life will be greatly changed." Do you agree? Explain.

PROJECTS AND REPORTS

1. Interview a farmer to get his or her ideas on farm problems today. What are some possible solutions? Present your findings in an oral report.
2. Compare and contrast modern farm machines with tools that were used for the same jobs in the 1800s. Present your information using photographs or drawings.
3. Listen to the media farm reports and keep a record of prices for one month. Show the trends on a graph and write a summary paragraph.
4. Gather newspaper articles on agriculture. Analyze them to determine what the main concerns of agribusiness are today. What legislation is working in favor of the farms? Which laws work against agriculture?
5. Gather information and report on how 4-H and Future Farmers of America organizations help young farmers.

MODERN OHIO MAJOR CITIES AND HIGHWAYS

N

0   20   40   60   80

CHAPTER 12

THE RISE OF CITIES AND INDUSTRY

MAIN POINTS

1. Early Ohio towns grew due to the effects of different types of transportation.
2. Transportation developments brought big changes to the state's economy and life style.
3. Ohio has one of the finest transportation systems in the nation today.
4. Ohio became a leading industrial state by the late nineteenth century.
5. Ohio has produced many leaders in industry.
6. Ohio's industrial growth has slowed in recent years.

Until 1900, most Ohioans lived in the country. Today three out of every four live in cities. Our state is one of the most urban states in the nation. How and why did this happen?

1. Early Ohio towns grew due to the effects of different types of transportation.

Some cities are as old as the state itself. Marietta, Cincinnati, and Cleveland were founded when Ohio was still part of the Northwest Territory. Most of the oldest towns are near Lake Erie or the Ohio River and its main branches. The reason for this is that water routes were an easy way for pioneers to enter the state.

Settlers from the South used the streams of Kentucky and Virginia to get to the Ohio Valley. Yankees from New England took the Mohawk River through New York and followed the shore of Lake Erie to northern Ohio. Once they reached the territory, pioneers found other rivers by which to reach the interior.

If a town became a county seat, it could be sure of a steady growth in business. What kinds of business would be done there? This is the Fayette County courthouse in Washington Court House.

Newark in Licking County. Look at a state map and find some reasons why the town developed in that location.

Location of early towns. The growth and spread of early towns is linked with the development of transportation. Towns built near rivers, roads, canals, or railroads became markets and supply centers.

The first towns competed with each other for special advantages. If a town became a county seat or the state capital, it could expect steady growth in business. Some towns were helped by having a federal land office, a state prison, or a military storehouse. A few were lucky enough to have a university or a college.

Expansion of cities. The 1820 federal *census* was the first one to give correct *statistics* (figures) on the growth of cities. It showed a new urban region spreading up the Miami Valley. There, new towns with one to two thousand persons each were growing. Some of them were Hamilton, Middletown, Dayton, Troy, and Piqua.

By 1830, the number of large towns had doubled from 13 to 26. Cincinnati, with 24,000 people, was the largest. Meanwhile, new towns of one to three thousand persons were springing up in the Scioto Valley. The main ones were Portsmouth, Circleville, and Delaware. Columbus, built as a capital city, was also there.

Still more settlements stretched to the north through the Mad River Valley north of Dayton.

These were Springfield, Urbana, and Bellefontaine. Elsewhere in the state, Steubenville near the upper Ohio River, and Mount Vernon in Knox County were new centers of population and business. A few of the new towns were laid out as *planned communities,* which are arranged around a circle or square. Circleville and Canfield are good examples of each type.

Origins of other Ohio towns. Towns were located in places for a number of reasons. Some, like Mansfield and Xenia, were the result of successful land *speculation.* Land speculators bought large sections of land and resold them for a profit. Other sites were near a good water source or had been old Indian towns on woodland trails (Defiance, Wooster, Coshocton, and Conneaut). Fremont and Zanesville developed near river falls to make use of water power. Sandusky was founded on a bay which is safe from Lake Erie storms. Other towns were founded at sites where land ridges join (Bowling Green and Norwalk), or where a ridge crosses a river (Tiffin). Several important cities grew up where early highways (Zane's Trace or the National Road) crossed major rivers. Cambridge, Lancaster, and Springfield were established near fords, ferries, or bridges. Akron was at a portage between rivers. Canals gave rise to still other towns (Canal Fulton, Dover, and Massillon).

Roads. The early roads in this state were just narrow, muddy passages through the woods. A few better ones were covered with logs or planks laid side by side. All roads were in constant need of repair.

Canals were a temporary improvement. In the 1830s this means of transporting people and goods became common in the state. Canal cities took on a new look with large brick and stone business blocks in place of the old wooden structures.

Cleveland, at the north end of the Ohio-Erie Canal, grew until it was the state's third largest city in the 1840s. Toledo, with 4,000 people by 1850, was the new business hub of the northwest. Cincinnati reached l00,000 *inhabitants* by 1850, mak-

ing it the nation's sixth largest city and the grandest city of the West.

Land speculation near proposed canal or highway routes ruined some *investors* who picked the wrong places, and made others rich in a short time. John Hunt at Maumee made more than $100,000 by buying land at $1 to $2.50 an acre. He later divided and sold it in small town lots for $200 to $400 each. Jessup W. Scott bought Toledo land for $12 an acre and saw it rise in value to $12,000. Under such conditions, cities grew quickly. The number of city dwellers jumped from 5% to 12% of the state's total during the 1840s.

Decline of the canals. In spite of all the hard work and business interest, the canal era did not last long. Canal shipping was cheap, but slow. It took 80 hours to travel the 308 miles from Cleveland to Portsmouth. Since the fare was just two cents a mile, it was hard to make a profit. In the winter months, the frozen canals brought a halt to business, and in the dry summer months there was often a lack of water. Public opinion against them and lack of funding led to the end of the canal system. A final blow came from the railroads.

2. Transportation developments brought big changes to the state's economy and life style.

Railroads planned at first to serve those towns beyond the reach of canals. They soon found that they could compete directly. The first railroad in the state was built in 1836 from Toledo to Adrian, Michigan. The start of the railroad era dates from 1845, and its greatest growth took place during the 1850s. The railroads took business from the canals with lower prices and faster service. So many new railroads started that, by 1860, Ohio was the leading railroad state in the nation.

What happened to the state's economy as the ways of travel changed from freight wagons to canals and riverboats, and finally to railroads?

New trade pattern. First, railroads changed the direction of the state's trade and business. Before

Railroad station in Mt. Victory on the New York Central Railroad.

1850, products were shipped south to market by way of the rivers. The railroads changed this pattern. They could cross rivers or tunnel through hills and mountains. Thus, trade with the South weakened as business with markets in the West and the East grew stronger.

Industry grew. Second, real estate and banking within the state began to draw eastern and foreign investors. With the railroads, this extra money speeded the growth of industry and helped to give a new character to the cities. After 1850, large factory cities like Cleveland and Toledo brought the state into an age of steam, smoke, and steel.

Rapid urban growth. Third, railroads helped cities to grow and created more jobs. Cities became a strong force in business and social life. Industry swelled the population of the cities. Ohio was 25% urban in 1870, but 10 years later the urban population was 33%, and it passed 40% by 1890. At the turn of the century, the state was almost half urban and half rural.

3. Ohio has one of the finest transportation systems in the nation today.

The region from the Great Lakes to the St. Lawrence River is known as the "Fourth Seacoast." Due to its good transportation *network,* our state is often called "The Transportation Center of America."

Ohio has a good location for trade. Fifty percent of all U.S. markets are within a 500-mile *radius* of the state. This makes our state a leading warehouse and *distribution* center.

OHIO IS THE CENTER OF AMERICA'S LARGEST MARKET

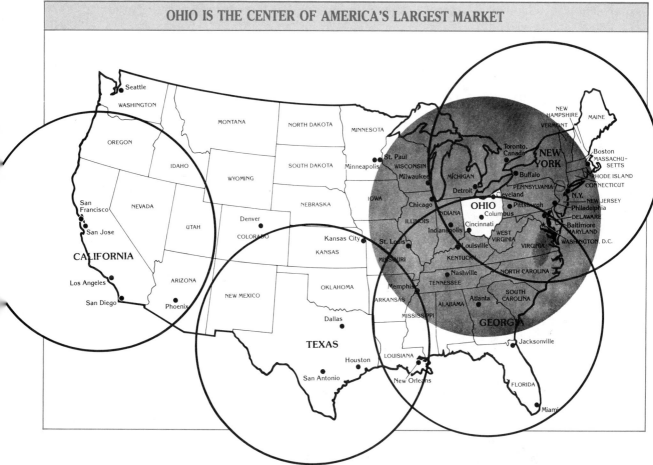

The systems of transportation brought the most important resource to the state. That resource is people. People from the East Coast traveled to Ohio, sometimes planning to pass through on their way west. But when they saw the lush forests and soils, many stayed.

The highway system in our state is now one of the best in the nation, ranking fifth in the miles of surfaced highways. If all our roads and streets were placed end to end, they would circle the earth four times! Super interstate highways give the state a fine travel system. I-70 follows the path of the old National Road through the middle of the state, and the Ohio Turnpike crosses the northern part. I-75 in the west and I-77 in the east provide two

In modern highway construction, concrete is mixed in batch plants and loaded into huge transport trucks to be hauled to the job site.

main north-south routes. I-71 joins Cincinnati, Columbus, and Cleveland.

Motor carriers handle 45% of the goods shipped in the state. At present, there are nearly one million trucks and truck trailers licensed here, and more than 300,000 people work in the motor freight business. With this heavy dependence on road transport, it is important to keep the highways in good shape. Trucking is the leading means of freight movement through the state.

Railroads have fallen on hard times. The airlines and cars have taken over most passenger travel. Cost factors have had a bad effect on the business of the railroads. Even the Amtrak system has not been a great success. The trend is to *merge* (join) railroad lines, such as the New York Central R.R. and the Pennsylvania R.R., to become part of Amtrak or Conrail. The merger of some lines has brought funds with which to update railroad prop-

erty. For instance, the new Buckeye Yard in Columbus helps move more trains faster and better than before. Much freight is still moved by rail, especially new cars, farm equipment, machinery, and coal.

Air traffic has gained a key place in our state since World War II. There are several large airlines and 11 major terminals serving 10 cities. But just 10% of our people travel by air, and less than 1% of the state's freight is shipped by air due to the high costs. Many new county airports have opened in recent years, and a commercial jet airport in northwest Ohio is being planned.

> What problems are the airlines going through in this decade? How will their difficulties affect people in your community over the next year?

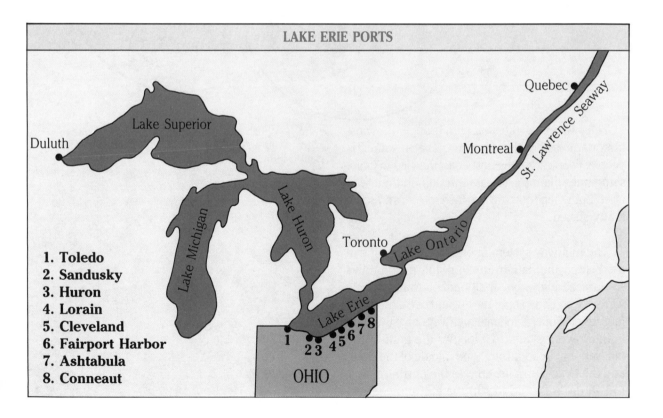

LAKE ERIE PORTS

1. Toledo
2. Sandusky
3. Huron
4. Lorain
5. Cleveland
6. Fairport Harbor
7. Ashtabula
8. Conneaut

Shipping on the Maumee River near Toledo.

Water travel is not as important as it was in the early days. Yet, a great deal of freight is still shipped on the Ohio River and on Lake Erie. There are more than 660 miles of *navigable* waters in and near Ohio. In fact, more tonnage is shipped on the Ohio River than passes between the Atlantic and Pacific oceans through the Panama Canal each year! Cincinnati is our largest port on the Ohio River and, as the "Queen City," handles more than nine million tons of *cargo* yearly.

Ohio has eight large Lake Erie ports. Toledo and Cleveland ship the most tonnage. Other ports are Ashtabula, Conneaut, Fairport Harbor, Lorain, Huron, and Sandusky. Cargoes passing through these ports include farm products, petroleum, coal, iron and steel products, automobiles, and glassware.

The St. Lawrence Seaway opened the Great Lakes to *international* trade routes. The seaway permits ships to pass from the Atlantic Ocean along the St. Lawrence River from Montreal, Canada, and through the Great Lakes as far as Duluth, Minnesota. The St. Lawrence Seaway has made Toledo a very busy fresh water port. It ranks second in foreign trade on the Great Lakes, and third in total tonnage. One advantage is that the port stays ice-free six weeks longer than any other on the lake. Toledo has the largest coal-handling port in the world. More than 100 million bushels of grain per year pass through there, as well. Toledo is a turn-around point for much of the seaway traffic. Most of the shipping from the Great Lakes ports goes from one lake port to another for distribution in the states.

The Rookwood pottery produced fine art pottery pieces in Cincinnati from 1800 until the 1940s.

Only a small amount reaches the St. Lawrence Seaway for transport to foreign markets. This is due in part to high tolls charged to use the seaway.

4. Ohio became a leading industrial state by the late nineteenth century.

After the Civil War, big business and the farming boom made the United States the richest nation in the world. Our state played a big part in all these events. While not quite as important as before, Ohio is still one of the nation's key industrial states.

Industrial products of the state. Ohio is first in the Midwest, and third in the nation, in the production of manufactured goods. Factories here make a wide range of products. Auto and aircraft parts, buses and trucks, motorcycles and trailers, machine tools, porcelain ware, plumbing fixtures, electrical machinery, glassware, and *fabricated* metals are common. We lead the nation in stone and clay products. The state is second in tableware, gray iron castings, dolls, advertising signs, and sporting and athletic goods. The state ranks third in furniture and fixtures, paper products, steel foundry products, hand tools, and electrical appliances.

Industrial centers of Ohio. A huge supply of resources and a strong transportation system led to the rise of most industrial centers here. Cincinnati was a leader in the early days. By the late 1800s Youngstown, Canton, Massillon, Cleveland, and Steubenville had become centers for iron and steel plants.

Other prime industries rose in the northeast. Akron became the world's rubber capital due to the leadership of Dr. Benjamin Goodrich, Frank Seiberling, and Harvey Firestone. Akron is a center for research in rubber and plastics. The first astronaut space suits were made there. Cleveland has become a leader in the oil refining industry through the work of John D. Rockefeller and his Standard Oil Company.

Western Ohio also had industrial growth. Galion became a leader in the production of heavy road building machinery. Toledo is the glass hub of the world, thanks to the work of glassmaker Edward Libbey and Michael Owens, a glassblower who invented machines for the industry. Three of the world's largest glass companies are found in Toledo.

Dayton is well known for its National Cash Register Company and the making of household appliances. Cincinnati holds the title of playing card capital of the world.

THE UNITED STATES PLAYING CARD COMPANY

THE next time someone says, "Deal them out," you can tell them that the playing cards being used are likely from Ohio. The United States Playing Card Company, largest in the world, is based in Cincinnati.

Cards were known in India and China more than 1,000 years ago. Fortune telling was the first use of the cards. Later crusaders took them to western Europe where card games were invented. During the 1500s, the four suits—spades, clubs, hearts, and diamonds—developed in France.

The first playing card makers in the state were the Longley Brothers in 1862. In 1873 their business became known as the Paper Fabrique Company. This firm joined with the *Cincinnati Enquirer* newspaper to form the United States Playing Card Company in 1894. In 1901 the company moved to its present site in Norwood.

The "Congress" and "Bicycle" decks are the best known trade names. At that time the bicycle was becoming popular, so a foreman suggested the name. The first Bicycle deck was sold in 1885.

Cards are made in six sizes, ranging from the giant size used for playing on the beach to the toy quarter size. To make the cards, products are shipped from faraway countries. Italy, Burma, Thailand, Argentina, and North Africa, as well as Death Valley in California, provide needed materials. Cotton and fiber from seven different trees are brought to Norwood. There they are processed with secret pastes to make sturdy playing cards.

During the Vietnam War thousands of aces of spades were shipped to American troops. Since Vietnamese believe the ace of spades is an *omen* (sign) of bad luck, these cards were scattered where the superstitious enemy would find them.

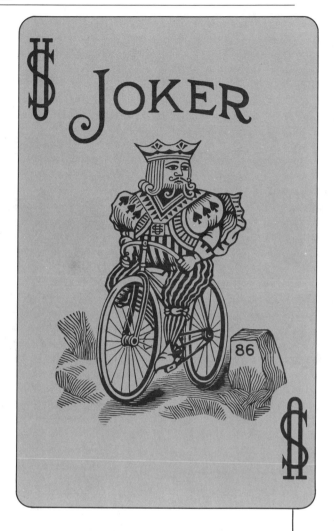

In 1969 the Diamond International Corporation merged with the Playing Card Company. Now Diamond International owns two well-known companies—the Diamond Match Company of Barberton and the United States Playing Card Company of Norwood.

—Adapted from an article by Kathryn M. Keller for Ohio Cues, *January 1980, a publication of the Maumee Valley Historical Society.*

In 1888, there was an oil boom in Findlay. Oil rigs appeared right in people's yards.

Natural resources fuel industry. The mineral resources of the state (discussed in Chapter One) are more scarce today, but are still important. The state ranks tenth in the nation in mineral production. Much of this business is centered in the southeast, a region less suited to farming.

Coal was, for many years, the key mineral industry. Coal mining declined in this century due to surpluses and competition from other kinds of fuel. After years of hardship caused by low demand and labor strikes, coal is making a comeback. The state's coal mines produce more than 50 million tons each year. It has been estimated that there are 40 billion tons of coal yet to be mined in this state. That's enough for 500 years of use.

Oil and natural gas have been vital to the state's industries. Oil has long been used to lubricate machines and vehicles. Fuels such as gasoline and kerosene are also made from it.

Oil found in Morgan, Washington, and Trumbull counties put our state in the oil business. New wells in the Lima field made this a key oil-producing state. Ohio became the oil *refining* capital of the nation in the late 1800s. Standard Oil controlled 90% of the nation's oil business.

In spite of competition from Texas and Oklahoma, a small oil boom came in the 1960s when oil was discovered in Morrow County. In some towns, like Mt. Gilead, oil rigs appeared in people's side yards.

The great natural gas fields were first opened in the 1880s near Findlay, Toledo, Bowling Green, and Fostoria. Dr. Charles Osterland was the leader in the development of this natural gas. The impact of gas and oil is still shown in Findlay, the home of the Marathon Petroleum Company.

> Ohio iron, clay, sand and gravel, limestone, and salt are the basis of many industries today. How many businesses in your county can you think of that use these products? Make a list on the chalkboard.

5. Ohio has produced many leaders in industry.

A strong force in the state's business success has been the leadership of gifted people who perfected processes or formed companies.

Electrical engineers. Several Ohioans are famous for their contributions as electrical *engineers.*

Best known is Thomas Alva Edison (1847-1931) of Milan who earned more than a thousand *patents* for his inventions. While still a young man he perfected the electric light bulb. At the age of 31, he went to Washington, D.C., to show his new phonograph to the American Academy of Science and the members of Congress. His last stop was at the White House. As Edison describes it in his journal:

"About 11 o'clock word was received from the President [Rutherford B. Hayes of Ohio] that he would be very pleased if I would come. . . . I was taken there and found Mr. Hayes and several others waiting, among them I remember Carl Schurz who was playing the piano. . . . The exhibition continued till about 12:30 A.M., when Mrs. Hayes and several other ladies who had been induced to get up and dress, appeared. I left at 3:30 A.M."

Edison improved generators, motors, and *dynamos.* He also helped to make electric railways, the telephone, and motion pictures more practical.

A Cleveland mining engineer, Charles F. Brush (1849-1929), invented the carbon arc lamp. It was used to light Cleveland's Public Square in 1879. He built a power station so the whole city could be

Harvey Firestone (left), Henry Ford (center) and Thomas Edison (right) at the funeral of President Warren G. Harding.

lighted by carbon rather than kerosene lamps. This made Cleveland the first city in the nation with the new electric street lights.

Elisha Gray (1835-1901) of Barnesville studied electricity at Oberlin College and made many improvements on the telegraph. His experiments led to the feat of transmitting the human voice. His patent application of 1876 was just a few hours too late. His rival, Alexander Graham Bell, applied for such a patent ahead of him. After a long court fight, Bell won credit for inventing the telephone.

In 1923, Garrett Morgan (1875-1963), a black inventor from Cleveland, built a device to control the traffic in cities and towns. The traffic light has been used ever since. Morgan sold his patent rights for the electric stop sign to General Electric Company for $40,000. Earlier he had invented the gas mask used by American soldiers in World War I. He won a gold medal from the city of Cleveland for using it to rescue workmen trapped in a tunnel under Lake Erie.

Charles F. Kettering invented many improvements for early automobiles.

Industrial inventors. Several others helped found corporations in the late nineteenth and early twentieth centuries.

Charles Martin Hall (1863-1914) of Thompson received a degree from Oberlin College in 1885. One of his teachers said that the person who could find a cheap way to separate aluminum from its ore would make a great gift to science. While still a student, Hall took the challenge. In a small shed on the edge of the campus, he perfected the process of *electrolysis.* This discovery led to the formation of the Aluminum Company of America. An aluminum statue of Hall now stands on the campus as a monument to his discovery and his gifts to the college. He gave more than $3,000,000 to Oberlin, which still receives royalties from the Aluminum Corporation of America.

Granville T. Woods (1856-1910), a black leader and inventor, was born in Columbus. At age 10 he worked in a machine shop. By age 16 he was a train engineer in Missouri. In 1880 he had his own repair shop in Cincinnati, where he also invented. At the time of his death in 1910, he had received more than 50 patents for his work. He made such things as a steam boiler furnace, three automatic air brakes, and a telegraph that could send messages between moving cars and trains. This device helped engineers know about other trains behind and in front of them.

Benjamin G. Lamme (1864-1924) was born on a farm near Springfield. He learned mechanical engineering at Ohio State University and became the chief engineer of the Westinghouse Electric Company in Dayton. His 162 patents included plans for streetcar motors and *rotary converters.* The first hydroelectric generators at Niagara Falls were one of his designs. Lamme also helped train young engineers and set up a school for this purpose.

Charles F. Kettering (1876-1958), of Loudonville, invented a quick-starting electric motor to open cash register drawers. He soon became more interested in automobiles. Kettering worked for a long time at the Dayton Electric Laboratories Company (Delco). Later he joined General Motors as an executive, engineer, and inventor. In his new job he added to the development of leaded gasoline, two-way shock absorbers, refrigeration, and air conditioning.

Dayton was the home of Wilbur (1867-1912) and Orville (1871-1948) Wright. They flew the first successful powered airplanes at Kitty Hawk, North Carolina, in 1903. The Wright brothers began as bicycle makers and repairmen in 1892. Reading about glider experiments drew their interest to flying. They built trial models and fixed errors in calculation. They finally got a patent for their airplane in 1906. A contract to build a plane for the United States War Department in 1908 gave approval to their invention and personal fame. The American Wright Company was formed in 1909.

Leaders in the auto industry. Cleveland was the nation's leading automobile center from the 1890s until about 1906. More than 80 models of cars were made there before 1932.

Alexander Winton (1860-1932) started the Cleveland automobile business and built the first standard model car in 1898. To show his cars were to be trusted, Winton twice drove from Cleveland to New York City. This helped his business and the rest of the industry, as well. In 1903, Winton made the first automobile trip from coast to coast. It took two months and cost $8,000.

James W. Packard (1863-1928) of Warren bought a Winton car in 1898. Not happy with some of its features, he founded his Packard Company which lasted more than 50 years. The steering wheel, in place of a single-lever "tiller," was developed jointly by Winton and Packard in 1901.

Products such as the automatic windshield wiper, shock absorbers, and the sealed-beam headlamp were first made in Ohio.

LEADERS IN THE SPACE INDUSTRY

SOME of the best examples of the pioneer spirit are found in the space industry. Ohio astronauts John Glenn (left), James A. Lovell, and Neil Armstrong (right) are well known for their flights in space.

On February 20, 1962, John Glenn of New Concord was the first person to circle the earth in space. Glenn was one of the first seven Mercury astronauts to be trained for space flight. On that first flight, Glenn traveled in his tiny capsule called *Friendship VII*. On a journey of 81,000 miles, he circled the earth three times in 4 hours and 56 minutes. His heroic mission set the stage for others to explore space.

James A. Lovell, Jr., was born in Cleveland in 1928. Lovell was in the astronaut program from 1962 to 1971. In December 1965, he and Frank Borman, in *Gemini VII*, set an *endurance* record of 14 days orbiting the earth. During the same flight, they made the first *rendezvous* with another space capsule, *Gemini VI*. In December 1968, in the spaceship *Apollo VIII*, Lovell, Borman, and William A. Anders were the first people to circle the moon. In April 1970, Lovell commanded the *Apollo XIII* mission, which was to be the second to land on the moon. However, an oxygen tank exploded shortly after takeoff, nearly taking the lives of Lovell and his two fellow astronauts. Lovell was able to guide the ship safely back to earth. James Lovell left the program in 1971 to become a deputy director for NASA.

Ohio and the nation felt a great surge of pride on July 20, 1969. It was on that day, at 10:56 EDT, that Neil Armstrong of Wapakoneta stepped from the *Apollo XI "Eagle"* to become the first person to walk on the moon. Armstrong remarked, "That's one small step for man, a giant leap for mankind!" A $1,000,000 museum has been built at Wapakoneta to serve as a memorial to Armstrong and Ohio's space leaders.

Other Ohio astronauts include Donn Eisele of Columbus, who flew in *Apollo VII* in 1968. Karl G. Henzie of Cincinnati, Charles A. Bassett, II, of Dayton, and Robert F. Overmeyer of Lorain work in the program while awaiting their space flight assignments.

A loading facility at the Port of Toledo.

6. Ohio's industrial growth has slowed in recent years.

The state has enjoyed good business growth for many years. Recent trends, however, show the state's economy is not keeping pace with the rate of national growth.

Ohio and the GNP. Ohio's share of the *gross national product* (GNP) has decreased steadily in the past 15 years. The GNP is an *index* of the nation's wealth. It measures the amount of goods and services used in the country and how much people spend for those things.

As of 1982, the state's share of the GNP had dropped from 6% to 5½%. One-half percent may not sound large, but the GNP is figured in billions of dollars, and ½% is a lot. The drop does not mean that our economic growth has stopped. In fact our *gross state product* has increased. The economies of other states at this time are growing faster than ours. As a result, they have gained a larger share of the GNP.

It is important to know why our state's economy is changing.

First, our nation's trade and growth is shifting to the states in the south and southwest, known as the sunbelt. Because of this shift, Ohio's east-west trade has decreased.

Second, our state has lost some of its former advantages. Natural resources, such as timber, farmland, and oil, are less plentiful. In turn, this has caused an increased cost of doing business. Labor costs are high in this state. Some of our plants and mills are outdated. Meanwhile, new factories and better transportation have helped other states to challenge Ohio.

Third, the state's human resources have changed, as well. The 1970 and 1980 census figures showed an increase at a rate lower than the national average. Many trained and skilled workers have left the state for other areas.

Overall, the economy is in a state of *transition* (change). Our state can remain strong if people choose wise leaders and work together to adapt to new conditions.

WORDS FOR STUDY

census	*omen*
statistics	*refine*
planned community	*engineer*
speculation	*patent*
inhabitant	*dynamo*
investor	*electrolysis*
network	*rotary converter*
radius	*endurance*
distribution	*rendezvous*
merge	*gross national product*
navigable	*(GNP)*
cargo	*index*
international	*gross state product*
fabricated	*transition*

QUESTIONS FOR REVIEW

1. What percentage of Ohioans live in cities?
2. Where were the earliest towns in Ohio located?
3. How did land speculation help build cities?
4. How did the railroads change the geographical direction of Ohio business?
5. What factors caused Ohio to be a leading industrial state?
6. What highway connects Cincinnati, Columbus, and Cleveland?
7. What is the most important transport method in the state today?
8. For what industry is Toledo famous?
9. How have mineral resources helped the state's industries?
10. Name three leaders in the field of electrical engineering and tell what their main contributions were.
11. For what is Granville T. Woods famous?
12. What inventions by Ohio leaders benefited the auto industry?

13. Name three Ohio astronauts and tell of one mission each completed.
14. What was Ohio's share of the GNP in 1982?
15. In what ways is the state's economy changing?

GOING FURTHER

1. Why were early Ohio towns located along water routes?
2. What are some reasons for the location of Ohio towns?
3. What was good and bad about canal transportation?
4. Why were railroads a better method of transportation than canals?
5. Why do you think Ohio is a leading warehouse and distribution center?
6. Why have railroads recently fallen on hard times?
7. What factor do you think is most important in keeping Ohio's economy from growing rapidly in the 1980s? Explain.

FOR THOUGHT AND DISCUSSION

1. If you were a state lawmaker, would you support a bill to finance a high speed rail line connecting the major cities? Explain.
2. If you were convincing prospective businesses to locate in Ohio, what arguments would you use?

PROJECTS AND REPORTS

1. Research the history of railroad lines in the state. Make a map to show routes traveled, names of railroad lines, and cities where stations were located.
2. Construct a chart which lists the advantages and disadvantatges of each of four methods of transportation—water, air, highway, and railroad.
3. Research and write a report on any of the following leaders in industry from the state: John B. Tytus (1875-1944), Ohio Columbus Barber (1841-1920), Benjamin Goodrich (1841-1888), George Oenslager (1873-1956), and John Henry Patterson (1844-1922).

Scene from *Trumpet in the Land*, a popular outdoor historical pageant presented each summer at New Philadelphia.

CHAPTER 13

OHIO'S CULTURAL HERITAGE

MAIN POINTS

1. The expressions of culture in our state can be grouped on three different levels.

2. Ohioans have been leaders in the field of literature.

3. Ohio artists have reflected American themes in their work.

4. Architecture in Ohio represents many American building styles.

5. Famous people in the fields of music and entertainment were from Ohio.

6. Many different sports have benefited from contributions of Ohioans.

1. The expressions of culture in our state can be grouped on three different levels.

As we learn more about culture, it will help to know that cultural activities fit into three categories—*high culture, popular culture,* and *folk culture.*

Elite or high culture includes the outstanding or best works in an artistic or creative field. A beautiful building by an architect or a fine painting by an artist would be an example of high culture. A ballet or an opera, too, would fit into this elite category of things which are likely to survive over a long period of time. They will be enjoyed by several generations of people.

Popular culture is what the average or ordinary people enjoy. This might be a popular hit song or a best-selling paperback novel. Popular culture may

have a more short-term appeal than high culture.

A third kind of culture is folk culture. This deals with native arts and crafts and traditions passed on from one generation to another. It is usually preserved by older people teaching younger ones the skills involved. *Oral* (spoken) *tradition* plays a big part in folk culture. American Indian culture is largely kept by oral methods.

Culture includes literature, music, art, architecture, sports, and amusements, among other things. Some would say that museums, libraries, and scientific achievements are also part of culture. We all take part in culture—either as participants or as the audience.

Cities are important as cultural centers that encourage and support the arts, literature, music, and science. All of Ohio's big cities are well known in this way.

Museums, libraries, performance halls, and sports stadiums are found in city centers. There, culture is preserved and carried on. The buildings themselves are part of our culture, for they are designed by architects and become landmarks for residents and visitors.

As a class project, gather information about cultural events and places in the city nearest you. Make a cultural events calendar for the month and display it on the bulletin board.

Restored auditorium of the Ohio Theatre in Columbus.

2. Ohioans have been leaders in the field of literature.

Ohio's cultural leaders represent a wide variety of backgrounds and interests. For this reason, culture in the state tends to be quite general in expression. It is more typical of the country, as a whole, than of a specific region. Ohio was settled by people from the 13 original states. It became a mixture of all of them.

Many Ohio artists and writers left the state for long periods to study or work in Europe or other parts of America. This kind of experience helped them develop a national outlook, rather than a narrow, regional point of view.

Ohio first gained cultural leadership in the field of literature. Starting in the 1850s, the state produced a group of writers whose humor, poetry, novels, and short stories became popular with Americans.

HUMORISTS

Abraham Lincoln enjoyed the humor of two Ohio newspapermen, **Charles Farrar Browne (1834-1867)** of the *Cleveland Plain Dealer* and **David Ross Locke (1833-1888)** of the *Toledo Blade*. Browne wrote under the name of "Artemus Ward" and poked fun at the serious side of life. Locke is remembered for his "Petroleum V. Nasby" letters which were full of funny dialects. Both men were popular with the general public.

James Thurber (1894-1961) is one of the best-known humorists of the 1900s. He was born in Columbus and was educated at Ohio State University. His fame came as a writer for the *New Yorker* magazine. People enjoyed his stories of his youth in Columbus, which he described in *My Life and Hard Times.* His book *The Secret Life of Walter Mitty* was made into a movie. Many of his works were collected into the *Thurber Album* from which a T.V. series appeared.

NOVELISTS

Harriet Beecher Stowe (1811-1896) lived for 18 years in Cincinnati, where she gathered the material for *Uncle Tom's Cabin* (1852). It sold 300,000 copies the first year and still is in print. The book led many people to form strong opinions against slavery.

William Dean Howells (1837-1920) was one of the most successful and influential Ohio writers. He came from Martin's Ferry, a river town. His Ohio upbringing furnished settings and characters for his later books. Howells left Ohio for the East to work as a magazine editor. Meanwhile, he wrote novels, short stories, poems, plays, and essays. He was the most active author of his time.

His *Hazard of New Fortunes* (1890) was one of the first novels to tell about the rise of the big city. Howells was so accurate in his portrayal of people, places, and events that he was called a *realist* writer. He founded a literary style called critical realism.

Sherwood Anderson (1876-1941), a twentieth-century Ohio author, was unhappy with his life as a successful paint manufacturer in Elyria, Ohio. So one day he quit work and went to Chicago to be a writer. *Winesburg, Ohio* (1919), his fourth book, tells the story of a small Sandusky County town. It draws heavily upon Anderson's boyhood in Clyde. The book has become one of the classics of American literature for its sharply critical picture of small-town life.

Zane Grey (1872-1939), "father of the adult western," wrote more than 70 novels which sold millions of copies. He was from Zanesville and was

William Dean Howells (above) and Sherwood Anderson, both Ohio natives, became successful novelists.

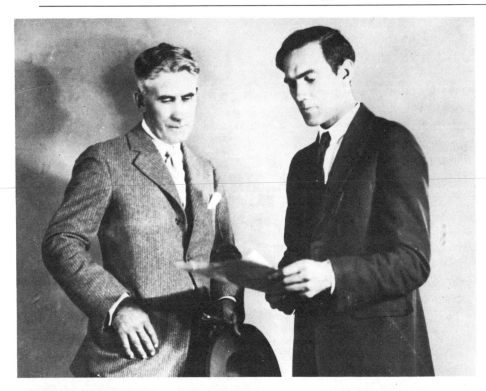

Zane Grey, from Zanesville, wrote more than 70 novels. Here he is shown with Lucian Hubbard, who wrote many of the screenplays when Grey's novels were made into movies.

Louis Bromfield was a novelist and early environmentalist. Visitors came from all over the world to see his successful experiment at Malabar Farm.

the grandson of Ebenezer Zane, who built Zane's Trace. Grey's first work in 1904 described the adventures of frontier heroine Betty Zane. She saved Fort Henry by carrying an apron full of gunpowder through enemy fire.

Grey's success dates from 1912 when he sold the literary rights of *Riders of the Purple Sage* to *Harper's Magazine*. Many of his stories were made into Hollywood movies.

Louis Bromfield (1896-1956), of Mansfield, started his career as a newspaperman and critic in New York. In his spare time he wrote novels. *The Green Bay Tree* (1924) earned him $1.5 million and made his reputation as a writer. Many of his books also became movies.

In 1938 Bromfield, an early environmentalist, bought three run-down farms near Mansfield which he combined and named Malabar Farm. He used his place as a model of how to reclaim and conserve the land. Visitors came from all over the world to see his successful experiment. Those who could not visit read about his work with the soil in books like *Pleasant Valley* (1945) and *Malabar Farm* (1948).

JOHN W. JAKES (1932-)

JOHN Jakes, who has lived in Dayton since 1961, has become one of the most popular authors in the country. Jakes's early work was in advertising, but he began writing popular history before he graduated from college.

Jakes has written books on many different subjects. His titles range from *Great Women Reporters* to *Conquest of the Planet of the Apes.*

Jakes is an author of versatile talent. In 1972, he had three plays published. He has also written the *lyrics* for six musicals.

Perhaps Jakes's most famous work has been his "American Bicentennial" series of historical novels. *The Bastard, The Rebels,* and *The Seekers* brought history alive for readers and T.V. viewers. The series is now called the "Kent Family Chronicles" and has carried the family into the twentieth century.

While Jakes does not claim to be an historian, he enjoys doing research for his novels. In an interview published in 1977, the author said he believes "everybody should read American history. It's a great restorer, a reminder that we've been through some rotten times in the past and survived them."

POETS

Alice (1820-1871) and Phoebe (1824-1871) Cary— the Cary sisters—were born on a family farm near Mount Healthy in Hamilton County. They used their birthplace as the setting for their "Clovernook" stories about early Ohio farm life. While still young, they wrote poetry and published it without pay. After 1849, they found a publisher, moved to New York, and issued a dozen more books of poetry. This was very uncommon at a time when few works by women authors were published. Their home was always open to literary friends. Here is a poem by Phoebe:

Don't Give Up

If you've tried and have not won,
Never stop for crying;
All that's great and good is done
Just by patient trying.
Though young birds, in flying, fall,
Still their wings grow stronger;
And the next time they can keep
Up a little longer.
Though the sturdy oak has known
Many a blast that bowed her,
She has risen again, and grown
Loftier and prouder.

If by easy work you beat,
Who the more will prize you?
Gaining victory from defeat,
That's the test that tries you!

> What is the message of the third stanza?
> Describe the "test" in your own words.

Paul Laurence Dunbar (1872-1906) was born in Dayton, the son of ex-slaves. He edited his high school paper, wrote the school song, and graduated with honors, but finding a job was hard. He worked as an elevator operator, a court messenger, and a Library of Congress clerk.

Dunbar published *Oak and Ivy* (1892) at his own expense and gave readings of his work to Midwest audiences. This established his reputation as a poet. Dunbar mastered six black dialects which he used in his verse. Before Dunbar's untimely death at 34, he wrote 18 other works of poetry and prose. Here is a sample of his work:

Sympathy

I know what the caged bird feels, alas!
When the sun is bright on the upland slopes;
When the wind stirs soft through the springing
* grass,*
And the river flows like a stream of glass;
And the faint perfume from its chalice steals—
I know what the caged bird feels!

I know why the caged bird beats his wing
Till its blood is red on the cruel bars;
For he must fly back to his perch and cling
When he fain would be on the bough a-swing;
And a pain still throbs in the old, old scars
And they pulse again with a keener sting—
I know why he beats his wing!

I know why the caged bird sings, ah me,
When his wing is bruised and his bosom sore—
When he beats his bars and he would be free;
It is not a carol of joy or glee,
But a prayer that he sends from his heart's deep
* core,*

But a plea, that upward to heaven he flings—
I know why the caged bird sings!

> 1. Why does the poet feel sympathy for the bird?
> 2. What events or conditions in Dunbar's own life allow him to have these deep feelings?

Hart Crane (1899-1932), of Garrettsville and Cleveland, met death by suicide after a sad and short life. This gifted poet published his first work at age 15, but his parents' divorce and a bitter quarrel with his father caused him to leave Ohio in 1916, for New York City. There, in spite of a bout with alcoholism, Crane published his first major poems. His best work, *The Bridge* (1930), remained unfinished at his death.

These and other writers from our state have strengthened the literary heritage of our country.

3. Ohio artists have reflected American themes in their work.

In addition to authors, Ohio's cultural heritage includes artists and sculptors. Their work is on display in art galleries in Cleveland, Toledo, Cincinnati, Columbus, Dayton, and Canton. Smaller art museums are located in Chillicothe, Massillon, Oberlin, Van Wert, Zanesville, and elsewhere.

PAINTERS

The state's strongest contribution to the *visual arts* is in the field of painting.

Frank Duveneck (1848-1919), of Cincinnati, was a leader in the field of painting. Trained in Germany, Holland, and Italy, he taught painting to others. His quality painting did much to make Cincinnati an art center.

Archibald M. Willard (1836-1918), of Bedford and Wellington, painted the nation's favorite patriotic picture, *The Spirit of '76.* The original painting hangs in the Western Reserve Historical Society's museum at Cleveland.

Is there a museum or historical society in your town? Ohio has dozens of fine art
and historical museums such as these in Dayton (above) and Canton.

Painter Robert Henri is the subject of this etching by artist John Sloan.

Robert Henri (1865-1929) was another outstanding Cincinnati artist. He became a leader of New York's "Ash Can School." He and other artists painted pictures of everyday life among common and poor people in the big city. This realism was like that which Howells used in his novels. Robert Henri excelled as a portrait painter of older people and children. He also taught painting to younger artists.

George Bellows (1882-1925) was a very gifted pupil of Henri. Bellows never studied art in Europe. He wanted to develop a purely American style of art. In Columbus he painted portraits and made *lithographs* of city scenes. In New York he followed the Ash Can tradition. His special talent was the portrayal of the action and excitement found in the

sports world. Bellows's ability to capture the feeling of a prize-fight, as in *Both Members of This Club*—was aided by personal experience. While a student at Ohio State, he won the amateur boxing championship.

Howard Chandler Christy (1873-1952), of Morgan County, won fame as a commercial artist and illustrator of books and magazine short stories. His best-known historical painting is *The Signing of the Treaty of Greene Ville*. It hangs in the rotunda of the State Capitol. He is also known for his pictures of women, nicknamed "Christy girls."

Charles Burchfield (1893-1967), of Ashtabula, lived briefly in Salem and studied at the Cleveland School of Art. He loved to paint the woods and wildflowers of Ohio. Later, he chose the "Main Street" life of small towns as his theme. No doubt, his work was influenced by Sherwood Anderson's book *Winesburg, Ohio*.

SCULPTORS

Two of the great American sculptors of the nineteenth century were Ohioans.

Hiram Powers (1805-1873) was a native of Vermont who grew up in Ohio and received his early training in Cincinnati. With the help of a *patron*, he studied in Italy and set up a studio in Washington, D.C. Daniel Webster and Andrew Jackson were two of his subjects.

Powers's most famous work is a nude statue called *Greek Slave*. It was so popular that six versions were made in marble. This made Powers very well known. He was the first American sculptor to win respect in Europe.

John Quincy Adams Ward (1830-1910), of Urbana, divided his career between Ohio and New York. Ward's chief strength as a sculptor was the creation of life-size bronze statues. Among his best works are *Indian Hunter* (Central Park, New York City) and *President Garfield* (Washington, D.C.). Ward was elected president of both the National Sculpture Society and the National Academy of Design.

Elijah Pierce, one of the finest folk artists in the country. Some of his works are displayed on the walls and on the desk.

Elijah Pierce (1892-1984) was born in Mississippi, the son of a former slave. Elijah moved to Columbus in the 1930s, where he worked as a barber for 50 years. As a hobby he carved wood sculptures and *reliefs* of animals, sports heroes, and especially scenes from the Bible. Pierce started to gain acclaim in 1971, and was known as one of the finest folk artists in the country. His workshop and gallery in Columbus is listed on the National Register of Historic Places. Masterpieces like his *Story of Job* and *Noah and the Ark* have been shown in major museums and exhibits.

4. Architecture in Ohio represents many American building styles.

Ohio has many examples of older American building styles. Some examples are shown here.

Jonathan Goldsmith (1783-1847) was a master architect-builder. He arrived in Painesville by covered wagon in 1811. His architectural taste and skill may be seen today in buildings he designed in the Lake County area over a 35-year period. The best-kept sample of Goldsmith's work is the Mathews House (1829) in Painesville.

Cass Gilbert (1859-1934), son of the first mayor of Zanesville, served as an *apprentice* in an eastern architectural firm. His own designs were often in the classical style. A good example of his work is the Supreme Court Building in Washington, D.C.

Throughout Ohio can be seen numerous interesting early architectural styles which were used for homes or public buildings. How can a style of architecture tell you something about the time when the building was built? Can you identify other building styles besides those pictured here?

Stage Coach Inn, McCutchenville—a Colonial-style building.

The Guthrie house in Zanesville is in the Greek Revival style. Can you give reasons why the style is called Greek Revival?

A Gothic Revival house near Homer. Notice the vertical siding and the decoration along the roof edge.

The Warner house in Wellington was built in 1868. It is an example of the Italianate Villa or "bracketed" style. Can you locate the brackets?

The house of Carey Brown in Wyandot County. This is a Victorian brick farmhouse with a mansard roof.

The Ohio governor's residence in Bexley is in the Tudor style.

An Octagonal house in Darke County. How many sides does it have?

The *Delta Queen* reminds us of earlier showboats where minstrel shows became popular.

5. Famous people in the fields of music and entertainment were from Ohio.

Ohio's musical heritage is rich in popular songs and the *performing arts*. The tradition began in the early nineteenth century and continues to the present day.

Early settlers brought folk music. During the 1830s-40s, minstrel showboat entertainment became popular in the state. Traveling tent shows reached the towns of the interior.

More serious, or classical music did not come on the scene until choral groups and symphony orchestras were started in the late 1800s. Cincinnati was the first place in the state where music was taught in elementary schools.

MUSICIANS

Daniel Decatur Emmett (1815-1904) helped develop the minstrel show. A minstrel show is a stage performance by white actors and singers who *impersonate* black people. They blacken their faces and use black speech and humor. Emmett wrote some of the best-loved minstrel songs like "Old Dan Tucker," "The Blue-Tail Fly," and "Dixie."

Stephen Collins Foster (1826-1864) spent several years in Cincinnati as a young man. He wrote many of his popular songs, such as "Oh, Susanna," while living there. He was employed first as a bookkeeper and later worked in a music publishing house.

Benjamin Hanby (1833-1867) is most famous for his Christmas song "Up on the House Top." Hanby lived in Fairfield County and Westerville and graduated from Otterbein College. He served briefly as a minister, but quit his church job to spend the rest of his life writing songs and teaching music to children.

Tell Taylor (1876-1937), a musical comedy singer, was born in Hancock County. He *composed* a song in 1910 which sold more than two million copies. The song was "Down by the Old Mill Stream," and it is still one of the favorites for barbershop quartets. The mill stream in the song was the Blanchard River that flows through Findlay, where Taylor was raised on a family farm.

Oley Speaks (1876-1948), of Canal Winchester, is another Ohio son who won national fame as a composer and singer. Speaks lived most of his life in Columbus and New York. He was a featured soloist in several large churches. During his life he wrote over 200 sacred and *secular* songs, including such favorites as "Prayer Perfect" and "On the Road to Mandalay."

ENTERTAINERS

Annie Oakley (1860-1926), whose real name was Phoebe Ann Moses (or Mozee), was from Darke County. Her nickname was "Little Miss Sure-Shot" because she was a world champion sharpshooter. She could hit a dime tossed into the air, or split playing cards held on edge—from 30 paces! Annie Oakley toured the show circuit with her husband, Frank Butler (also a marksman), until 1885. Then she joined Buffalo Bill's "Wild West Show" as a star for 17 years.

Roy Rogers (1912-) of Duck Run and Cincinnati, starred in 89 western films and was on radio and T.V. many times. Along with his wife, Dale Evans, he also performed at rodeos and fairs.

Frohman Brothers. In the theatre business of the late nineteenth and early twentieth centuries, the three Frohman brothers from Sandusky achieved great success. They worked to develop "stars" (outstanding performers) and a system called "booking," to arrange tours by star performers.

Other stage stars who spent part of their lives in this state include Lillian and Dorothy Gish, Doris Day, Clark Gable, Bob Hope, and Phyllis Diller. Each had a wonderful career and left a heritage of *classic* films that are still shown today. One of the biggest movies of all time was *Gone With the Wind* starring Clark Gable. These entertainers, and many more from Ohio, have brought happiness to millions of people all over the world.

6. Many different sports have benefited from contributions of Ohioans.

In the fields of racing, baseball, football, and other sports, people from this state have won honors and made improvements on some games.

Eddie Arcaro (1916-), one of America's great horse jockeys, was born and raised in Cincinnati. In 31 years, he won 4,779 races. This is the second-best score of all American riders. The horses which Arcaro rode earned over $30 million for their owners. Twice (in 1941 on Whirlaway, and again in 1948 on Citation) Arcaro won all three big races: the Kentucky Derby, the Preakness, and the Belmont Stakes.

Barney Oldfield (1878-1946), of Wauseon, raced cars in the old days. He was the first person ever to drive a mile a minute. That was in 1903. In 1910, he drove 131 miles per hour, a record which lasted for nearly 10 years.

Jesse Owens (1913-1980) was a racer of another sort. He starred in track at East Technical High School in Cleveland and at Ohio State University. The height of his career came in 1936 at the Olympic Games in Berlin. Owens won four gold medals. Voters in a 1950 newspaper poll named him as the greatest track and field athlete of the early twentieth century.

Baseball records were set by several Ohioans. Several star Cleveland Indian pitchers are pictured in the National Baseball Hall of Fame at Cooperstown, New York. Among them are Cy Young and Bob Feller.

Entertainers like Bob Hope (left) and Clark Gable bring happiness to millions of people during long and successful careers.

DENTON TRUE (CY) YOUNG (1867-1955)

WHEN Cy Young began pitching for the Cleveland Spiders in 1890, the pitcher's box was just 50 feet away from home plate. The pitcher would release the baseball from a flat area and the catcher wore no glove. By 1911—Young's last season—pitchers were throwing from a mound 60 feet, 6 inches from the plate to a catcher suited up in armor.

Young grew up in Ohio's hill country and became a strong farmer and expert rail splitter. He was earning $10 a month on his father's farm when he received an offer of $60 a month to pitch for Canton in the Tri-State League. He earned the nickname "Cy," short for cyclone, while pitching at Canton.

He went on to win 511 games in the major leagues, a record no one has ever approached. Pitching many times with only one or two days' rest, Young appeared in over 900 games. Cy averaged more than eight innings a game for 22 years.

Although he admitted his arm became tired, he claimed never to have a sore arm. He credited his health to off-season running and hard work all winter on the farm.

Cy's top annual salary was $5,000, but he worked his farm until his wife's death in 1933. He moved in with friends and neighbors, actively farming until he was over 80 years of age.

Cy was inducted into the Baseball Hall of Fame in its first year, 1939. Today the outstanding pitchers in both leagues are given the annual Cy Young award for pitching excellence.

Bob Feller (1918-) had many good years as a pitcher for the Cleveland Indians. In one year he struck out 348 batters. Seven times he led the American League in strikeouts. He also pitched three no-hitters and 12 one-hitters in his career. His best pitches were a fast ball, a sharp-breaking curve, and a good slider.

Branch Rickey (1881-1965), of Stockdale, became a baseball catcher and manager. He developed the farm system as a way of preparing players for the major leagues.

Larry Doby (1924-), outfielder for the Cleveland Indians, was the first black player in the American League in 1947.

Football leagues got the benefits of two great coaches from Ohio.

Paul Brown (1909-), of Norwalk and Massillon, now is an owner of the Cincinnati Bengals professional team. In his long career as a coach, he was the first coach to call plays from the sidelines, the first to grade his players, the first to use movies of games, and the first to use helmet face guards.

Wayne Woodrow "Woody" Hayes (1913-) was the coach of the Ohio State University Buckeyes. For more than 25 years he guided his teams to winning seasons and championships.

Golf is a big sport in this state. There are over 300 golf courses in Ohio, including some of the most difficult ones in the nation.

Jack Nicklaus (1940-), from Upper Arlington in Columbus, is America's all-time golf money winner and title holder. He has won the Ohio Open, the U.S. Open, the British Open, and Masters and PGA Championships.

The many people listed in this chapter are only some of those from our state who have made contributions to the several fields of culture. There likely are people from your own community who are famous there, in the state, or in the nation for records set, performances, or improvements to their field.

We can be proud of the cultural heritage in our state—both high culture and popular culture. The next chapter will remind us of the rich folk culture in our state.

The Cincinnati Bengals play the Cleveland Browns in an exciting football contest. What other Ohio professional sports teams can you name?

Jack Nicklaus, from Upper Arlington, is the nation's all-time golf money winner.

WORDS FOR STUDY

high culture	*folk culture*	*realist*
popular culture	*oral tradition*	*lyrics*

visual arts   *apprentice*   *compose*
lithograph   *performing arts*   *secular*
patron   *impersonate*   *classic*
relief

QUESTIONS FOR REVIEW

1. What are the three kinds of culture? Give an example of each.

2. What book was one of the first to tell about the rise of big cities? Who was its author?

3. What kind of literature did Zane Grey write?

4. For what series of historical novels is John Jakes famous?

5. What was unusual about the careers of Alice and Phoebe Carey?

6. Who is the author of the poem "Sympathy"?

7. What Ohio artist painted *The Spirit of '76?*

8. Name two famous sculptors from our state.

9. What building today is a good example of the work of architect Jonathan Goldsmith? of Cass Gilbert?

10. Name three songs that were written in Ohio, and identify their composers.

11. For what was Annie Oakley famous?

12. What contributions did the Frohman brothers make to the field of theater?

13. Name five movie stars who were from Ohio.

14. What sports event was Jesse Owens's specialty? What honors did he win?

15. How did Cy Young get his nickname? What position did he play in baseball?

16. Name two famous football coaches from this state.

17. What is Jack Nicklaus's sport? What contests has he won?

GOING FURTHER

1. In what ways do Ohio cities serve as centers of culture?

2. Why is there not an Ohio style in literature, art, or architecture?

3. What subject matter did Robert Henri and George. Bellows have in common in their paintings?

4. How did Daniel Emmet, Stephen Foster, and Benjamin Hanby make people's lives richer?

5. Why can Paul Brown be called one of the most innovative football coaches?

6. In what way have authors from this state preserved its history and culture?

FOR THOUGHT AND DISCUSSION

1. What is culture?

2. Would you say that authors from Ohio have written popular literature or classic work?

3. In what ways have writers, painters, sculptors, musicians, and entertainers from our state been leaders in their fields?

PROJECTS AND REPORTS

1. Attend a "high" cultural event and share your feelings about it with the class.

2. Skim-read a book, or several articles, to gather biographical information on any Ohio movie star. Summarize the person's life and contributions to his or her field in a written report.

3. Find examples in your community of different architectural styles. Take photographs of the buildings and make a bulletin board display, labeling each photo.

4. Learn any song composed by an Ohioan and perform it for the class.

5. Give a report on any one of these or other Ohio scientists, and tell how he or she contributed to the state's culture: Daniel Drake (1785-1852), Jared P. Kirtland (1793-1877), Charles Whittlesey (1808-1886), Ormsby M. Mitchel (1809-1862), Cleveland Abbé (1838-1916), Karl Compton (1887-1954), Arthur Compton (1892-1961).

6. Attend your favorite sporting event and write a report telling how that sport has contributed to Ohio culture through the years.

7. Find out how the Ash Can school of art got its name. Who were the artists in this group?

The Leiderhosen 5 is a German performing band.

CHAPTER 14

OUR ETHNIC HERITAGE

MAIN POINTS

1. Ohio has been built by many ethnic and religious groups.

2. Several small religious sects helped settle early Ohio and added to its culture.

3. The first major ethnic groups to settle in Ohio were from western and northwestern Europe.

4. Immigrants after 1880 came largely from eastern and southern Europe.

5. Immigrants from Asia have contributed to the richness of Ohio culture.

6. The largest minority group in Ohio today is the black community.

7. Mexican-Americans are the second most numerous minority in the state and the nation.

8. The United States began to restrict immigration in 1890, but exceptions have allowed political and war refugees to settle here since World War II.

9. Cleveland has one of the most ethnic populations of any city in the nation.

1. Ohio has been built by many ethnic and religious groups.

Ethnic heritage. Ours is a state rich and varied in its *ethnic* heritage. A look at place names on a road map, or family names in a phone book will quickly show the many backgrounds of Ohio people. Some 70 different national groups live in Cleveland alone. This mix of people is called "ethnic heritage." An ethnic group is one which shares common national roots, customs, language, or religion.

Black-Americans, Japanese-Americans, and Jewish-Americans are types of ethnic groups. Cities like Cleveland have distinct ethnic neighborhoods—"Little Italy" on the east side and the "Cosmo Wards" on the west side. Ethnic groups preserve their identity in other ways, too. Often they support a foreign language press, speak the native language in their homes and neighborhood, or belong to a social club with others of the same background. On holidays or at festival times, ethnic peoples dress, eat, and celebrate as their parents or grandparents did in another country. Language schools and churches help them to keep their traditions alive. So do arts and crafts and ethnic foods, passed down from one generation to the next.

We are a product of many ethnic cultures which have helped to make Ohio strong.

Religious heritage. Some groups that are important in the development of the state are the many church organizations. The main Protestant groups active today are the United Methodist Church, Presbyterians, Lutherans, the United Church of Christ, Episcopalians, Evangelical United Brethren, and Baptists. There are nearly 100 Jewish congregations, as well. However, the largest single religion in Ohio today is the Roman Catholic Church, with more than two million members.

POPULATION OF OHIO

1970 Population	1980 Population	Percent Change
10,657,423	10,797,630	+1.3

White		9,597,458
Black		1,076,748
American Indian		11,985
Eskimo		167
Aleut		87
Asian and Pacific Islander		47,820
Other		63,365
Total		10,797,630

---

2. Several small religious sects helped settle early Ohio and added to its culture.

The Amish, who came from Germany and Switzerland, went first to rural Pennsylvania. Around 1810, they moved to Holmes County, south of Cleveland, where they still live today. One belief of their faith is to oppose war. With their plain dress and simple horse-and-buggy transportation, they offer a sharp contrast to most twentieth-century people. Travelers who pass through Amish districts like Darby Plains near Plain City can see their well-run farms.

Mennonites are also found in Holmes County, as well as Wayne, Medina, and Allen counties. Although *receptive* to some modern ways, they live simple lives and are conscientious objectors to armed service. Bluffton College, in the northwest part of the state, is a Mennonite school.

Mormons, fleeing from *persecution* in upstate New York, settled at Kirtland in 1830. Under the leadership of their founder, Joseph Smith, they built the first Mormon temple there in 1836. Several years later, because of anti-Mormon feelings (partly due to a poorly managed Mormon bank), they were forced to flee to Missouri. The group finally settled in Utah, now the headquarters for its more than five million members.

Quakers built one of the most historic buildings (1814) which is still preserved in eastern Ohio. This is the 2,000-seat Friend's Meeting House at the Quaker settlement of Mount Pleasant in Jefferson County. It was planned that the beautiful little town would become a center for the Quaker faith in Ohio.

An auction of chinaware, melons, and sunbonnets among the Amish people in Berlin, around 1940.

This did happen. Quakers there were strongly opposed to slavery. They published two anti-slavery papers and ran a station on the Underground Railroad.

The Shakers, founded in England by "Mother" Ann Lee, also lived simply. Since they did not practice marriage, adult converts and orphaned children brought new members for the group. The Shakers are well known for their skills and crafts. These included farming, furniture and cabinet making, and building construction. The Shakers designed many simple, but practical devices such as a circular saw, clothespins, and a washing machine. Their herb medicines were another contribution to our culture. In this state, four distinct Shaker communities were founded: Union Village near Lebanon; North Union, now Shaker Heights;

Shaker hats, waistcoat, and trousers.

The German experimental colony of Zoar in 1885.

Watervleit, near Dayton; and Whitewater in Hamilton County.

Zoarites lived in Tuscarawas County. Zoar was a German experimental colony founded in 1817 by Joseph Bimeler and others. The sect survived until 1898, when the colony was dissolved and its money divided among the members. It proved too hard for young people to follow the strict life style. They left the colony for land of their own and many other opportunities nearby. Visitors to Zoar may see restored buildings, a central square, and some beautiful gardens.

3. The first major ethnic groups to settle in Ohio were from western and northwestern Europe.

The first major groups of settlers in the early period were the Scotch-Irish and the English, who migrated west from the older seaboard states. Marietta was founded by people from Massachusetts, and a group from Connecticut settled the Western Reserve.

Scotch-Irish farmers and pioneers from the backwoods of Virginia and Kentucky founded communities in southern and eastern Ohio. The Scotch-Irish are people whose families lived in northern Ireland before coming to this land. They copied the log cabin from the Finns and Swedes and made it the typical frontier home. A practical and hardy people, they were one of the main groups in the state by 1850. Those living in Appalachia today are mainly of Scotch-Irish descent. Their customs and life style have changed little over 150 years. Their folk art, music, and crafts are a key part of our state's heritage.

The Scotch-Irish are noted for their strong interest in religion and education. In Ohio they founded many Presbyterian churches and backed public schools and private colleges. In rural parts of the state, they earned a reputation for making strangers welcome at cornhuskings, house or barn raisings, and quilting bees.

The English people gave us our basic form of government. Their influence upon architecture and town planning is also great. Most early English settlers were farmers or craftsmen with skills needed for frontier life. After the Civil War, those who came from England tended to be factory workers. Other persons of English background became outstanding in business and commerce. Four of Ohio's eight presidents—William Henry Harrison, James A. Garfield, Benjamin Harrison, and William Howard Taft—were of English ancestry.

Germans were the white ethnic group that made the greatest impact on the state's history. In fact, German is the ancestry that leads in 61 of the state's 88 counties.

Germans from Pennsylvania came here in the early 1800s and soon settled the east-central counties. One whole group from Lancaster, Pennsylvania, settled in Lancaster, Ohio. After 1830, a great number of Germans came here directly from Europe. They drained the Black Swamp, then set up productive farms and ethnic communities in such places as New Bremen, New Knoxville, and Minster. Meanwhile, other Germans settled in big cities. They became a major force in Cleveland, Columbus, and Cincinnati politics. They founded many churches (Lutheran, Reformed, Evangelical, Catholic), and colleges (Ashland, Capital, Heidel-

A bagpiper reminds us of the Scottish influence in Ohio.

berg, Wittenberg), besides German-language newspapers. They built breweries and gyms; they supported music and the theatre.

Popular German foods include breaded pork or veal, sausage, sauerkraut, and pastries served with coffee. In earlier times, a German father often took his family on picnics, where they played games and sang old world songs. Other Americans have

These Irish gentlemen are enjoying a traditional St. Patrick's Day parade.

adopted the German Christmas custom of beautifully decorated trees.

Irish moved here in large numbers before the Civil War. Many who helped build the Erie Canal in New York (1817-1825) came to dig more canals here. Later they helped build the state's first railroads.

The Irish came to America in three waves. The first came to get the canal jobs in the 1820s and 1830s. The second sought to escape the potato famine (crop failure) in Ireland in the 1840s. The

third arrived after the Civil War to work in industries. Their Catholic religion and competition in the labor market sometimes led to problems with native-born Protestant workers, but the Irish held their own. In some cities they became leaders in local government.

The Irish love to sing and dance their jigs and reels. Irish plays are still popular, and long parades on St. Patrick's Day are fun for all who march along or just watch.

The Welsh (from Wales) were a small ethnic group who reached Ohio in the early 1800s. Some of their descendants now live in the Granville area. The Welsh developed the salt and iron resources of Jackson County. They are well known for their music festival called the Eistedfodd, which is held each year.

Finns (from Finland) came here in the 1860s and settled in Ashtabula, Conneaut, and Fairport Harbor. They stressed strong family ties and published their own newspapers to help preserve their culture. Finns also organized cooperative and temperance groups. Hard workers, many of the Finns found jobs on the ore boats of the Great Lakes. Today their numbers are declining in the state.

4. Immigrants after 1880 came largely from eastern and southern Europe.

The ethnic people mentioned so far belonged to the "old immigrants" group. About 1880, the type of European immigrants to America changed. Instead of mainly Protestant, middle-class persons from northwest Europe, the "new immigrants" were of Catholic, Jewish, or Eastern Orthodox belief. They came from central, southern, and eastern Europe. Most of them belonged to the poverty-stricken lower class.

The new immigrants came in very large numbers. Up to a million people a year came to the United States. This swift growth of immigrants and their diverse cultures gave our country a new character. It became the most ethnic nation in the world. Large numbers of the new immigrants chose not to live in the East, but went directly to the inland states like Ohio. Here, they quickly found jobs and more social and economic security. This is how Cleveland got such a blend of ethnic people from 1880 to 1920. These new immigrants were a key factor in the labor force that helped the rapid industrial growth in the state.

Who were the new immigrants? Italians and Poles made up the largest groups in the state. There were Czechs, Slovaks, Hungarians, Russians, Slovenes, Croatians, Serbians, Greeks, and people from the Baltic states. Most of them settled in northern Ohio.

Many Jews also came in the 1880s to escape persecution in central and eastern Europe. Their kinfolk had formed communities in Cleveland and Cincinnati and built synagogues there. They established a Jewish newspaper and Hebrew Union College in Cincinnati to help preserve their culture. Taking low-paid jobs at first, the Jewish people gradually entered other fields of work, such as marketing, law, and medicine. Over 70,000 Jews now reside in or near Cleveland. Few of them live in the inner city, but most in suburbs like Shaker Heights and Beechwood. In Columbus, the main center of Jewish culture is the community of Bexley, which is 45% Jewish.

Italian immigrants at first took pick-and-shovel and factory jobs. Others were skilled *artisans.* Some Italians started groceries. They felt great pride in running family-owned businesses. Meanwhile, they founded Italian churches, societies, and mutual aid groups. They emphasized family discipline and thrift. Often their sons and daughters became teachers, doctors, lawyers, dentists, labor leaders, and skilled workers.

Many Italians who settled on the west side of Columbus worked in stone quarries. Stone masons, who had learned their trade in Europe, cut the stone used to build the Ohio Statehouse.

Italian-Americans sometimes celebrate by staging religious parades or shooting off fireworks. Co-

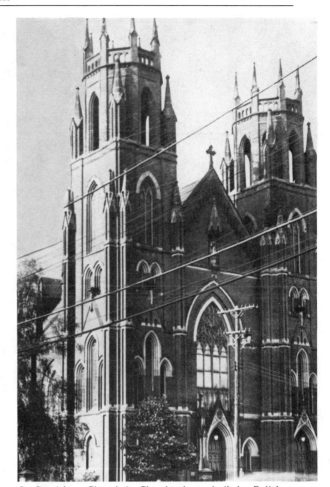

St. Stanislaus Church in Cleveland was built by Polish immigrants in 1891. It was one of the largest churches in the state at that time.

lumbus Day is always a special occasion for them. Italians have made major contributions in opera and in violin music.

The Poles arrived after the Civil War, although a few were here as early as the 1840s. They found jobs in steel mills, oil refineries, and the building trades. They set up churches, newspapers, and social halls to keep their Polish traditions alive. Some 30,000 foreign-born Poles lived in Cleveland by 1920. The heart of their community was the East 65th-Forman Avenue neighborhood called War-

George Szell, who for many years conducted the Cleveland Symphony Orchestra, came to the United States as an immigrant from Hungary.

zawa. Here they built a great church—St. Stanislaus—in 1891. It was one of the largest in the state up to that time.

A peak Polish migration in the 1920s-1940s brought another 50,000 to 80,000 Poles to Cleveland. Clevelanders of Polish descent are leaders in every phase of the city's business, cultural, political, and professional life.

Polish people are very friendly and enjoy church fairs, religious feast days, and big wedding celebrations. Some of their favorite foods are keilbasa (pork sausage) and babka (a cake made from many eggs and nuts or raisins.)

The Czechs and Slovaks live mostly in Cleveland, Youngstown, Akron, and Cincinnati. The Czechs first came here in the 1850s from the industrial sections of Moravia and Bohemia in central Europe. Most were skilled workers who found good jobs in factories, the garment industry, and the needle trade. The Slovaks, on the other hand, *emigrated* from the southern rural part of their homeland. They took factory jobs in the cities as unskilled workers until, by hard work and study, they gained better jobs and wages.

Beer taverns were social centers for early Czech immigrants. The saloon was a place to discuss politics with friends or to get help for those in need.

Favorite Czech foods are houska and kolach (both sweet breads) and vegetable-meat stews. Slovak dishes include sweet and sour cabbage and ginger cookies.

The Hungarians emigrated mainly in the 1880s-1920s. Ohio is one of the chief centers for Hungarian people in the nation. Hungarians founded many *fraternal,* mutual aid, religious, and charitable groups. They built both Protestant and

Catholic churches. They are known for their newspapers and singing clubs. After World War II, Hungarian political refugees—mostly *intellectuals* and professional people—fled their homeland to find a new freedom in America. Fritz Reiner and George Szell, who conducted the Cincinnati and Cleveland orchestras, are two such immigrants.

Hungarian dishes are popular with many Ohioans. Chicken paprika, beef goulash, stuffed cabbage, and pork with sauerkraut make delicious meals. For dessert, a Hungarian torte or a cherry strudel is a special treat.

Hungarians stage colorful harvest festivals, and they also enjoy a lively dance called the Czardas. Gypsy music is a popular type of folk music from Hungary.

Slovenes, Croatians, and Serbians fled from poverty and political *oppression*. By 1960, Ohio led the nation in the number of South Slavs in the state, with the largest portion of them living in the Cleveland area. Other South Slavic communities are located in Lorain, Akron, Youngstown, Canton, Mansfield, Columbus, and Cincinnati.

The Slovenes were the first of this group to come, arriving in the late nineteenth century. Held back by a poor knowledge of English, they often took low wages and hard jobs in factories and mines. Cleveland is the largest Slovenian center in the nation. One well-known member of their group is Frank J. Lausche, a former mayor of the city. He was the state's only five-term governor, and has since served two terms as a U.S. senator.

Favorite Slovenian foods include hearty soups and delicate pastries like potica (a nut roll) and krofi (donuts).

Greeks came to northern Ohio in the early 1900s. They spread to such cities as Cleveland, Akron, Toledo, Canton, and Columbus. Some Greeks opened small restaurants, sweet shops, shoe repair stores, and dry cleaning shops. Greek descendants often chose the *professions* of teacher, lawyer, doctor, and dentist. There are some 22 Greek Orthodox churches in the state.

Popular Greek foods are lamb—either roasted, stewed, or skewered (shish kabob)—and baked eggplant slices called moussaka. At Greek picnics, a whole lamb may be roasted over a spit while the people dance. Marinated olives are also common. Baklava is a nutty Greek dessert drenched in a honey syrup.

"Ricemilk" (as this pudding is called in Greece) is a traditional Greek favorite.

Rice Pudding
Yield: 8 to 10 6-oz. servings

2 quarts milk (8 cups) ½ cup rice (long cooking) ½ cup sugar ¼ cup butter	Combine in a heavy saucepan and bring to a boil, stirring constantly to avoid scorching. Reduce heat and cook at a high simmer, uncovered, until the rice is thoroughly cooked (about one hour), stirring occasionally. Remove from heat.
1 tablespoon vanilla	Stir into the rice. (Also stir in the skim.)
1 egg, separated	Beat egg white until stiff, then blend in the yolk. Carefully dilute the egg with 4-5 tablespoons of hot pudding, beating constantly to keep the egg from coagulating. Slowly add egg mixture to pudding, stirring until it thickens.
Ground cinnamon	Sprinkle cinnamon over individual dishes of pudding. Serve warm or cold.

Brightly painted eggs are a tradition of Ukrainian and Russian folk art.

Ukrainians and Russians have brought their lively folk arts to the state. Ukrainians moved to Cleveland in the late 1800s and settled on the near west side. Their children have moved south to the suburb of Parma. Ukrainian folk art is shown in embroidered blouses, beautifully painted Easter eggs, wood carvings, and ceramics. A number of choirs and small groups perform their folk music.

A group of Russian-Germans from the Black Sea region reached Ohio in 1847-48. These people settled on Kelley's Island in Lake Erie and started *vineyards*. After the Civil War, most Russians coming to the United States were single men who were unskilled and poor. They took jobs in the soft coal mines and steel mills of Ohio.

In Cleveland, Russians built the impressive St. Theodosius Church in 1911. Modeled like Our Savior Church in Moscow, it stands as a striking

symbol of Eastern European culture. Other Russians came after 1915 as political refugees.

Baltic people—Lithuanians, Latvians, and Estonians—number over 20,000 here today. Their ancestors came from the eastern shores of the Baltic Sea, a place often invaded by foreign armies. Uprisings during times of war caused many Baltic people to move to America. Cleveland is the center for these nationality groups. Those who have come since World War II keep alive the Baltic language and culture in our state.

Parish dinners and bake sales are important parts of Lithuanian community life. Special foods are kugelis (a crusty pudding of grated potatoes baked with milk) and cabbage squares (pastry filled with cabbage, hard-cooked eggs, and onions) served with soup. If the pastry square is filled with fruit, it may be served as a dessert.

5. Immigrants from Asia have contributed to the richness of Ohio culture.

The new immigrants include some from Asia who now live in this state. In 1970, there were about 5,000 each of Chinese and Japanese foreign-born residents here. Roughly 25-30% of these lived in Cleveland. The 1980 census showed nearly 10,000 Chinese in Ohio, more than 7,200 Filipinos and Koreans each, and about 3,500 Vietnamese.

The Chinese, at first associated with food and laundry shops, now work in many fields, including the professions and the arts. The Chinese are a good example of those who preserve the best of two cultures. They keep alive their ancient traditions through groups like the Chinese-American Cultural Association. At the same time, they change to the American life style of business, dress, and homes.

Japanese immigrants moved to the state in the years from 1880 to 1907. Then a policy to restrict their coming was started by President Theodore Roosevelt. In recent years, some Japanese have moved here from the western states. Many were taken from their homes and held in *relocation camps* in the Rocky Mountain states while the U.S. was at war with Japan during during World War II. This was because they were wrongly suspected of being disloyal to the United States. This practice was later declared unconstitutional. A small group of Japanese entered the state after the war as brides of our servicemen.

A Japanese steak house in Columbus. What ethnic restaurants are located in your area? What kinds of food do they serve?

6. The largest minority group in Ohio today is the black community.

Ohio's black people today number more than one million, or about 10% of the state's population. The size of the black community in the state grew slowly until the Civil War. Then it rose 75% in 10 years, but slowed down again. It reached 111,500 persons by 1910. A rapid increase brought a 200% gain by 1940. Both World Wars created a chance for southern blacks to seek better jobs and housing in northern industrial states. The trend continued after World War II. The increase of blacks in the state showed a 23.5% gain in the sixties and another 10% by 1980.

The official state policy toward blacks in the early 1800s was to prevent slavery here, to keep blacks out, to degrade those already living here, and to permit slavery to continue in the South. After years of struggle, blacks gained some rights and began to have status in several fields by 1870.

Carthagena in Mercer County preserves some examples of the black community which began there in 1842.

Robert S. Duncanson of Cincinnati was a painter; John Mercer Langston of Lorain County became a teacher and a diplomat; Granville T. Woods of Columbus was an inventor; and George Washington Williams of Hamilton County wrote a history of black people.

By 1900 blacks had the right to travel, to enter the state freely, and to hold and sell property. They were lawful citizens with the right to attend public schools. However, *de facto* segregation kept black students from a quality education. Busing is a recent move to correct this problem.

Most blacks live in cities such as Cleveland, Cincinnati, Columbus, Dayton, Youngstown, Toledo, Akron, and Springfield. Historically, they moved into central city neighborhoods formerly lived in by low-income ethnic groups who left as their education and income improved. The vacant homes, once nice places to live, had decayed to the point of misery and poverty. It was a poor place for anyone to inherit.

In recent years, many blacks have overcome social and educational problems. Many are skilled workers or professional people. Some have won honors for military service. Many are property owners or key public officials. Former Mayor Carl Stokes of Cleveland and his brother, Louis, a Congressman from Cleveland, are examples of this *mobility*.

Many black Ohioans are leaders in cultural, social, and political life. Poets and novelists include Nikki Giovanni and Virginia Hamilton. Leontyne Price and Nancy Wilson are famous singers. Dorian Harewood and Greg Morris are T.V. stars. Woodcarver Elijah Pierce and artist Willis Bing Davis have excelled in the visual arts.

Nathanial R. Jones is a judge of the Sixth U.S. Circuit Court of Appeals in Cincinnati. The state legislature has more than a dozen black members. The late Daniel "Chappie" James was the first black four-star general.

In 1983 the new National Afro-American Museum and Cultural Center was underway in Wilberforce to tell the history of black Americans.

7. Mexican-Americans are the second most numerous minority in the state and the nation.

During World War I, Mexican laborers were brought in to work in coal mines and steel mills. The 1980 census showed that more than 53,000 foreign-born Mexicans lived here. Nearly 1% of the state's population is Hispanic. These people live in all of the big cities of the state, with large groups in Toledo, Findlay, and Bowling Green. The contributions of Hispanics are rich in literature, music, painting, and dance. Most Mexican-Americans are Roman Catholics. The Catholic Church is important to them both as a religious and as a social institution which lends welfare aid to poor families. A private group called *La Raza Unida* also gives help to Spanish-speaking people.

The Hispanic culture includes colorful *fiestas,* dances, and folk music. From our Spanish-speaking neighbors we have learned to enjoy enchiladas, tamales, and tortillas.

Migrant workers have been very important to the state's farm economy. Some 30,000 migrant workers trek to the northwest part of the state each year, mainly from Texas. There are around 500 migrant farm labor camps in Ohio. The workers arrive early in May and stay until October. They plant, cultivate, and harvest sugar beets, strawberries, cucumbers, beans, corn, cabbage, and tomatoes.

The migrants live in poor, simple housing, and do back-breaking work for low pay. Children work long hours in the fields beside their parents and other relatives. Their schooling is *disrupted* and limited.

The migrant family is usually paid as a unit rather than individually for their work. Some of their pay is often held back until the final week of the season to make sure they stay and finish a job. Since their work is seasonal, and work in Texas during the winter months is uncertain, many families are caught in an endless cycle of poverty.

Leontyne Price became a famous opera singer.

It is difficult for them to get proper medical care, nutrition, education, or housing.

8. The United States began to restrict immigration in 1890, but exceptions have allowed political and war refugees to settle here since World War II.

Since 1890, and especially during the 1920s, the federal government has limited the number of immigrants who could come to America. A quota system was set up so that each country could send only a few of its people to the United States each year.

Until the 1950s, few changes were made in the U.S. immigration policy. Since that time special laws have been passed by Congress to allow for groups

THE UPS AND DOWNS OF U.S. IMMIGRATION

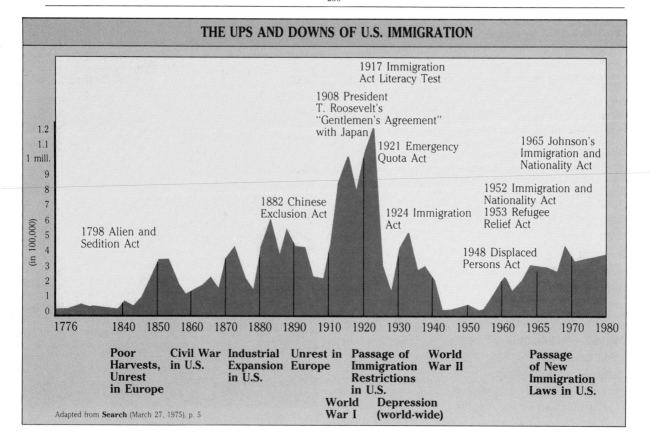

1917 Immigration Act Literacy Test

1908 President T. Roosevelt's "Gentlemen's Agreement" with Japan

1921 Emergency Quota Act

1965 Johnson's Immigration and Nationality Act

1882 Chinese Exclusion Act

1924 Immigration Act

1952 Immigration and Nationality Act
1953 Refugee Relief Act

1798 Alien and Sedition Act

1948 Displaced Persons Act

| Poor Harvests, Unrest in Europe | Civil War in U.S. | Industrial Expansion in U.S. | Unrest in Europe | Passage of Immigration Restrictions in U.S. | World War II | Passage of New Immigration Laws in U.S. |

World War I   Depression (world-wide)

Adapted from **Search** (March 27, 1975), p. 5

of political refugees. The most recent of these have come from Cuba and Vietnam.

Most of these later groups have found it difficult to adjust to life here. The climate and life style are so different from what they left behind.

Because they seldom speak English, they have trouble finding jobs and making friends in their new homes. Some progress has been made to make these refugees feel welcome, but much remains to be done.

In what ways would a newcomer to your school, from another city or state, feel like an immigrant? What is your role in making newcomers feel welcome? Work with classmates to make a plan to help new students in the school feel more comfortable.

9. Cleveland has one of the most ethnic populations of any city in the nation.

In this chapter, the city of Cleveland has often been cited as a *haven* for many ethnic groups. A fitting reminder of the city's heritage are the Cultural Gardens in Rockefeller Park. This unique series of memorials celebrates the arts and traditions of peoples from 20 different nations. The first garden, in honor of the English author William Shakespeare, took form in 1916. Ten years later, the Hebrew Garden was added and, by 1939, a whole cluster of gardens was dedicated. Together, the Cultural Gardens represent the many peoples of Ohio. They serve as a symbol of our ethnic heritage.

At the Cultural Gardens in Cleveland's Rockefeller Park, memorials celebrate the cultures of people from 20 different nations. How do they serve as a symbol of our ethnic heritage?

WORDS FOR STUDY

ethnic	*oppression*
receptive	*professions*
persecution	*vineyard*
artisan	*relocation camp*
emigrate	*mobility*
fraternal	*disrupt*
intellectual	*haven*

QUESTIONS FOR REVIEW

1. How many nationalities live in Ohio?
2. What parts of life does ethnic heritage affect?
3. Name four religious groups that contributed to the state's culture, and give examples.
4. From where did the old immigrants come? the new immigrants?
5. What was the official Ohio policy toward blacks in the early nineteenth century?
6. What work do migrant workers find in Ohio?
7. What is the purpose of *La Raza Unida*?
8. Why have the recent immigrants come from Cuba and Vietnam?

GOING FURTHER

1. What were reasons for early settlers coming to America, compared with recent arrivals in the state?
2. What is similar and different about the beliefs and practices of the Amish and the Mennonites?
3. What evidence is there to prove that the Mount Pleasant Quakers were opposed to slavery?
4. What impact did the Shakers have on American culture?
5. Why did the Irish come to America?
6. Why did many eastern and southern Europeans settle in Ohio?
7. Why did many blacks move to Ohio cities during and after World War II?

FOR THOUGHT AND DISCUSSION

1. How would you go about maintaining a specific ethnic tradition? Give specific suggestions.
2. Carl Wittke called his history of immigrants *We Who Built America.* How have the various immigrant groups enriched our state?
3. What problems do immigrants face today? What are some possible solutions?
4. What are the advantages to immigrants of adopting the American life style? What are the advantages of keeping their own traditions?

PROJECTS AND REPORTS

1. Make a chart to show the ethnic breakdown of students in your school.
2. Prepare and demonstrate for the class a bit of ethnic culture.
3. Have an ethnic day in class, showing costumes, food, music, and other cultural customs.
4. Trace the ethnic origin of your favorite holiday traditions.
5. Write a report on any religious group that helped build Ohio. Identify their cultural contributions.
6. Write a report on the Amish and the Mennonites, comparing their cultures.
7. Write a report on a utopian community in Ohio. Share your findings with the class in an oral report.

The State Capitol building at Columbus. The stone for this beautiful building was quarried by stone masons who had immigrated to Ohio from Italy.

CHAPTER 15

OUR STATE AND LOCAL GOVERNMENT

MAIN POINTS

1. The responsibilities of government are carried out at different levels and are divided among three branches: legislative, executive, and judicial.
2. The Ohio State Constitution gives the legislative branch the most power in state government.
3. Special interest groups play a role in the legislative process.
4. The state executive branch is responsible to enforce and to administer the laws of state government.
5. The state judicial branch is made up of three levels of courts.
6. Ohio's local governments provide many services for the people.
7. As a responsible citizen, you may help shape and influence government.

Every society in the world has developed some form of government. Why? When people live together they need a way to make decisions that affect the whole group. They also need a way to settle disputes that may arise.

As societies get more complex because of more and more people living together, the government grows more complex. More laws must be made to handle the changing relationships among members of society.

> Can you think of any new laws that likely did not exist 10 years ago? 50 years ago? 100 years ago? For each one you list, what reasons do you think led to the changes in law?

The type of government in the United States is called a representative democracy. The majority rules by means of elected representatives. Early Indian tribes had this type of government. A chief was the head of the tribe, and he was assisted by an elected council. Together they would decide such issues as when to move to new hunting grounds and whether or not to engage in war with their neighbors.

Another role of government is to provide services that individual people cannot take care of themselves. For instance, local governments often supply fresh water through a system of pipes. This service is necessary for people who live in cities, because they cannot dig wells to get their own water. (Why not?) Another local service is fire protection. It would be very unsafe if each person who experienced a fire tried to put it out with a garden hose, and it would be expensive to pay the thousands of dollars it costs the fire department to put it out. By sharing the cost of such services through taxes, everyone can use the services when needed.

ORGANIZATION OF OHIO STATE GOVERNMENT

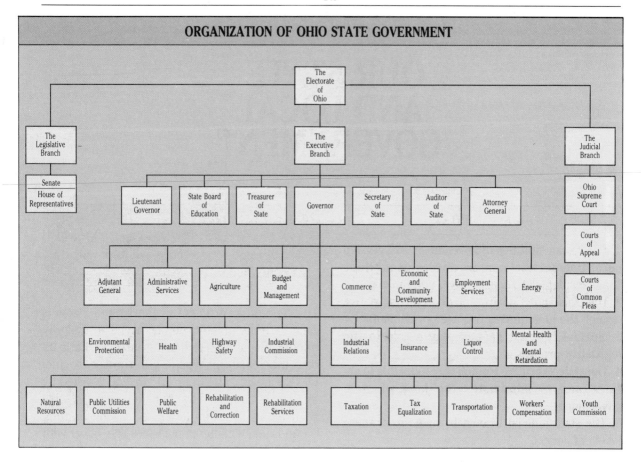

1. The responsibilities of government are carried out at different levels and are divided among three branches: legislative, executive, and judicial.

Levels of government. We live under the rules of several governments: federal; state; county; city, township, or village; school; family. Each one operates on a different level. While a family government may make rules for everyone who lives in the house, it cannot make rules for the neighborhood. A state government cannot make rules for the whole nation. Neither can the federal government make rules that control the home life of a family.

Each level of government handles different services. Make a list of some offered by the federal government, the state government, and the county government.

We might compare governments to the human body. All of the levels mentioned above make up a system in America. Just as your heart is more important to your life than a hand is, some governments are more important than others. The national government is very important because it does things others cannot do. The national government can maintain an army and a navy for national defense. However, township governments have lit-

The Ohio House of Representatives meeting in the house chamber. How many members sit in the house of representatives? How many sit in the senate?

tle power to make rules and usually provide few services.

State governments are very important. They can respond to the particular needs and problems of their people. The state also acts to carry out many programs and services which the federal government has established. The welfare assistance program is in this category. The money comes from the federal government, but the state does the work and keeps the records.

Branches of government. The tasks of government are divided among three branches, or divisions. The *legislative branch* makes the laws. The *executive branch* enforces, or carries out, the laws. The *judicial branch* interprets the laws, or decides how they affect people in certain cases.

One advantage of this system is that it creates a *balance of power.* No one branch of government can act on its own to take over all the authority of government. The branches must work together to get the job done. As we discover how state government works in Ohio, we will be able to compare it with other levels. By getting this broad view of government, we can learn how to take part as responsible citizens in our state and communities.

2. The Ohio State Constitution gives the legislative branch the most power in state government.

The basic law for any state is its constitution. You might think of this document as a blueprint for building a government. The Ohio Constitution sets forth how the state government is to be organized. It also guarantees certain freedoms in a bill of rights. It provides for counties, townships, and *municipalities.* It calls for taxes and public schools, and it puts limits on the state debt (the amount of money the state may borrow and owe).

If the people want to change their constitution, they may vote for certain amendments. The amended 1851 state constitution is the basic law at this time.

The job of the legislature. Ohio's founding fathers gave the legislature great power to control the state monies. Although the governor develops a state budget to distribute the money, the assembly must approve the plan before money can be spent. This "power of the purse" is the most important power the legislature has.

The other job of the legislature is to make the laws.

Representatives and senators are elected from geographic districts within the state. Citizens in each district vote for one representative to serve a two-year term and one senator to serve a four-year term. There are 99 house districts and 33 senate districts in the state. Senate districts are made by combining house districts. Look at the map to find which district you live in.

Article II of the state constitution describes the qualification for legislators: they must live in the districts from which they are elected for one year prior to the election. Terms in office for these and other state officials begin in January following the election.

Compared to other states, Ohio's legislators are paid quite well. Senators and representatives each recieve $30,152 a year. The senate majority leader and the speaker of the house each get $47,000. The senate minority leader gets $42,883, while the house minority leader receives $42,883. In addition, members of the house receive travel expense money enough to make one round trip a week from their homes to Columbus.

Organization in the legislature is determined by political parties. Each house is organized to get the work done. The leader of the house of representatives is called the speaker. The leader of the senate is called the president. Both leaders are chosen by the political party which has the majority of members in each house.

These leaders have much influence in deciding which bills will be chosen for debate and a vote.

They also appoint members to serve on committees which study the bills. In this way, the majority party has great strength.

The minority party also elects a leader in each house, whose job it is to help the party push through legislation it favors.

Committees are set up in each house to study various issues. Some are *standing committees* (permanent and ready to work). They deal with specific types of problems. In a recent session of the legislature, the house had 15 standing committees and the senate had 11. Those in the house were agriculture, commerce and labor, education, environment and natural resources, finance-appropriation, health and welfare, insurance, utilities and financial institutions, interstate cooperation, judiciary, local government and urban affairs, reference, rules, state government, transporation, ways and means.

The senate committees were agriculture, conservation and environment, applied technology and local services, commerce and labor, education and health, finance, financial institutions, insurance and elections, judiciary, rules, ways and means.

A bill in the house of representatives, for instance, that deals with public education would go to the standing committee on education for discussion and research. The committee would present its findings to the general body and try to get members to vote on the bill according to the committee's opinion.

Party membership plays a big role in deciding the make-up of the committees. Each senate committee has eight or nine members. House committees have 15 to 20 members. The majority party has more of its members on each committee. Therefore, if all members of the majority party on a committee agree on a bill, they can recommend it be passed.

While a bill is being studied, citizens who are either for or against it can appear before the committee and state their opinions. That is, they *testify* on the bill. After the committee work is done, it

OHIO HOUSE DISTRICTS

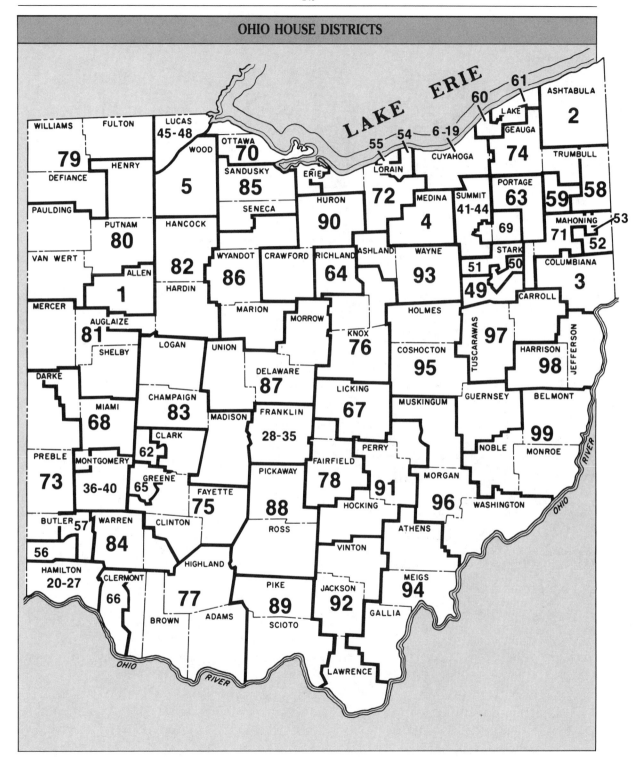

OHIO SENATE DISTRICTS

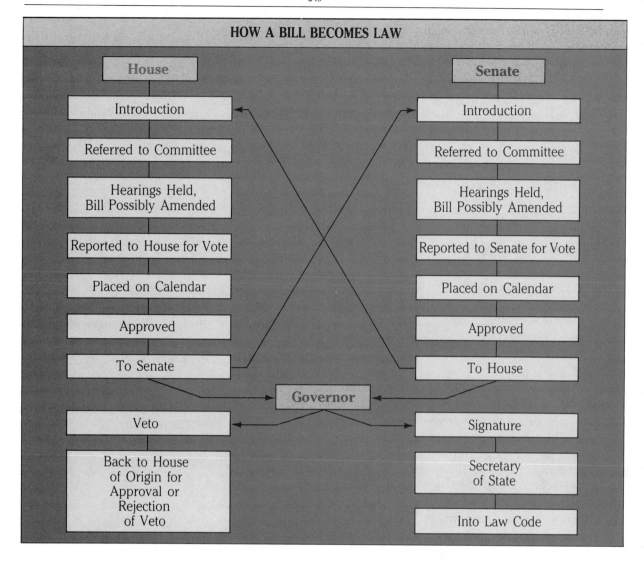

HOW A BILL BECOMES LAW

House	Senate
Introduction	Introduction
Referred to Committee	Referred to Committee
Hearings Held, Bill Possibly Amended	Hearings Held, Bill Possibly Amended
Reported to House for Vote	Reported to Senate for Vote
Placed on Calendar	Placed on Calendar
Approved	Approved
To Senate	To House
Governor	
Veto	Signature
Back to House of Origin for Approval or Rejection of Veto	Secretary of State
	Into Law Code

can either recommend the bill to the main body for a "yes" vote or kill the bill. A bill which is killed stays in committee. It is not likely that such a bill will ever be presented for a vote. Most bills are killed. In this way, much of the work of the legislature is actually done by the committees.

How a bill becomes law. A bill may be introduced by members of either house. The clerk of the house reads aloud the number, title, and sponsor of the bill. The presiding officer of the house then assigns the bill to a committee, where it is studied. When the bill comes out of committee, it goes to the powerful Rules Committee which decides if the bill will be placed on the legislative calendar. (A bill may be delayed for a long time if the Rules Committee does not put it on the calendar.) When the bill comes up on the calendar, it is read before the house. Amendments may be added to it at that time, and then the bill is voted upon.

The Ohio House of Representatives members vote by an electric voting board. Members press a "yes" or a "no" button to record their votes. The senate votes by a voice roll call. A majority of legislators must approve a bill if it is to pass. While 17 votes is a majority in the senate, 50 votes are needed in the house. For special emergency legislation, two-thirds approval of each house is needed. (An example of this would be to approve funds to help clean up a disaster caused by harsh weather.) Constitutional amendments must be approved by a three-fifths majority in each house.

An approved bill is sent to the other house and follows the same procedure. If both houses pass it with exactly the same wording, it is sent to the governor for approval or veto. (In the case that a bill is passed in each house with different wording, a Conference Committee is assigned the task to decide on a final version. Members from each house serve on this committee. Then the bill is sent back to the main bodies for another vote.)

If the governor signs the bill, it becomes law in 90 days. (Emergency legislation takes effect immediately.) If the governor vetoes the bill, it is sent back to the legislature, where a three-fifths majority in both houses may override the veto.

Two service groups help legislators do research. The Legislative Service Commission was created in 1953 to do research and write up bills. This group makes studies of issues as requested by the legislators. It has a full-time director who oversees the work of a paid research staff. Staff reports are given to the state legislators and are available to the public, as well.

Another service to lawmakers is provided by the Legislative Reference Bureau, established in 1910. The governor and the clerks of the house and the senate are the members of this bureau. It has a paid staff to do research for legislators who are preparing bills. The bureau also has a library where all *resolutions* (bills) since 1800 and acts passed since 1913 are kept.

3. Special interest groups play a role in the legislative process.

While many bills pass through the system without a contest, others attract special interest from groups who are either for or against them. For instance, a bill may affect a specific industry or citizens who live in a certain area, or it may affect school teachers more than other people. This causes members of the interested groups to take note of the proposed law and to try to get legislators to vote their way.

When the groups are organized to make their wishes known, they are called special interest groups. Each group tries to convince the legislators to pass laws which will benefit its members by providing information on the issues. The group may also promise to work to get the representative re-elected. The group often gives money to the election campaigns of candidates it likes, and sometimes threatens to vote against those who do not support its interests.

Learn more about special interest groups in your area from current news sources. Find an example of a special interest group and describe the bill in which they have a special interest at this time.

Popular legislation, or initiative, is a tool often used by special interest groups to promote laws that favor their members. The initiative is outlined in Article II, Section 1a of the state constitution. Voters may *draft* (write) a bill and present it to the General Assembly. The bill must be backed by a petition signed by 3% of the state's voters from the last election.

If the assembly fails to pass the initiative, it may be put on the ballot for a vote by the public in the next general election. However, an additional 3% of the voters must sign a petition to demand the vote. If the voters pass it, the governor may not exercise a veto in the matter.

The governor meets with many people in an effort to solve problems and to cooperate with special interest groups.

Special interest groups may bypass the legislature in the initiative process and take the proposal directly to the voters. To do this, a petition signed by 10% of the eligible voters in the state must be presented to the secretary of state. The petition must clearly explain exactly what the proposed law will do. If the voters pass it by a majority plus one, it becomes an amendment to the constitution.

Popular veto, or referendum, is another measure used by special interest groups. Referendum is described in Article II, Section 1a. It requires that 6% of the voters from the last election sign a petition and present it to the secretary of state within 90 days from the date the legislature has *adjourned* (quit for the year). Then the bill (which has already been voted on by the legislature) goes to the public for a vote. The decision of the public is the final word in the matter. Emergency laws are not subject to referendum.

The General Assembly may also call for the referendum process. They can present a bill to the public at the next general election rather than voting on it themselves.

These are ways the public can have a direct effect on lawmaking. Special interest groups take a role in getting these processes started.

4. The state executive branch is responsible to enforce and to administer the laws of state government.

The executive branch consists of a number of elected officials, as outlined in the state constitution. The term in office for each position is four years. The governor is the head of this branch and is limited to two *consecutive* (one right after the other) terms.

The governor is considered the most important person in state government due to powers of the office. The governor earns $65,000 a year for performing the following duties:

1. Propose laws.

Because many activities of government are under the control of this office, the governor is in a good position to know about problems which face the state. Each year in a State of the State speech

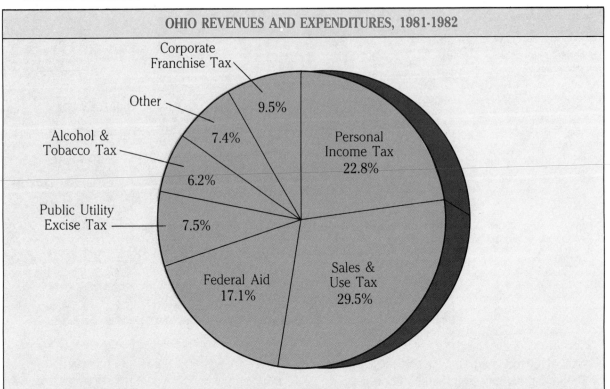

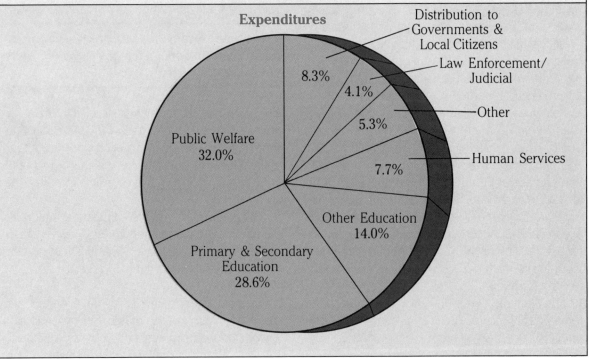

The Ohio National Guard is Ohio's state militia. Here guardsmen are shown on a training exercise.

to the General Assembly, the governor may talk about these problems and suggest ways to solve them. Many of the proposals are later sent to the legislature as bills.

One more job of the governor is to prepare, each year, a budget which suggests how many state tax dollars to spend for each government program.

2. Chief administrator.

It is the job of the governor to be sure that all laws passed by the legislature are carried out. Since this is a big job, there are departments which act under the governor's direction. The highway patrol is one of these. Other departments also help to carry out the laws of the state and to spend the annual budget. Some of the departments build and maintain highways, operate state parks, regulate the sale of insurance, and provide help for the physically handicapped or mentally ill. Others collect state taxes.

The governor appoints department heads to take care of day-to-day management. (These people must be approved by the senate.) Each department head is directly accountable to the governor. In this way,

the governor is able to keep track of and be responsible for the huge state government.

As the commander of the state militia and naval forces, the governor may call out the National Guard to preserve law and order in the event of an emergency in the state.

3. Party leader.

In addition to the above powers, the governor is usually a key person in his or her political party. The governor's support of certain issues may influence people either to support or to oppose the governor's political party during elections.

Legislators often find it an advantage to be on the same side of the issues as the governor. To show appreciation for this support, the governor may recommend that projects be built or money be spent in the home district of a legislator. Or the governor may appoint some of the legislator's friends to office. In this way, the legislator also gains favor in his or her political party.

4. Ceremonial leader.

One role which takes up much of the governor's time is that of representing the state government

Governor Rhodes acts as Ohio's chief host to foreign representatives at the Ohio State Fair. Receiving visitors to the state is an important part of the governor's job.

at ceremonies of all sorts. He or she attends many public events and welcomes important visitors to the state. The governor may also *endorse* (lend his or her name by means of advertisement) the fund drives of various volunteer groups, thereby supporting their causes.

5. Special powers.

Among the special powers that the governor has is the right to pardon (excuse), *reprieve* (postpone), or *commute* (lessen) the sentence of a convicted criminal. Advice to carry out such acts must come from the Department of Rehabilitation and Corrections.

With all these duties, it is obvious that the governor needs help. There are other officials in the executive branch who help take care of certain jobs.

The **lieutenant governor's** role is to "perform such duties in the executive department as are assigned to him by the governor and as prescribed by law." For instance, in 1983, Governor Richard F. Celeste chose Lieutenant Governor Myrl Shoemaker to be the director of the Department of Natural Resources.

The only other role of the lieutenant governor, whose salary is $35,000 a year, is to assume the duties of the governor should the governor die in office or otherwise be unable to perform his or her duties.

The **secretary of state** is the chief elections officer. As such, he or she appoints members of the Board of Elections in each county. This board sees that elections are properly carried out. The secretary of state, salaried at $50,000 a year, keeps election records for state offices and approves election forms. He or she must also approve official newspaper advertisements that are placed to inform the public about proposed constitutional amendments.

State agencies which adopt rules to carry out state laws must report to the secretary of state. Any organization, whether a business or a *nonprofit* group, must file papers in the secretary's office. All laws passed by the legislature must be on file there, as well.

The **state treasurer** is responsible to collect all the state *revenue* (income) from taxes, fees, and licenses. This office also keeps records of the state's money and pays the bills. The treasurer is the chairperson of the Board of Deposit, which decides how to invest the state's money. The state treasurer earns $50,000 a year.

The **state auditor** might be viewed as the chief bookkeeper. This office keeps a record of all money deposited in the state treasury. Bills may not be paid by the treasurer until the auditor approves payment.

Another function of this office is to *audit* (examine) the accounts of more than 6,000 governmental units in the state. In this way, the auditor can be sure the money is being spent legally. The auditor receives $50,000 a year.

The **attorney general** may be thought of as the chief lawyer for the state. The attorney general's office advises other state or local agencies on questions of state law. It also assists such agencies in the case of a lawsuit.

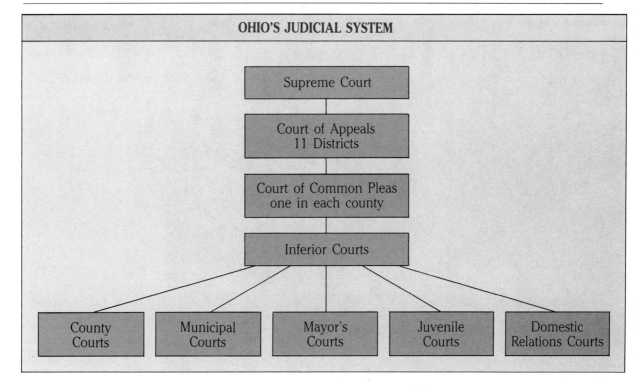

OHIO'S JUDICIAL SYSTEM

Supreme Court

Court of Appeals
11 Districts

Court of Common Pleas
one in each county

Inferior Courts

County Courts — Municipal Courts — Mayor's Courts — Juvenile Courts — Domestic Relations Courts

The attorney general's office gets involved in tax issues and buying land for highways. It reviews business practices to see that there is no price fixing or unfair business dealings. It investigates consumer complaints about business. The attorney general has a staff of over 125 lawyers. The annual salary of the attorney general is $50,000.

The governor's cabinet is made up of many aides who head various departments under the governor. Cabinet members are appointed by the governor, and some of them must be approved by the senate.

At this time there are 27 departments to aid the governor. Some of them are: economic and community development, education, energy, highway safety, liquor control, mental health and retardation, Public Utilities Commission, taxation, transportation, and Youth Commission.

These and many other departments help the governor keep aware of and solve problems with various parts of our society. Each department head must report directly to the governor. In this way, the governor maintains control over the operations of government.

5. The state judicial branch is made up of three levels of courts.

The judicial branch has three main functions: to settle disputes between individuals, to interpret the law if questions are raised, and to determine whether or not a person has broken a law.

The types of cases which courts handle are of two types: civil and criminal. A civil case is one which involves debts or contracts or property rights. An example of this type might be that after a contractor finished building a house for Mr. Smith, the garage collapsed. Mr. Smith has the right to sue the contractor to try to get back some or all of the money for the garage. The court must decide whether the garage actually collapsed and if it was the fault of the builder.

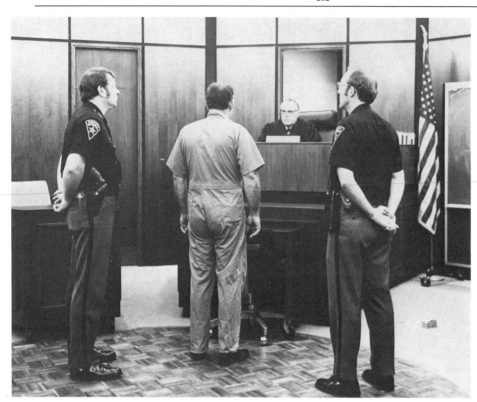

A judge of the court of common pleas calls a prisoner before the court to hear the charges against him.

An example of a criminal case would be a felony, such as an armed robbery, or a misdemeanor (not punishable by a prison term), such as disturbing the peace. The court would have to determine whether the person actually committed the crime and, if so, what the punishment would be.

Juries play an important role in the court system. They are made up of citizens (jurors) called at random to serve for a short time.

One type of jury is the grand jury. Its job is to examine the evidence provided by the *prosecution* (the one making the charge). Then it must decide whether there is enough evidence to formally *indict* (accuse) someone of a crime. If seven of the nine grand jury members feel there is enough evidence, then the person is put on trial. If not, the person goes free and may not be tried. The grand jury process is a good protection, for it prevents police from taking a person to trial without evidence that he or she committed the crime.

The petit jury has the job of deciding the guilt or innocence of the accused. This jury is made up of 12 citizens who hear all the evidence in the trial. They then meet privately to decide whether the person is guilty or innocent. In a criminal case (such as a robbery), all 12 jurors must agree that the person is guilty. If all do not agree, they can recommend either that a new trial be held or that the person be *acquitted* (go free). In a civil case (such as the homeowner vs. the contractor), there are only eight jurors and only six must agree on the decision.

The courts. Let us now look at the types of courts in the state and the issues with which they deal. The state constitution creates a supreme court, courts of appeals, and courts of common pleas. The legislature is allowed to create other courts as

The seven Ohio Supreme Court justices, with Chief Justice Celebrezze in the center. How does the number of justices on the Ohio court compare with the number on the U.S. Supreme Court?

needed. There are lower courts which are called inferior courts because they have limited jurisdiction (power to hear cases). They are county courts, municipal courts, mayors courts, juvenile courts, domestic relations courts, and police courts.

These lower courts deal with civil cases involving amounts of money less than $10,000 or criminal misdemeanors. The juvenile courts involve people under 18 years of age. Domestic relations courts handle divorces.

The court of common pleas is the general trial court in the state. Each of the 88 counties has a court of common pleas with at least one judge who lives in the county. Larger counties have several judges. A judge's term of office is six years, and the yearly salary is $48,500.

It is in the common pleas court that serious crimes and civil cases involving sums of money over $10,000 are tried. These courts have *original jurisdiction* (the case begins in that court) in some civil cases. They handle cases where the sum of money or the crime involved is beyond the limits of inferior courts. They also hear *appeals* (cases referred to higher courts) from the inferior courts in their own counties.

The two examples given—the homeowner vs. contractor and the armed robbery charge—would both be tried in a court of common pleas.

Three of the inferior courts are divisions of the court of common pleas. Probate courts have power to settle wills, administer *estates* (property of deceased people), issue marriage licenses, regulate child adoptions, and determine mental incompetence. Domestic relations courts hear cases involving divorce matters. They also hear juvenile cases unless the county has a juvenile court.

The court of appeals was created to relieve the case load of the supreme court. The court of appeals usually does not hear trials and has original jurisdiction in only a few situations. In the case of an appeal from a common pleas court, the court of appeals determines if the lower courts followed proper procedure and interpreted the law correctly.

The state is split into 11 appellate districts, with a court of appeals for each. Three judges, elected for six-year terms, make up each court. The judges, who make $61,000 a year, must have been attorneys for six years prior to their election. There is no jury in the court of appeals; the three judges decide the appeal. They must hold court at least once a year in each county in their district.

The supreme court is the highest court in the state. It is made up of six justices and a chief justice, each elected for six-year terms. Each justice gets $70,500 a year, while the chief justice earns $75,000. The supreme court must meet at least once a year.

The county courthouse is the center of county government activities. This is the Lorain County courthouse in Elyria.

This court has original jurisdiction in very few matters. It is mainly an appeals court which hears cases involving interpretation of the state and U.S. constitutions.

The supreme court acts as a check on the governor and the legislature. The court reviews actions of the executive agencies and it checks to see that laws passed by the General Assembly are constitutional. By interpreting the laws and ruling that some are unconstitutional, the court may have strong influence in state policy.

Since 1968, the supreme court has had authority over all the courts in the state.

6. Ohio's local governments provide many services for the people.

The local governments include the county, township, and various municipal (city or town) governments.

County government. Ohio is divided into 88 counties, each with a county seat where the offices of the county government are located. Most of these offices are in a building called the county courthouse. The voters in each county elect three commissioners, an auditor, a treasurer, a sheriff, and other officers to carry out the duties of county government. Except for the judges, the term of each office is four years.

County government plays a role as the agent to carry out policies of state law. The county also serves as the unit to provide some federal programs. Much of our state judicial system is based in the county. This means the county is involved in law enforcement and prosecuting criminals. The county also collects taxes, keeps records, and maintains the county roads.

Commissioners make up the executive and the legislative branches of county government, though their power is very limited. They form what is called the Board of Commissioners.

The board controls all county business which is not the legal responsibility of other elected county officers. The commissioners' key role is concerned with finance. They propose and approve the county budget. They may arrange to construct county buildings, oversee the highways, and adopt rules which allow the county to take part in the many federal programs available. They may also set up rules to protect the health of the people, operate airports and transit systems, and even run a zoo.

Should a new county jail be built for a million dollars? Should a bridge be closed which is thought to be unsafe? Should a new rule about sewers in the county be adopted? These types of issues may directly affect county residents. That is why voters are so interested in county government.

The county auditor, as the financial officer, must keep current records of all monies that belong to the county. As in state government, money paid out by the county treasurer must be approved by the auditor.

At the local level, property tax is a main source of revenue. The amount of taxes paid is determined by the *appraised* value of property. It is the auditor's job to appraise real estate for tax purposes and to keep a record of all real estate in the county.

The county treasurer has three main duties: to collect money due the county through taxes, fines, and licenses; to keep an accurate record of that money; to pay the county's bills and distribute money to other agencies as directed by the auditor.

The county recorder keeps records of mortgages, deeds, and other documents about the sale or transfer of land ownership. Lawyers and real estate agents use these records to be sure that properties offered for sale are free from claims by other people.

The clerk of the common pleas court keeps the records of all trials. He or she also records licenses, certifies (vouches for truthfulness of) motor vehicle titles, and reports on all fines collected by the court.

Counties provide many services which directly affect their citizens. They may build roads, sewers, or public buildings, such as this Justice Complex in Franklin County, among other things.

The sheriff is the chief law enforcement agent for the county. This is the Franklin County Sheriff's Department.

The **prosecuting attorney** is the legal advisor to all government offices within the county. He or she also investigates crimes within the county and follows them through the court system. Because there is often a lot of publicity that comes with the trials, the job of prosecuting attorney is attractive to lawyers who later hope to be elected to a higher public office.

The **county sheriff** is the chief law enforcement officer. The sheriff may hire a number of deputies to help in this work.

The **county engineer** has the job of supervising all building, maintenance, and repair work on county highways and bridges. He or she must be a registered engineer and surveyor.

The **coroner** must be a doctor licensed for two years in Ohio. He or she investigates to determine the cause of death of anyone who died in a violent manner—either by accident or murder.

Should all county officers be elected? A number of government experts suggest that county officers should be appointed rather than elected. Under this plan, the county legislators would hire a manager to run the county. The manager would then hire people to fill the various positions. Other experts feel strongly that most county officials should be elected, as they are now.

What do you feel are the advantages and the disadvantages of each plan? Join a discussion group to talk about this question.

Townships originally had a role in governing areas of the state, but now they have a very limited role. They basically maintain township roads. In some urban areas, however, townships provide services which would usually be provided by the town or city government.

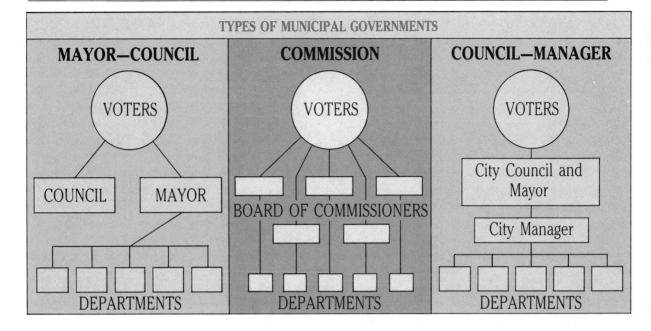

TYPES OF MUNICIPAL GOVERNMENTS

MAYOR—COUNCIL

VOTERS

COUNCIL   MAYOR

DEPARTMENTS

COMMISSION

VOTERS

BOARD OF COMMISSIONERS

DEPARTMENTS

COUNCIL—MANAGER

VOTERS

City Council and Mayor

City Manager

DEPARTMENTS

Municipal corporations are formed by the local citizens to have legal power which the county and the township do not have. This means the municipal government may provide services which the other levels of government do not cover.

A municipality is a form of local government called a village if there are fewer than 5,000 people, or a city if there are more than 5,000.

Suppose you lived in a small community which is not part of a municipality. Any services would be provided by the county and township. Most likely, everyone's water supply comes from wells, the streets probably would not be paved, there would be little police protection, and fire protection likely would not exist.

By forming a municipal corporation, the state law allows the citizens to have their own government. They can then tax themselves to pay for the services they want. The range of services is almost limitless if the citizens are willing to pay higher taxes. What services are provided by your municipality, or one near you?

A village is organized when 30 people in an area sign a petition to *incorporate*. The township then holds a vote, and if a majority of the residents approve it, the village is established.

The village then elects its officers, beginning with a six-member council. The council members serve four years. The council is the legislative body of the village. It adopts *ordinances* (local laws) to govern the village.

A mayor is also elected to serve four years. She or he may appoint a village marshall, someone to oversee street maintenance, and other positions the council may create.

The mayor-council form of city government is the one used by most cities. Under this system, the city has a council (legislative branch), and a mayor (executive branch), an elected president of the council, an auditor, a treasurer, and a *solicitor* (city attorney). The mayor serves for either two or four years. The number of people on the council varies from 5 to 33.

Columbus has a mayor-council form of government.
This is a meeting of the Columbus city council.

The city council meets at least once a month. In larger cities it meets once a week or more. The council adopts policies for the city, but the mayor has veto power, which the council may override. The mayor divides the city duties among the various appointed department heads.

The council-manager form of city government is used by a few cities in the state. Dayton was the first city in the nation to use this form. An elected city council hires a qualified person to manage the business of the city. This person is called a city manager, and he or she serves at the pleasure of the city council. This means the manager may be fired at any time. The idea behind this form of government is that the council makes city policy, and the trained manager carries it out.

Although there is a mayor under this system, the office carries little responsibility. The mayor does appoint people to fill all other positions in the city government.

OHIO'S VOTING REQUIREMENTS
You may vote in Ohio if:
1. You are a citizen of the United States.
2. You are at least 18 years old on the day of the election at which you seek to vote.
3. You have been a resident of Ohio for at least 30 days before the election.
4. You have been registered to vote at least 30 days before the election.

The commission plan of city government is not in wide use today. Few cities in the state have this form. The elected commissioners serve much the same as a city council. In addition, each commissioner manages some department of city government. One commissioner is appointed to be mayor, but has no more authority than the others. In this plan, the legislative and executive jobs of government are under one body, so it lacks the balance that most other forms have. This is one reason it is not a popular form.

7. As a responsible citizen, you may help shape and influence government.

Local governments—such as city, town, and county—are the closest governments to the people. They can be more responsive to the needs and wishes of the citizens. For this reason, participating in local elections and council meetings is a good way to get involved in government. After all, rules adopted by city and town officials can have a direct impact on how you live.

Local matters might involve raising taxes to build a new swimming pool or buying buses for a city transportation system. They might concern the placement of traffic lights or street lamps. Matters like these create conflict between citizens. That is why each person should be active in government and express opinions in matters being considered. The citizens' votes are the final word in most matters.

Your role is to become a responsible citizen. There are many ways you can prepare to do your part. As a teenager, you might choose to help in someone's campaign for office by donating your services in passing out fliers or folding literature. You might volunteer some time in a city cleanup project or circulate a petition for an issue you favor.

You could help organize a neighborhood watch program to prevent crime.

The most important way to prepare for citizenship responsibilities is to be informed about the issues. This comes from reading the newspaper and talking with people about their viewpoints. By getting a broad exposure to ideas and issues, you will develop a strong background to help you make decisions.

> Try this case study to see if you are a responsible citizen: A group of business people in your city are trying to change a piece of property in the center of your neighborhood from residential to commercial zoning. This means they would like to set up some businesses. What is your role as a citizen in the community? What are your options?

WORDS FOR STUDY

legislative branch
executive branch
judicial branch
balance of power
municipality
standing committee
testify
resolution
draft
adjourn
consecutive
endorse
reprieve
commute
nonprofit
revenue
audit
prosecution
indict
acquit
original jurisdiction
appeal
estate
appraise
incorporate
ordinance
solicitor

QUESTIONS FOR REVIEW

1. Why do we need government?

2. What type of government do we have in this country and in our state?

3. What are the three branches of government, and what is the job of each?

4. Which groups make up the legislative branch of our state government?

5. What is the title of the majority party leader in the senate? in the house of representatives?

6. What steps are required for a bill to become law?

7. What two service groups help legislators gather information on bills?

8. What part do special interest groups play in the legislative process?

9. Who heads the executive branch in state government?

10. What are the five duties of the governor?

11. What system makes up the judicial branch of government?

12. What are the three types of courts in the state court system? What are the various types of inferior courts?

13. What are the two types of cases a court may handle?

14. Name eight jobs of county government.

15. What is the number of people that determines whether a municipal corporation is a village or a city?

16. Name the three types of city government that are used in Ohio.

17. Why should you become involved in your local government now?

GOING FURTHER

1. What powers does state government have that no other levels have?

2. What roles do political parties play in state government? in local government?

3. Why are the positions of speaker of the house and president of the senate considered powerful?

4. In what way do the three separate branches of government create a balance of power? Is any one branch more powerful than the others?

5. How does a grand jury differ from a petit jury?

6. In a lawsuit between a citizen and a business that involves $1,500, which court would have original jurisdiction?

7. What is the relationship between county and state government?

8. Why is it an advantage to form a municipal corporation?

FOR THOUGHT AND DISCUSSION

1. How do you feel about the part government plays in your life? Is there too much government control? Not enough? Explain your answer and support with specific examples.

2. Which level of government do you feel is the most important? Why?

3. In the November 1983 election, a referendum gave Ohioans a chance to repeal a state income tax increase that had been passed by the legislature. (The referendum failed.) Do you think voters should have this power? Explain.

4. What are the advantages and the disadvantages of the jury system?

5. What is the difference between initiative and referendum?

PROJECTS AND REPORTS

1. Make a chart of your municipal government showing its organization. Fill in the names of people who serve in each position.

2. Attend a city council meeting or a Board of Commissioners meeting and take notes on all the matters discussed. Write a page describing your impressions of government in action.

3. Write a letter to your state representative or senator to express your view on a particular matter or to compliment his or her work.

4. Interview a law enforcement officer and give an oral report on the duties of this job.

5. Learn the basic rules of parliamentary procedure. Then organize and participate in a mock legislative session.

The Cincinnati skyline with Riverfront Stadium in the foreground. New futuristic development is taking place in Ohio's cities, making them more beautiful and livable.

CHAPTER 16

LOOKING TO THE FUTURE

MAIN POINTS

1. Changes in the future will create new needs and problems for Ohio and its communities.

2. Ohio has many strengths to help solve the problems of the future.

3. You have an important role in the future of the state and your community.

Throughout the state's history, one common theme has been active in all time periods—change. As an old saying goes, "The only thing that is constant is change." People have had to alter ways of meeting their needs. What changes did the prehistoric Indians face? What major changes came to our state as it joined the new nation? What kinds of changes were caused by wars and by times of peace?

1. Changes in the future will create new needs and problems for Ohio and its communities.

Move to suburbia. A major population shift has been taking place in the state for the past 20 years. Many people are moving to the *suburbs,* a trend that had its start back in the 1920s. This change puts a bigger burden on local governments to provide services such as sewer, clean water, and police and fire protection.

In recent years many Ohioans have moved from farms and inner cities to suburbs and small towns. For example, Cleveland's population fell 25% in the 1970s. Youngstown was down 19%, Dayton 17%, Cincinnati 15%, and Akron 14% in the same decade. Columbus, with its varied economy and low unemployment rate, was the only city in the whole American Midwest to gain population in its inner city. Already it is as big as Cleveland and will likely be the state's largest city by the mid-1980s.

A lot of things attract people to the suburbs. Single family homes, new shopping centers, good schools, and jobs are some of the draws. Most who move from the city feel they are escaping the high crime rate and the decay of older buildings.

Those who can afford to make a greater change have moved beyond the city limits to small towns. A good highway system and fast *commuter* bus lines make it possible to live in the country or a small town and work in an *urban* area. Medina County, below Cleveland and west of Akron, is a good example of this newer life style. Population in this county jumped by 27% between 1970 and 1980, while the state as a whole gained just over 1%. Another cause of population shifts is *outmigration.* This means that more people move out than move in. This is a real problem for the southeastern region of Ohio called Appalachia. The main industry there is coal, and it does not provide enough jobs for all who need work. So people leave in search of a better life.

Another reason for outmigration is the desire to move to the sunbelt states of the South and Southwest. There the climate is warm year round

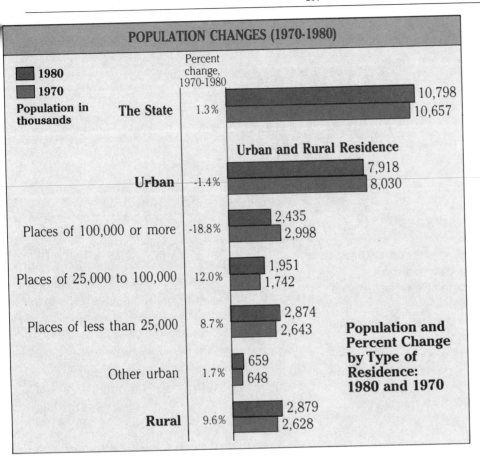

POPULATION CHANGES (1970-1980)

	Percent change, 1970-1980	1980 / 1970 (Population in thousands)
■ 1980 ■ 1970 Population in thousands		
The State	1.3%	10,798 / 10,657
Urban and Rural Residence		
Urban	-1.4%	7,918 / 8,030
Places of 100,000 or more	-18.8%	2,435 / 2,998
Places of 25,000 to 100,000	12.0%	1,951 / 1,742
Places of less than 25,000	8.7%	2,874 / 2,643
Other urban	1.7%	659 / 648
Rural	9.6%	2,879 / 2,628

Population and Percent Change by Type of Residence: 1980 and 1970

and there are more new job opportunities. Young families and older people alike are attracted to this region.

This shift in population creates major problems for our state. Skilled workers in search of new jobs take their skills to other states. With fewer workers here, less tax money is collected for the state. Federal grant money is also cut back, since it is usually based on population.

The growing senior citizen population of Ohio has special needs that must be met. This change has been brought about mainly by improved health care which helps people live longer. The result is that by 1990, *senior citizens* (those age 65 and above) are expected to number 1,348,000. This is 35% higher than in 1970.

What will happen to the quality of life for this group of citizens? Recent studies show that the main problems which older people face involve income, transportation, housing, safety, and health. Most seniors have a *fixed income* (limited amount of money each month) which comes from government social security or some other retirement *pension* plan. When inflation goes up, the pension may not. This makes it hard for people on fixed incomes to meet the basic living expenses of food, shelter, and clothing.

Many older people cannot afford to own a car because costs are so high. This means they must use buses and taxis to get around. Finding transportation is even harder when people live in rural areas.

An aerial view of Bluffton and the surrounding countryside, with Interstate 75 and the Bluffton airport. Excellent transportation systems allow people to live in rural regions and work in urban areas.

High technology industry has replaced many early heavy industries, such as iron and steel plants. This is NASA's Lewis Research Center in Cleveland, with the Hopkins Airport in the background.

The Honda plant at Marysville.

Talk with some senior citizens in your neighborhood to get a better idea of their concerns for the future. How do you think their needs can be met?

Heavy industries out, high technology in. For over 100 years, Ohio was a center for industries based on large iron and steel plants. The main products were machines, tools, auto parts, and household appliances. The picture has changed. At least 20% of the state's factories are too old to compete with more modern plants in other states and foreign countries. Many companies have closed or moved out and have taken jobs with them.

For instance, the number of factory jobs in Akron alone fell 20% from 1970 to 1980. Not enough new jobs and businesses have moved in to take up the slack. Unemployment was especially bad in "one-industry towns" like Akron (rubber) and Youngstown (steel). The struggle for control of Findlay's Marathon Oil Company in 1981-82 shows how even a small city can depend on a single employer with 2,000 jobs. United States Steel won control over Mobil Oil, which wanted to move the Marathon headquarters out of Findlay. Local citizens lobbied hard and held street demonstrations to protect their jobs and to save the town's economy.

In the 1970s, central Ohio did gain some new businesses, like American Electric Power in Columbus and new Honda motorcycle and automobile plants at Marysville. But more are needed.

How do you feel the new high technology industries like electronics and computers will affect

Beaver Creek is a beautiful natural area. Many groups have formed to work for the protection of natural recreation and wildlife areas.

the economy of your own community in the next years?

Changes in education will be needed. How to finance the public schools is just one problem facing public education. Another issue is *desegregation*. Cleveland has struggled with the matter. In spite of court orders, busing of students, and the work of some new leaders, there is still a problem with racial prejudice. Progress has been made, but a final solution is not yet in sight.

What are some other problems in education today? Talk with other students, teachers, and parents to find out. How do you think the problems will be solved?

One more area where changes will come is in concern for the environment. The natural environment includes air, land, water, mineral resources, forests, wildlife, and scenic beauty. The early Indians who lived here had great respect for nature, taking from the land only what they needed. The white settlers who came later were not so careful. People came to know that they could harm the balance of nature. Now, in the 1980s, some real progress is being made in solving environmental problems, such as cleaning up air quality.

Another major issue is land use. Every year, approximately 100 square miles of good Ohio cropland are lost to other uses. What if a grove of 100-year-old trees were cut down for lumber to build homes and furniture? What would happen to the wildlife and the watershed? What might happen to the sound of wind and traffic in rural areas?

Other environmental issues deal with land

A problem of the future is how to balance the ugly scars of strip mining with the need for coal. In 1982, Ohio passed the nation's toughest requirements for reclaiming strip-mined land.

beautification. A serious problem has been caused by the strip mining of coal. Coal mine operators would strip the soil away until they reached the coal deposits. Some companies planted trees and grass once they finished mining an area, but usually nothing was done to cover up the ugly scars left on the countryside. The result was soil erosion by wind and rain. In 1982, Ohio passed the nation's toughest strip mining law to renew the land.

Acid rain is an issue which affects our state. It occurs mainly when sulfur dioxide and other chemicals mix with moisture in the air. The sulfur in the air comes from a variety of sources. It can come from volcanic eruptions, forest fires, burning coal, and auto *emissions*. Acid rain pollutes streams and may cause the breakdown of minerals which fertilize the soil. It can also slowly eat away at buildings. What might happen if nothing is done to prevent acid rainfall?

Ohio has a basic problem because its electric utilities use coal for 95% of their energy. American Electric Power says the cost to reduce the sulfur emissions to the legal limit will be quite high. It will boost the cost of electricity bills.

> What do you think about the acid rain issue? What are some solutions to the problem?

One more area of concern is wildlife protection. Some birds are now on the *endangered species* list.

The Davis-Besse nuclear plant near Port Clinton. What are the advantages and disadvantages of using nuclear power to create energy? Do you feel that other plants such as Davis-Besse should be constructed? Why or why not?

Owls and herons are two of these. Conservation work is being done at the bird *sanctuary* and research center at Crane Creek and Magee Marsh on Lake Erie's western shore.

> Discuss this question with classmates and your teacher: Is there a need to protect wildlife in your area? If so, which species? Support your opinion with evidence.

Energy demands. As the fifth largest user of energy in the nation, Ohio has a need to guard *energy sources*. We must buy extra fuel such as natural gas from other states. As prices rise and supplies dwindle, there is a need to find alternate energy sources. A lot of companies and private citizens are experimenting with solar energy and wind power. What do you think will be the energy source of the future?

Much of the job of meeting the needs of the future will fall on government. Now, the state's combined state and local taxes are among the lowest in the nation. For instance, in 1983 the state relied upon federal aid, a 5% sales tax, personal and corporate income taxes, and a state lottery to finance its basic operations. Even so, this did not yield enough money to pay for all of the services the people needed. Governor Richard F. Celeste won approval of a new $17 billion dollar state

Richard F. Celeste, of Cleveland, was elected governor in 1982.

budget, up 27% from the year before. Part of the plan raised the personal income tax by 90%.

> Do you think higher tax is a trend of the future? How do you see government's role in meeting the needs of people? Will private organizations help share this burden? Join a small discussion group to answer these questions.

2. Ohio has many strengths to help solve the problems of the future.

Transportation strengths. In facing the issues of the 1980s and beyond, Ohio has strengths to draw upon. Location is still of much value. With Lake Erie to the north and the Ohio River to the south, the state has ideal waterways for trade. In the future, the Great Lakes-St. Lawrence Seaway could be a stronger link to international markets.

Also, the nation's interstate highway system crisscrosses the state. Trucking is a very big business, and our state is at the center of a large trucking market.

Every county in the state now has its own airport. Air, ground, and water transportation systems are important for a good economic future.

Fresh water access. Ohio has access to one-fourth of the world's fresh water reserves. This is a strength in a world where pollution and population growth are working to limit the supply of water.

Agriculture is another strong point. Farming is still the state's largest economic activity although less than 3% of Ohio people are full-time farmers.

Human resources. The best strength our state has is its people. There is a highly skilled labor force to work in the state's many industries. Moreover, a blend of many cultures is another asset. It brings long experience and a rich heritage of varied leadership to our state.

Favored in all these ways and more, we may surely face the future with hope and confidence in our ability to meet the challenge of change.

Ohio has strong transportation links to national and international markets. The highways are excellent, with freeway systems criss-crossing the state. Here I-71 crosses Route 97 at Lexington.

3. You have an important role in the future of the state and your community.

In a few years, you will help make the decisions in your community. You will plan its government and help make changes.

History is a valuable tool in managing the future. You will be able to keep Ohio's heritage in mind and remember mistakes from the past. Likewise, you will recall the things that helped the state and its communities prosper and grow. There will be examples from the past of how similar problems were solved.

Your role is to start now to help build the communities and state that you want to inherit.

Learning to regulate the changes that will take place is an exciting prospect. By studying the history of the state and seeing how your community has changed over the years, you have already begun this process.

Ohio's best strength is its people. Ohio people—all of us—give our state hope and confidence to face the future.

WORDS FOR STUDY

suburbs
commuter
urban
outmigration
senior citizen
fixed income
pension
desegregation
emissions
endangered species
sanctuary
energy sources

QUESTIONS FOR REVIEW

1. What has been a common theme throughout the state's history?
2. Why is the population of communities and our state changing?
3. What special needs do senior citizens have?
4. How will the state's industries change in the near future?
5. What is a "one-industry town"? Name one.
6. How will the needs for education change?
7. What are the environmental concerns of the eighties?
8. What is acid rain?
9. Ohio is the _____ largest user of energy in the nation.
10. Name at least four strengths the state has to help solve the problems of the future.

GOING FURTHER

1. Why is change constant?
2. How does outmigration affect our state?
3. Why is there a need for new high technology industries?
4. Why and how will education become more important for the future?
5. Why are people concerned about the environment?

6. In what way is agriculture a strong point for solving future needs?

FOR THOUGHT AND DISCUSSION

1. What changes do you think you will see in your lifetime in economics? in politics? in health care? in technology?
2. How do you see the role of government in providing for the needs of senior citizens? How do you see the role of society in meeting their needs?
3. Do you agree with the authors that "the best strength our state has is its people"? Explain.

PROJECTS AND REPORTS

1. Plan a community of the future. It may be a type that does not exist now, such as interplanetary, underwater, underground, in orbit. Tell what daily life would be like. Plan the type of government that would provide for services and growth. Illustrate your ideas with charts, pictures, or models.

GLOSSARY

Many of the words in this glossary have more than one meaning. The definition given here applies to the word's use in the context of this textbook.

abolition, *v.* doing away with

abolitionist, *n.* against slavery

acquit, *v.* to free from a charge of wrongdoing

adjourn, *v.* to end or close a meeting

advocate, *v.* to speak in favor of

agent, *n.* a person who acts for another

agribusiness, *n.* producing and selling farm products

agronomy, *n.* the art and science of crop production; management of farm land

ally, *n.* a person or nation united with another in a common purpose

anarchist, *n.* one who rebels against authority, particularly government

anthropologist, *n.* one who studies human cultures, past and present

antitrust, *adj.* opposed to, or regulating business monopolies

apathy, *n.* lack of interest

appeal, *n.v.* to take action to have a legal case considered by a higher court

appraise, *v.* judge the value of, or set a value on (for instance, a house)

apprentice, *n.* a person who is learning a trade or art by actual experience under a skilled worker

arbitrate, *v.* to settle a dispute after hearing and considering arguments on both sides

archaeologist, *n.* a person who studies past human life as shown by artifacts and relics left by ancient people

arsenal, *n.* a place where military equipment is stored

artifacts, *n.* things made by human work

artisan, *n.* a person who works at a trade which requires skill with hands

audit, *v.* to examine financial accounts

balance of power, *n.* in government, a limiting of powers in each branch; a system where each branch checks the work of the others

banish, *v.* to force, by authority, a person to leave one's own country

bedrock, *n.* the solid rock underlying the surface soil

bill, *n.* a proposed law

bond, *n.* a certificate issued by the government or a business promising to pay the holder a set amount of money, plus a fixed interest, on a set date

brewer, *n.* a person who makes beer

campaign, *n.* planned action, such as in a war operation

cargo, *n.* the goods carried in a vehicle, as a ship

cash crop, *n.* crops which farmers can sell on the market for cash, as opposed to those which they use to support the farm (i.e. feed to their own animals)

cavalry, *n.* soldiers on horseback

census, *n.* count of people

champion, *n.* one who defends or speaks in behalf of a cause

charge, *n.* a person given to another to look after

charnel house, *n.* a place for bones of the dead

charter, *v.* to officially grant rights and privileges to a town or city

circuit, *n.* a series of stops along a travel route

circuit rider, *n.* one who travels a circuit, stopping at each place along the way

civic, *adj.* of or pertaining to a city

civilian, *n.* not military

civil servant, *n.* a person who works for the government

clan, *n.* related families (especially Indian)

classic, *adj.* of high quality; notable as the best or most typical example of its kind

co-educational, *adj.* pertaining to the education of students of both sexes in the same class

collective bargaining, *n.* cooperation between labor and management to settle disputes

colonialism, *n.* a practice or system of extending territory

common, *adj.* used or shared by everybody

commute, *v.* to travel back and forth regularly

commuter, *n.* one who travels to work

compose, *v.* to form by putting together; to write music

compromise, *n.* settlement of a dispute where both sides give in part way

confederation, *n.* a union or joining together in a league or alliance

conglomerate, *n.* in geology, a mass of rock formed by fragments from various sources

conscientious objector, *n.* a person who objects to warfare because he believes it is wrong to kill

consecutive, *adj.* following in order, one right after another

conservation, *n.* the act of guarding or protecting from decay or loss

conservative, *adj.* favoring a policy of keeping things as they are; resisting or opposing change

conserve, *v.* to save or protect

constitutional, *adj.* in accordance with the laws of the constitution

consumer, *n.* a buyer and user

convert, *v.* to change beliefs

corrupt, *adj.* morally bad; carrying on improper conduct

council, *n.* a lawmaking or discussion group

critic, *n.* a person who judges the value, worth, beauty, or excellence of something

crucial, *adj.* being very important or decisive

culture, *n.* a civilization and its way of life

de facto, *adj.* in fact; actually happens or exists

de jure, *adj.* by law

delegate, *n.* a person sent with power to act for another

demonstration, *n.* a parade or gathering to show public feeling

depression, *n.* a business slump

desegregate, *v.* to open to all races; to free of any laws or practices which set apart members of a particular race

desegregation, *n.* racial unity

deserter, *n.* a person who runs away from duty (as military)

devastated, *adj.* ruined or laid waste

devout, *adj.* devoted to, and sincere about, religion

direct primary, *n.* the election of candidates by party members to run against candidates from other parties

discriminate, *v.* to show preference in favor of one over another (as one race over another)

dispute, *n.* an argument

disrupt, *v.* to break up; to throw into disorder

distribution, *n.* the act of spreading around (as sending products to other locations)

dividend, *n.* a sum of money divided among holders of shares of stock

draft, *n.* a condition of being chosen for duty;

draft, *v.* to draw, or draw up

dynamo, *n.* a machine for producing electricity

earthworks, *n.* a construction made by hauling and piling up dirt

efficiency, *n.* ability to work without waste (as of time or resources)

effigy, *n.* image or likeness of a form or person

electoral college, *n.* formal voters of the U.S. who elect the president and vice president

electrolysis, *n.* the producing of chemical changes by passage of an electric current through a liquid

emigrate, *v.* to leave a country to settle somewhere else

emission, *n.* substance sent out or put forth (as auto exhaust fumes and particles)

empire, *n.* an area of one's rule or power

endangered species, *n.* a class or kind of plant or animal put in jeopardy or peril of extinction

endorse, *v.* to give one's support

endurance, *n.* the ability to withstand strain or suffering; power to continue on

energy resources, *n.* those natural forces which have ability to produce power

engineer, *n.* a person who designs or builds machines

environment, *n.* surroundings; all influences affecting development of an organism

environmentalist, *n.* a person who works to solve problems of the environment, such as water and air pollution

erosion, *n.* wearing away

estate, *n.* property of a person

ethnic, *adj.* relating to races or large groups of people classed by common traits or customs

executive branch, *n.* the part of government that puts law into action

expedition, *n.* a journey for a particular purpose (as to explore)

extended family, *n.* a social unit made up of parents and children along with other relatives such as grandparents, aunts, uncles, and cousins

fabricate, *v.* to make or manufacture

fail, *v.* to lose strength; to become bankrupt

feeder canal, *n.* one that leads into another (usually a smaller one leading to a larger, or main canal)

fertile, *adj.* capable of producing plentiful crops

fixed income, *n.* established or set amount of money coming in each month or pay period

fixed percent, *n.* a firm, set rate in every hundred

folk culture, *n.* activities and handmade products of the common people

fossil, *n.* a print or remains of a plant or animal of a past age preserved in earth or rock

foundry, *n.* a factory where metals are cast or molded

fraternal, *adj.* composed of members banded together like brothers

fringe, *n.* edge; border

frontier, *n.* the edge of a settled part of a country

geology, *n.* a science that deals with the history of the earth and its life

girdle, *v.* to strip a ring of bark from a tree trunk; encircle

glaciated, *adj.* changed by glacial action

glean, *v.* to gather little by little

grid, *n.* a network of horizontal and vertical lines

gross national product, *n.* total value of goods and services produced in a country (usually measured yearly)

gross state product, *n.* total value of goods and services produced in a state (usually measured yearly)

haven, *n.* a place of shelter; harbor

high culture, *n.* activities or works of superior quality; classic in nature

Hispanic, *adj.* belonging to a Spanish language group

historic, *adj.* belongs to the past; famous in history

home rule, *n.* local self-government

horticulture, *n.* the science and art of growing fruit, flower, and garden crops

immigrate, *v.* to come into a new country or region

impeach, *v.* to officialy charge a person in public office with wrongdoing

impersonate, *v.* pretend to be; act the part of

import, *v.* to bring into a country

incorporate, *v.* to form a legal body

index, *n.* the relation of one amount to another

indict, *v.* charge with an offense

industrialization, *n.* the establishment of industry in a place

industry, *n.* manufacturing activity

inflation, *n.* a sharp and sudden fall in the value of money

inhabitant, *n.* one who lives permanently in a place

initiative, *n.* the right of citizens or the legislature to introduce a matter for legislation either to the legislative body or directly to the citizens

integrate, *v.* bring races together

intellectual, *n.* a person who is a thinker; one who strives to develop his or her intelligence

interest, *n.* the money paid by a borrower for the use of borrowed money

international, *adj.* relating to, or affecting two or more countries

interrelated, *adj.* having a close connection with each other

intimidate, *v.* frighten

investment capital, *n.* money used to improve a business's ability to make money

investor, *n.* one who invests money

issue, *n.* a point, matter, or problem to be decided

judicial branch, *n.* the part of government that makes the laws

leisure, *adj.* free time

liberate, *v.* set free; remove restrictions

liberated, *adj.* the condition of being free or unrestricted

lithograph, *n.* a kind of print made by a method of fusing ink with grease on a metal or stone plate

lottery, *n.* a way to distribute prizes by chance

lyrics, *n.* words for songs

malleable, *adj.* able to be shaped or molded

management, *adj.* those who direct or supervise (as managers in business)

maneuverability, *n.* quality of being skillfully guided

mean, *n.* middle point

mechanization, *n.* quality of being equipped with machinery or made automatic

merge, *v.* unite or combine, causing one to be swallowed up by the other

methodically, *adj.* in a systematic or organized manner; in a step-by-step method

migrant, *n.* one who passes periodically from one region to another

migrate, *v.* move from one region or country to another

migration, *n.* the act of moving to another place

militarism, *n.* an aggressive policy of maintaining strong armed forces and being willing to use them

militia, *n.* citizen soldiers called to action in an emergency

minority, *n.* a part less than half of any population different from other groups in some ways and sometimes discriminated against

mobility, *n.* a condition of being easily moved

moderator, *n.* one who controls or presides over a group (as at a meeting)

monopoly *n.* a company that controls the entire supply of a service or product in a given market

morality, *n.* moral qualities of character; pertaining to what is right and wrong in human behavior

mortar and pestle, *n.* a bowl (mortar) and pounding utensil (pestle) used to grind substances into powder

Moundbuilders, *n.* early North American prehistoric Indians who built burial mounds and fortifications

municipality, *n.* a town or city

nationalism, *n.* a policy that national interests are more important than international considerations

Native Americans, *n.* Indians

natural foods, *n.* those without chemicals added

natural resources, *n.* those things found in nature that are valuable to humans

navigable, *adj.* able to be traveled

network, *n.* system of lines

non-profit, *adj.* not operated for the purpose of making a profit

notorious, *adj.* widely and unfavorably known; having a bad reputation

nuclear family, *n.* a social unit made up of parent/s and their children living in one household

omen, *n.* sign or warning of a future event

oppression, *n.* unjust use of power; burden; condition of being crushed by harsh rule

oral tradition, *n.* a method of passing down customs from one generation to another by spoken language

ordinance, *n.* law made by a town or city government

ore, *n.* a mineral from which metal can be extracted

original jurisdiction, *n.* authority to start the legal process

outmigration, *n.* a condition of more people moving out of than into a region

outspoken, *adj.* direct in speech or discussion; frank; blunt

overbearing, *adj.* acting in a proud or domineering way toward other people

overproduce, *v.* to create a supply of a product greater than the demand for it

parcel, *n.* section of land

pardon, *n.* a freeing from penalty for a crime

patent, *n.* official document that gives an inventor exclusive right to make and sell his/her invention for a certain number of years

patron, *n.* a person who donates or supports something

pension, *n.* fixed sum paid to a retired person

performing arts, *n.* those arts presented for an audience, specifically music, opera, dance, drama

persecution, *n.* pursued for the purpose of being harmed or having property destroyed

petroglyph, *n.* prehistoric carvings cut into rock cliffs or stone

philanthropist, *n.* a person who makes charitable gifts to society

planned community, *n.* one whose growth and development is modeled after an organized design

plantation, *n.* a large farm growing cultivated crops (especially in the South)

pollute, *v.* make dirty or impure

popular, *adj.* representing the whole body of people

popular culture, *n.* activities and customs enjoyed by many people

popular government, *n.* government responsive to and representative of the people

prehistoric, *adj.* before written history

prejudice, *n.* favoring or dislike of one over another without good reason

premonition, *n.* a forewarning

prosecution, *n.* the state's lawyers in a criminal case; the one bringing charges against the accused

preservation, *n.* keeping from injury, loss, or decay

preservative, *n.* a substance added to food to keep it from spoiling

preserve, *v.* keep safe

producer, *n.* maker of a product

professions, *n.* those careers and occupations that require advanced training in liberal arts or science, usually involving mental work

progressive, *adj.* favoring political change and social improvement by government action

prohibit, *v.* forbid by law or authority

protest, *n.* complaint or objection against an idea or action

quaint, *adj.* pleasingly old-fashioned

quarry, *v.* to dig building stone from its excavation site

quota, *n.* required share or part

radius, *n.* the circular area defined by the sweeping of a line that exends from the center to the edge of a circle

raw materials, *n.* those things found in nature from which other things can be made

realist, *n.* a person who portrays nature and people in art or literature as they really are

recall, *v.* remove an official from public office by popular vote

receptive, *adj.* able to accept new ideas

referendum, *n.* issue handed to the people by the legislature for approval or rejection

refine, *v.* make pure

reform *v.* make better

reformer, *n.* a person who works to make improvements in society

relief, *n.* projection of figures from a flat surface so they stand out (as in sculpture)

relocation camp, *n.* place to where people are moved and held captive

rendezvous, *n.* planned meeting

repeal, *v.* do away with

representative democracy, *n.* a type of government in which the majority rules by the action of elected representatives

reprieve, *n.* a temporary delay of a penalty or sentence (especially the death penalty)

resolution, *n.* a statement voted on

resource, *n.* a supply of something that can be used to take care of a need

restore, *v.* put back into a former original state

revenue, *n.* income

revival, *n.* public religious gathering

rout, *n.* an overwhelming defeat

sanctuary, *n.* a place of refuge or safety

scarce, *adj.* in short supply

secede, *v.* withdraw

secular, *adj.* not sacred or religious

segregation, *n.* separation or isolation by discrimination

self-sustaining, *adj.* able to support oneself

senior citizen, *n.* a person over 65 years of age

shelf life, *n.* length of time a food product will retain its maximum nutritional value

siege, *n.* a continued attack

slogan, *n.* word or phrase used by a group or product to call attention; a motto

solicitor, *n.* a lawyer serving as an official law officer for a government or a division of government

specialize, *v.* limit one's business or activity to a narrow field

spectacular, *n.*a musical production with extravagant costumes and scenery, involving large chorus scenes

speculate, *v.* engage in a business deal in which a large profit may be made, but where a high risk is involved

speculator, *n.* an investor who takes high risks

spring house, *n.* a small building enclosing a brook or spring for the purpose of cooling milk and food

squatter, *n.* a person who settles on land without rights

standing committee, *n.* a permanent legislative committee, ready to work

statistics, *n.* data and their interpretations

stock, *n.* shares in a company

stock certificate, *n.* a paper telling how many shares a person owns

stock market, *n.* buying and selling of shares

strata, *n.* layers

strike, *n.* work stoppage

suburban, *adj.* close to the city

suburbs, *n.* residential area just outside the city

suffrage, *n.* right to vote

surplus, *n.* extra amount

survey, *v.* taking exact land measurements

temperance, *n.* non-use or limited use of alcoholic beverages

tenant farmer, *n.* one who is allowed to work a piece of land owned by another in exchange for a share of the crop yield

tenement, *n.* low-grade apartment housing

testify, *v.* give evidence

thrift, *n.* careful management, especially of money

till, *n.* stiff, stony material, deposited by glaciers, that does not let water penetrate

tillage, *n.* cultivation (plowed, planted, and worked)

township, *n.* unit of land

transition, *n.* condition of change

treaty, *n.* an agreement negotiated between two or more countries or rulers

trilobite, *n.* a type of fossil whose body is made up of three parts

tuition, *n.* money paid for schooling

Underground Railroad, *n.* a system of transporting and hiding slaves to help them escape to freedom

unglaciated, *adj.* not affected by glacial action

urban, *adj.* relating to a city

vast, *adj.* very large in extent

veto, *v.* to refuse to agree, as to a legislative bill, causing it to be reconsidered or canceled

vineyard, *n.* a crop of grapes; place where grapes are grown

visual arts, *n.* those art mediums that are viewed, such as painting and sculpture

workman's compensation, *n.* government insurance for workers who are injured on the job

APPENDICES

GOVERNORS OF OHIO

D = Democrat **F** = Federalist
R = Republican **W** = Whig

Name	Term in Office
Edward Tiffin (resigned) D	1803-1807
Thomas Kirker D	1807-1808
Samuel Huntington D	1808-1810
Return J. Meigs, Jr. (resigned) D	1810-1814
Othniel Looker D	1814
Thomas Worthington D	1814-1818
Ethan Allan Brown (resigned) D	1818-1822
Allen Trimble F	1822
Jeremiah Morrow D	1822-1826
Allen Trimble F	1826-1830
Duncan McArthur F	1830-1832
Robert Lucas D	1832-1836
Joseph Vance W	1836-1838
Wilson Shannon D	1838-1840
Thomas Corwin W	1840-1842
Wilson Shannon (resigned) D	1842-1844
Thomas Bartley D	1844
Mordecai Bartley W	1844-1846
William Bebb W	1846-1848
Seabury Ford W	1848-1850
Reuben Wood (resigned) D	1850-1853
William Medill D	1853-1856
Salmon P. Chase R	1856-1860
William Dennison R	1860-1862
David Tod R	1862-1864
John Brough (died) R	1864-1865
Charles Anderson R	1865-1866
Jacob D. Cox R	1866-1868
Rutherford B. Hayes R	1868-1872
Edward F. Noyes R	1872-1874
William Allen D	1874-1876
Rutherford B. Hayes (resigned) R	1876-1877
Thomas L. Young R	1877-1878
Richard M. Bishop D	1878-1880
Charles Foster R	1880-1884
George Hoadly D	1884-1886
Joseph B. Foraker R	1886-1890
James E. Campbell D	1890-1892
William McKinley R	1892-1896
Asa Bushnell R	1896-1900
George K. Nash R	1900-1904
Myron T. Herrick R	1904-1906
John M. Pattison (died) D	1906
Andrew L. Harris R	1906-1909
Judson Harmon D	1909-1913
James M. Cox D	1913-1915
Frank B. Willis R	1915-1917
James M. Cox D	1917-1921
Harry L. Davis R	1921-1923
A. Victor Donahey D	1923-1929
Myers Y. Cooper R	1929-1931
George White D	1931-1935
Martin L. Davey D	1935-1939
John W. Bricker R	1939-1945
Frank J. Lausche D	1945-1947
Thomas J. Herbert R	1947-1949
Frank J. Lausche (resigned) D	1949-1957
John W. Brown R	1957
C. William O'Neill R	1957-1959
Michael V. DiSalle D	1959-1963
James A. Rhodes R	1963-1971
John J. Gilligan D	1971-1975
James A. Rhodes R	1975-1983
Richard F. Celeste D	1983-

1980 POPULATION

County	Population
WILLIAMS	36,369
FULTON	37,751
LUCAS	471,741
OTTAWA	40,076
ASHTABULA	104,215
LAKE	212,801
GEAUGA	74,474
DEFIANCE	39,987
HENRY	28,383
WOOD	107,372
SANDUSKY	63,267
ERIE	79,655
LORAIN	274,909
CUYAHOGA	1,498,295
TRUMBULL	241,863
PAULDING	21,302
PUTNAM	32,991
HANCOCK	64,581
SENECA	61,901
HURON	54,608
MEDINA	113,150
SUMMIT	524,472
PORTAGE	135,856
MAHONING	289,487
VAN WERT	30,458
ALLEN	112,241
HARDIN	32,719
WYANDOT	22,651
CRAWFORD	50,075
RICHLAND	131,205
ASHLAND	46,178
WAYNE	97,408
STARK	378,823
COLUMBIANA	113,572
MERCER	38,334
AUGLAIZE	42,554
SHELBY	43,089
LOGAN	39,155
MARION	67,974
MORROW	26,480
KNOX	46,309
HOLMES	29,416
TUSCARAWAS	84,614
CARROLL	25,598
JEFFERSON	91,564
HARRISON	18,152
DARKE	55,096
MIAMI	90,381
CHAMPAIGN	33,649
UNION	29,536
DELAWARE	53,840
LICKING	120,981
COSHOCTON	36,024
GUERNSEY	42,024
BELMONT	82,569
PREBLE	38,223
MONTGOMERY	571,697
CLARK	150,236
MADISON	33,004
FRANKLIN	869,109
FAIRFIELD	93,678
PERRY	31,032
MUSKINGUM	80,340
NOBLE	11,310
MONROE	17,382
BUTLER	258,787
WARREN	99,276
GREENE	129,769
FAYETTE	27,467
PICKAWAY	43,662
MORGAN	14,241
WASHINGTON	64,266
HAMILTON	873,136
CLERMONT	128,483
CLINTON	34,603
HIGHLAND	33,477
ROSS	65,004
HOCKING	24,304
VINTON	11,584
ATHENS	56,399
MEIGS	23,641
BROWN	31,920
ADAMS	24,328
PIKE	22,802
SCIOTO	84,545
JACKSON	30,592
GALLIA	30,098
LAWRENCE	63,840

State - 10,797,419

Lost Population 1970-1980

Gained Population 1970-1980

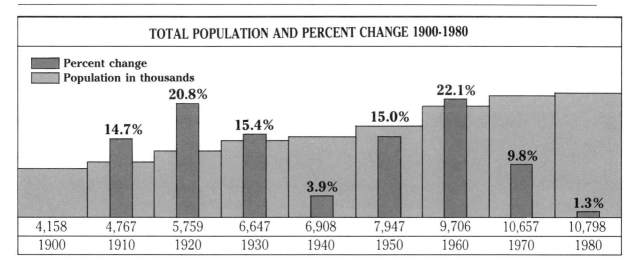

POPULATION OF OHIO CITIES

(1980 Census)

Over 200,000

City	Population	Percent Change, 1970-1980
Cleveland	573,822	-23.6
Columbus	564,871	+ 4.6
Cincinnati	385,457	-15.0
Toledo	354,635	-7.4
Akron	237,177	-13.9
Dayton	203,588	-16.2

50,000 to 200,000

City	Population	Percent Change, 1970-1980
Youngstown	115,436	-18.1
Canton	94,730	-13.9
Parma	92,548	-7.7
Lorain	75,416	-3.5
Springfield	72,563	-11.4

Hamilton	63,189	-6.9
Lakewood	61,963	-11.7
Kettering	61,186	-14.9
Euclid	59,999	-16.1
Elyria	57,504	+7.6
Warren	56,629	-10.8
Cleveland Heights	56,438	-7.1
Mansfield	53,927	-2.0

25,000 to 50,000

City	Population	Percent Change 1970-1980
Lima	47,381	-11.8
Middletown	43,719	-10.4
Cuyahoga Falls	43,710	-12.3
Mentor	42,065	+14.0
Newark	41,200	-1.5
Marion	37,040	-4.2
East Cleveland	36,957	-6.7
North Olmsted	36,486	+4.7
Upper Arlington	35,648	-8.0
Findlay	35,594	-0.6
Lancaster	34,953	+6.2
Garfield Heights	33,380	-19.4
Shaker Heights	32,487	-10.5
Beavercreek	31,589	-
Sandusky	31,360	-4.0
Fairfield	30,777	+109.7
Massillon	30,557	-6.1
Barberton	29,751	-10.0
Maple Heights	29,735	-12.8
Fairborn	29,702	-7.9
Zanesville	28,655	-13.3
Strongsville	28,577	+88.2
Brunswick	27,689	+74.7
Steubenville	26,400	-14.2
Norwood	26,342	-13.4
Brook Park	26,195	-14.9
Kent	26,164	-7.2
Portsmouth	25,943	-6.1
Bowling Green	25,728	+75.5
South Euclid	25,713	-13.1
Stow	25,503	+26.1

SELECTED PRODUCTS OF RURAL OHIO

Archbold	Chinese food
Brown County	Tobacco
Burton	Maple sugar
Butler	Camping trailers
Caldwell	Apples
Celeryville	Grass sod
Hancock County	Beet sugar
Kenton	Candy
Knox County	Sheep
Lake Erie Islands	Grapes and wine
Marion County	Popcorn
Marysville	Grass seed and lawn supplies
Mercer County	Turkeys
Millersburg	Buggies
New Lexington	Roofing tile
New London	Uniforms
Northwest Ohio	Tomatoes
Ottawa	Television picture tubes
Rio Grande	Sausage
Scio	Pottery
St. Paris	Ice cream and frozen desserts
Sugarcreek	Swiss cheese
Upper Sandusky	Burial vaults
Van Wert	Work clothing

SELECTED PRODUCTS OF URBAN OHIO

Akron	Rubber
Ashland	Toy balloons
Barberton	Matches
Bucyrus	Copper kettles
Canton	Roller bearings; vacuum cleaners
Celina	Tables
Chillicothe	Paper
Cincinnati	Machine tools; playing cards; soap
Cleveland	Automobile parts; iron and steel; paint
Columbus	Research and development
Dayton	Cash registers; computers; refrigerators
Elyria	Furnaces and air conditioners
Euclid	Airplane parts
Hamilton	Safes; printing presses
Lancaster	Glass
Lima	School busses
Lorain	Clothing
Mansfield	Electrical equipment
Marion	Power shovels
Medina	Beeswax and beekeeper's supplies
Middletown	Paper boards and boxes
Newark	Missile guidance systems
Tiffin	Bathroom fixtures
Toledo	Glass; oil refining
Troy	Kitchen mixers and dishwashers
Warren	Automobile parts
Youngstown	Iron and steel

GREAT OHIOANS HALL OF FAME

The Great Ohioans Hall of Fame is located in the Ohio Historical Center in Columbus, Ohio. It honors Ohio men and women recognized by the Ohio Historical Society for their productive lives and inspiring achievements.

The Trailblazers

FLORENCE E. ALLEN (1884-1966, Cleveland)
First lady judge of a court of general jurisdiction and the U. S. Circuit Court of Appeals

CHRISTOPHER GIST (1706-1759)
First English-American explorer of the Ohio country

BENJAMIN GOODRICH (1841-1888, Akron)
Ohio's pioneer rubber industrialist

THOMAS HUTCHINS (1730-1789)
Geographer who began the rectangular land survey in Ohio

NATHANIEL MASSIE (1763-1813, Ross County)
Irrepressible town founder in southern Ohio

ROBERT PATTERSON (1753-1827, Cincinnati, Dayton)
Indian fighter who helped found two great cities

RUFUS PUTNAM (1738-1824, Marietta)
Pioneer who made our first permanent settlement successful

JOHN CLEVES SYMMES (1724-1814, North Bend)
Pioneer land proprietor between the Miamis

BEZALEEL WELLS (1763-1846, Steubenville)
Founder of Canton and Steubenville; made Ohio a wool state

EBENEZER ZANE (1747-1812, eastern Ohio)
Pioneer who blazed Ohio's first road

DAVID ZEISBERGER (1721-1808, Schoenbrunn)
Missionary who believed Indians were worth teaching and saving

The Legends

JOHN BROWN (1800-1859, Akron)
Shepherd who aroused nation's passion by Harpers Ferry raid to free slaves

JOHN CHAPMAN "Johnny Appleseed" (1775-1845)
Itinerant who planted wild apple seedlings and weeds but whose humility captured America's heart

JOHN CLEM (1851-1937, Newark)
Drummer-boy of Shiloh

SIMON KENTON (1775-1836, Clark, Champaign counties)
Ohio's symbolic frontiersman

JAMES LOGAN (1725-1780, Pickaway County)
Mingo chief whose "morsel of eloquence" aroused pity for the Indian

PIERRE NAVARRE (1790-1874, Toledo)
Fur trader who became the heroic scout of War of 1812

ANNIE OAKLEY (1860-1926, Darke County)
Sharpshooter who won fame in a man's world

PONTIAC (d. 1769, northwestern Ohio)
Ottawa chief who resisted English possession of the Northwest

LEWIS WETZEL (1764-1808)
Best known, most trusted scout in the Ohio country

The Valiant

HENRY BOUQUET (1719-1765, Coshocton)
British colonel who cowed Indians without firing a shot

GEORGE ROGERS CLARK (1752-1818, Clark County)
Militiaman who conquered the Northwest for U.S.

GEORGE CROGHAN (1791-1849, Fremont)
Heroic defender of Fort Stephenson in the War of 1812

GEORGE A. CUSTER (1839-1876, New Rumley)
> Controversial figure in American military history whose career ended at Little Big Horn

FREDERICK FUNSTON (1865-1917, New Carlisle)
> General who captured Philippine rebel Aguinaldo

ERNEST J. KING (1878-1956, Lorain)
> World War II commander of U.S. Fleet

THE FIGHTING McCOOKS (Carrollton, Steubenville)
> Major Daniel and his nine sons; Dr. John's five sons

OLIVER H. PERRY (1785-1819, Put-in-Bay)
> Routed British fleet in Battle of Lake Erie

PHILIP H. SHERIDAN (1831-1888, Somerset)
> Greatest cavalry officer of Civil War

WILLIAM TECUMSEH SHERMAN (1820-1891, Lancaster)
> Professional soldier who marched to the sea and called war "Hell"

TECUMSEH (1768-1813)
> Shawnee warrior who united Indian tribes to keep settlers at bay

"MAD" ANTHONY WAYNE (1745-1796, Greenville)
> Soldier who restored confidence to American arms at Fallen Timbers

The Ingenious

CHARLES F. BRUSH (1849-1929, Cleveland)
> Mining engineer who lighted city streets electrically

GEORGE W. CRILE (1864-1943, Cleveland)
> Surgeon who pioneered in blood transfusion and nerve-block anesthesia

HARVEY W. CUSHING (1869-1939, Cleveland)
> One of America's most accomplished neuro-surgeons

THOMAS A. EDISON (1847-1931, Milan)
> America's pre-eminent inventor

JOHN EISENMANN (Cleveland)
> Engineer who designed Cleveland arcade and state flag

CHARLES FLEISCHMANN (1834-1897, Cincinnati)
> Nation's first producer and marketer of compressed yeast

CHARLES M. HALL (1863-1914, Oberlin)
> Professor who found the way to make aluminum a common metal

CHARLES F. KETTERING (1876-1958, Kettering)
> Inventor of electric starter

A. ROY KNABENSHUE (1876-1960, Bryan and Toledo)
> Aeronaut who spanned balloon and airplane eras

JAMES LEFFEL (1806-1866, Springfield)
> Manufacturer who harnessed water-power with turbine

ALEXANDER W. LIVINGSTON (1822-1898, Reynoldsburg)
> Seed merchant who made the tomato popular

DAYTON C. MILLER (1866-1941, Cleveland)
> Professor who harnessed the X-ray for medicine

EDWARD W. MORLEY (1869-1903, Cleveland)
> Scientist who first determined atomic weights of oxygen and nitrogen

JOHN B. TYTUS (1875-1944, Middletown)
> Invented continuous steel rolling mill

ALEXANDER WINTON (1860-1932, Cleveland)
> Bicycle repairman who made and sold first reliable auto

WILBUR and ORVIILLE WRIGHT (1867-1912, 1871-1948, Dayton)
> First to fly heavier-than-air craft

DENTON T. (CY) YOUNG (1867-1955,
Tuscarawas County)
  Baseball's winningest pitcher

The Builders

SETH ADAMS (d. 1852, Muskingum County)
  First to import purebred sheep to nation
  and later to Ohio

DANIEL DRAKE (1785-1852, Cincinnati)
  "Father of Ohio physicians" and founder of
  Ohio's first museum

THOMAS EWING (1789-1871, Lancaster)
  "Logician of the West," who was U.S.
  senator and served in cabinets of three
  presidents

EDWARD D. FENWICK (1768-1832,
Cincinnati)
  Bishop-missionary who laid foundation for
  Catholicism in Ohio

JOHN HARRIS (1798-1848, Bainbridge)
  Physician who professionalized dentistry

NICHOLAS LONGWORTH (1782-1863,
Cincinnati)
  Lawyer and horticulturalist who introduced
  commercial grape culture to Ohio

MICHAEL J. OWENS (1859-1932, Toledo)
  Glassblower whose inventions made Toledo
  the glass capital

FELIX RENICK (1770-1848, Ross County)
  Pioneer cattleman who imported the shorthorn to America

BRANCH RICKEY (1881-1965, Stockdale)
  Manager who developed baseball farm
  system and put blacks on the ballfield

ARTHUR ST. CLAIR (1736-1818, Marietta and
Cincinnati)
  Soldier who gave the Northwest Territory its
  first government and laws

EPHRAIM G. SQUIER and EDWIN H. HARRIS
(1821-1888, 1811-1888, Chillicothe)
  Ohio's first accomplished archaeologists

EDWARD TIFFIN (1766-1829, Chillicothe)
  Physician-preacher who led fight for Ohio
  statehood and became its first governor

TIMOTHY WALKER (1802-1856, Cincinnati)
  Co-founder of first Ohio law school and
  author of first Ohio legal text

THOMAS WORTHINGTON (1773-1827,
Chillicothe)
  Lobbyist in Washington for statehood

The Organizers

NEWTON D. BAKER (1871-1937, Cleveland)
  Secretary of war who directed nation's
  military might in World War I

JAMES BENNETT (East Liverpool)
  Launched mass production of commercial
  ceramics in Ohio

JOE CARR (1880-1937, Columbus)
  Coach who helped weld National Football
  League as its first president

JAY COOKE (1821-1905, Sandusky)
  Financial genius of Union cause in Civil
  War

HARVEY S. FIRESTONE (1868-1938, Akron)
  Inventor of balloon tire; molded a rubber
  empire

OREN J. FOLLETT (1798-1894, Sandusky)
  Publisher who organized and served as
  chairman of Republican party

ALBERT B. GRAHAM (1868-1960, Champaign
County)
  Educational heretic who promoted school
  consolidation and founded 4-H Club

WILLIAM GREEN (1870-1952, Coshocton)
  Mineworker who fostered labor unions and
  became president of A.F. of L.

MARCUS A. HANNA (1837-1904, Cleveland)
  Industrialist, political genius who produced
  a president

WILLIAM R. HARPER (1856-1906, New Concord)
Educational pacemaker, creative president of University of Chicago

ALFRED E. KELLEY (1789-1859, Cleveland, Columbus)
Community builder who fathered transportation and banking systems

SAMUEL P. LEWIS (1799-1854, Cincinnati)
Carpenter-lawyer who founded and nurtured Ohio public school system

EDWARD D. LIBBEY (1854-1925, Toledo)
Modern glassmaker who founded an art museum

WILLIAM McKENDREE (1757-1835)
First American-born bishop who spread Methodism in Ohio

JAMES W. PACKARD (1863-1928, Warren)
Manufacturer who produced quality auto of his day

WILLIAM C. PROCTOR and JAMES N. GAMBLE (1862-1934, 1836-1932, Cincinnati)
Candle and soapmakers who made Ivory a top name in soap

JOHN D. ROCKEFELLER (1839-1937, Cleveland)
Clerk who founded an oil dynasty and devised the modern trust

AMOS I. ROOT (1839-1923, Medina)
Developed beekeeping into national commercial industry

FRANK A. SEIBERLING (1859-1954, Akron)
Founder of two successive rubber empires

EDWIN M. STANTON (1814-1869, Steubenville)
Lincoln's secretary of war

GUS SUN (1868-1959, Springfield)
Juggler who discovered and promoted some of nation's leading theatrical talents

LOUIS J. TABER (1878-1960, Barnesville)
Welded Grange into national force for agricultural improvement

ELISHA WHITTLESEY (1783-1863, Canfield)
Founder of Whig party, first comptroller of U.S. Treasury

ISAAC M. WISE (1819-1900, Cincinnati)
Foremost figure in American Jewish religious life in his day

The Reformers

WILLIAM M. AWL (1779-1876, Columbus)
Secured state care for mentally ill, blind, and retarded

SALMON P. CHASE (1808-1873, Cincinnati)
Outspoken foe of human slavery who managed Union's fiscal cause

THOMAS CORWIN (1794-1865, Lebanon)
Orator who eloquently thundered opposition to Mexican War

JAMES M. COX (1870-1957, Dayton)
Implemented more reform legislation than any other Ohio governor

JACOB S. COXEY (1854-1951, Massillon)
Championed unemployed with Coxey's armies

FRANCES DANA GAGE (1808-1884, McConnelsville)
Eloquent female voice in battle for temperance and women's rights

JOSHUA REED GIDDINGS (1795-1864, Jefferson)
Congressman whose opposition to slave trade won him censure

WASHINGTON GLADDEN (1836-1918, Columbus)
Clergyman, hymnist who preached urban reform

SAMUEL HUNTINGTON (1765-1817, Painesville)
Achieved the right of state supreme court to nullify laws of Ohio

TOM L. JOHNSON (1854-1911, Cleveland)
Street railway operator who became Ohio's greatest reform mayor

SAMUEL "GOLDEN RULE" JONES (1846-1904, Toledo)
Manufacturer who urged collective ownership of industry and reformed city government

BENJAMIN LUNDY (1789-1839, St. Clairsville)
Saddler who organized first antislavery society

GEORGE H. PENDLETON (1825-1889, Cincinnati)
Senator who dealt blow to spoils system by sponsoring U.S. Civil Service Commission

JOHN SHERMAN (1823-1900, Mansfield)
Statesman who dominated national fiscal policy after Civil War

JOSEPH SMITH, Jr. (1805-1844, Kirtland)
Prophet who established Church of Jesus Christ of Latter-day Saints

BENJAMIN F. WADE (1800-1878, Jefferson)
Antislavery leader and intensely patriotic U.S. senator

WAYNE B. WHEELER (1869-1927, Brookfield)
Leader of "mighty edifice," The Anti-Saloon League of America

BRAND WHITLOCK (1869-1934, Toledo)
Mayor who crusaded for fair deal for working man

The Communicators

CHARLES F. BROWNE (1834-1867, Cleveland)
"Artemus Ward," who with pen or on platform, made America laugh at itself

CLARENCE S. DARROW (1857-1938, Kinsman)
Irreverent trial lawyer whose acid wit and drawling speech won him international fame

JAMES W. FAULKNER (1863-1923, Cincinnati, Columbus)
Foremost observer and writer of Ohio political scene of his era

CLARK GABLE (1910-1960, Cadiz)
Idol of cinema whose handsome visage graced 67 motion pictures in 29 years of stardom

ZANE GREY (1872-1939, Zanesville)
Popular writer who wove epics from the American saga

ELSIE JANIS (1889-1956, Columbus)
Child star who became "sweetheart of the A.E.F." in World War I

DAVID ROSS LOCKE (1833-1888, Findlay, Toledo)
Journalist who tickled Lincoln's and America's ribs with satirical letters of Petroleum V. Nasby

HORACE MANN (1796-1859, Yellow Springs)
Educator who led common school revival in U.S.

JULIA MARLOWE (1870-1950, Cincinnati)
Actress whose Shakespearean roles won her world acclaim

WILLIAM MAXWELL (1755-1809, Cincinnati)
Printer who launched first newspaper and printed first book in territory

WILLIAM H. McGUFFY (1800-1873, Oxford)
Professor whose "eclectic Readers" taught and influenced generations of youth

OSCAR O. McINTYRE (1844-1938, Gallipolis)
Columnist who made Broadway and Main Street "a dual highway"

JOSEPH RAY (1807-1865, Cincinnati)
Mathematician who made arithmetic understandable

WHITELAW REID (1837-1912, Columbus)
Reporter whose analysis of Civil War era made those turbulent times intelligible

PLATT R. SPENCER (1800-1864, Ashtabula County)
Penmanship teacher whose embellished handwriting became standard in American schools for decades

BURTON E. STEVENSON (1872-1962, Chillicothe)
Librarian, author who rescued immortal words from obscurity

HARRIET BEECHER STOWE (1812-1896, Cincinnati)
Author of most influential antislavery novel

JAMES G. THURBER (1894-1961, Columbus)
Ungainly scribe who became top American humorist of his time

HARRY E. WARNER (1876-1941, Elyria)
Impresario who introduced Ohio to the motion picture

The Conservers

CALEB ATWATER (1778-1867, Circleville)
Intellectual pioneer, first Ohio historian and first forest conservationist

LOUIS BROMFIELD (1896-1956, Richland County)
Bard of virtues of rural life and of conservation

HENRY HOWE (1816-1893, Columbus)
Chronicler who first awoke popular interest and pride in Ohio and its history

JARED P. KIRTLAND (1793-1877, Cleveland)
Physician who became Ohio's first nationally reputable naturalist and horticulturalist

JOHN LOCKE (1792-1856, Cincinnati)
Geologist, inventor who was among first in the nation to advocate soil conservation

EMILIUS O. RANDALL (1850-1919, Columbus)
Attorney whose exhaustive chronicles were milestone in state historiography

EDMUND SECREST (1882-1949, Wooster)
Ohio's first state forester who implemented reforestation

ROBERT A. TAFT (1889-1953, Cincinnati)
"Mr. Republican" who sought to preserve traditional American ideals tempered with sound social welfare programs

CHARLES E. THORNE (1846-1936, Greene County, Wooster)
Agriculturalist who unlocked secrets of our soils

CHARLES WHITTLESEY (1808-1886, Cleveland)
Ohio's first great geologist who early recommended crop rotation

The Creators

SHERWOOD ANDERSON (1876-1941, Elyria and Clyde)
Businessman who realistically immortalized small town Ohio life

DANIEL C. BEARD (1850-1914, Cincinnati)
Illustrator who helped found Boy Scouts

HART CRANE (1899-1932, Cleveland and Akron)
Ohio poet of undisputed greatness

PAUL L. DUNBAR (1872-1906, Dayton)
"Poet laureate" of his race who probed both pathos of past and restlessness of future

FRANK DUVENECK (1848-1919, Cincinnati)
Artist whose naturalistic styles and personal influence inspired a generation of artists

DANIEL D. EMMETT (1815-1904, Mt. Vernon)
Minstrel trouper who gave South its war song, "Dixie"

STEPHEN C. FOSTER (1826-1864, Cincinnati)
Bookkeeper whose folk songs gave expression to sad status of slaves

CASS GILBERT (1859-1934, Zanesville)
Strong-willed architect whose public buildings adorn our landscapes

JONATHAN GOLDSMITH (1784-1847, Painesville)
Architect-builder who studded northeastern Ohio with his gems

BENJAMIN R. HANBY (1833-1867, Westerville)
Teacher who wrote some of most widely sung popular tunes of any era

ROBERT HENRI (1865-1929, Cincinnati)
Artist whose works are in 30 museums

WILLIAM D. HOWELLS (1837-1920, Columbus)
Journalist who became dean of American letters

WILLIAM S. PORTER (1862-1910, Columbus)
O. Henry, who as a prison inmate mastered short story form

ARCHIBALD M. WILLARD (1836-1918, Wellington)
Carriage painter who created popular patriotic painting, *Spirit of '76*

OHIO WOMEN'S HALL OF FAME

Established in 1978, the Ohio Women's Hall of Fame is administered by the Women's Services Division and the Women's Advisory Council of the Ohio Bureau of Employment Services.

Hall of Fame inductees are selected on the basis of contributions that have provided statewide, national or international impact. Nominees must be native-born Ohioans or currently living in the state (a 10-year residency is required). Contributions by women both living and deceased are considered.

AKELEY, MARY L. JOBE (1878-1966, b. Tappan, Ohio)
Explorer of Canadian northwest

ALLEN, JUDGE FLORENCE E. (1884-1966, Cleveland)
First woman judge of a court of general jurisdiction and the U.S. Circuit Court of Appeals

BAYER, MILDRED (1908- , b. Weston)
Advocate of health care to developing countries who developed Health Clinics International

BERLIN, GRACE F. (1897- , B. Monclova)
Ecologist

BICKERDYKE, MARY ANN BALL (1817-1901, b. Knox County)
Civil War nurse

BISCHOFF, TINA MARIE (1958- , b. Columbus)
Long-distance swimmer and title holder

BLACK, HELEN CHATFIELD (1924- , Indian Hill)
Conservationist

BOLTON, FRANCES PAYNE (1885-1977, b. Cleveland)
First woman from Ohio in U.S. House of Representatives

BOMBECK, ERMA, L. (1927- , b. Dayton)
Author and syndicated humor columnist

BOYER, ELIZABETH M. (1913- , Novelty)
Founder and first president of Women's
Equity Action League

BRACKEN, HARRIET (1919- , Columbus)
Vice-president of a Columbus bank

BYRNE, PATRICIA M. (1925- , b. Cleveland)
Career foreign service officer

CLEVELAND, BEATRICE (1920- , b.
Delaware)
4-H leader

COOPER, MARTHA KINNEY (1874-1964,
Cincinnati)
Founder of Ohioana Library Association

CORNELIUS, DOROTHY (1918- ,
Reynoldsburg)
Executive director of Ohio Nurses Associa-
tion, and editor of *Ohio Nurses Review*, and
past president of International Council of
Nurses

CRAWFORD, RUTH PORTER (1901-1953, b.
East Liverpool)
Composer, pianist, musicologist and collec-
tor of folk music

DAY, DORIS (1924- , b. Cincinnati)
Actress and singer

DILLER, PHYLLIS (1917- , b. Lima)
Comedienne and author

DONAHEY, GERTRUDE W. (1908- , b.
Tuscarawas County)
Treasurer, State of Ohio—first woman
elected to a statewide public office

EARLEY, CHARITY EDNA (1918- , Dayton)
Educator, administrator, and volunteer
worker

FAST, LOUISA K. (1878-1979, Tiffin)
Women's rights activist and League of
Women Voters organizer

FULDHEIM, DOROTHY (1894- , Cleveland)
Actress, lecturer, and television news analyst

GISH, LILLIAN (1896- , b. Springfield)
Actress

GREISHEIMER, DR. ESTHER M. (1891- ,
Chillicothe)
Pioneer in medical education

HUNKINS, EUSEBIA (1902-1980, b. Troy)
Musician and composer, specialist in Appalachian folk music

HUNTER, JANE EDNA (1882-1971, Cleveland)
Established Phyllis Wheatley Association

JAMMAL, ELEANOR (1925- , b. Cleveland)
Vice-president of Ashtabula Rubber
Company

KELLER, EDITH M. (1880-1978, b. Blooming
Grove)
Music educator

KITCHEN, TELLA (1902- , Adelphi)
Folk painter

KLINE, SISTER M. CONSOLATA (1916- ,
Youngstown)
Hospital administrator

KOCHAN, BERNICE (1926- , Cleveland)
Artist

KRUPANSKY, JUDGE BLANCHE (1915- ,
Cleveland)
Associate Justice of Ohio Supreme Court—
first woman on high court

KUNKLE, VIRGINIA L. (1915- , Columbus)
Author, teacher, and Assistant Superintendent of Public Instruction in Ohio

LARLHAM, HATTIE LENA (1914- , St. Marys)
Nurse and administrator of better care for
handicapped children

LEEDY, EMILY L. (1921- , b. Jackson)
Educator and administrator, and state official

LYONS, RUTH (?- , Cincinnati)
Television and radio broadcaster; originator of Christmas Fund for children's hospitals

McCLELLAND, HELEN GRACE (?- , Fredericktown)
Nurse who won Distinguished Service Cross in World War I

MAHONEY, MARGARET A. (1894-1981, b. Cleveland)
Lawyer, state legislator, and majority leader of Ohio Senate

MERRITT, AGNES S. (1899- . Columbus)
Author of *Ohio Government Digest* and youth worker

MOCK, JERRIE L. (1925- , b. Newark)
First woman to fly solo around the world

NEMETH, MARY LOUISE SOLTES (1932- , Solon)
Vice-president of marketing for a business publishing company)

NORTON, ANDRE (ALICE MARY) (1912- , b. Cleveland)
Science fiction writer and author of 47 books for young adults

OAKLEY, ANNIE (1860-1926, b. Darke County)
World's best woman marksman

PAPIER, ROSE L. (1908- , Columbus)
Leader in medical care for the elderly

PHALER, EMMA (1882- , Columbus)
Bowling leader in promoting Women's International Bowling Congress

RANDOLPH, LOTTIE (1887-1968, b. Rushville)
First woman to serve as assistant director of a state department of agriculture in U.S.

REDINGER, RACHEL (1920- , Dover)
Founder and producer of Ohio Outdoor Historical Drama Association, Inc. and *Trumpet in the Land*

STERNE, BOBBIE (1919- , b. Moran)
Cincinnati's first elected woman mayor

STEWART, ELLA P. (1893- , Toledo)
Leader in women's affairs and world affairs lecturer

SWANBECK, ETHEL G. (1895- , Huron)
Served ten terms in Ohio General Assembly

UNTERMEYER, JEAN STARR (1866-1970, b. Zanesville)
Celebrated poet and translator

UPTON, HARRIET TAYLOR (1853-1945, b. Ravenna)
Suffragette and first woman appointed vice-chairman of Republican National Executive Committee

VALIQUETTE, MARIGENE (1924- , b. Toledo)
Member of Ohio House of Representatives and State Senate since 1962

WALKER, ANN B. (?- , Columbus)
Television director and first woman to cover the Ohio General Assembly for broadcasting

WALSH, STELLA (1911-1980, Cleveland)
Outstanding athlete and Olympic track star

WEBER, DORIS MARTHA (1898- , Hinckley)
Internationally-known photographer

WEISENBORN, CLARA E. (1907- , Dayton)
Member of Ohio General Assembly for 22 years

WELLS, MARION S. (?- , b. Licking County)
Leader in Ohio Society for Crippled Children and Ohio Mental Health Association

WHITEMAN, MARJORIE (1898- , Liberty Center)
Authority on international law

WILSON, NANCY (1937- . b. Chillicothe)
Singer and entertainer

BLACK LEADERS IN OHIO HISTORY

BRYANT, ELIZA (1827-1907, Cleveland)
Founder of Home for Aged Colored People supported by blacks

CHESNUTT, CHARLES WADDELL (1857-1932, Cleveland)
First nationally-known black writer of novels and short stories

DAY, WILLIAM HOWARD (1825-1900, Cleveland)
Librarian, newspaper editor, civil rights leader

DUNCANSON, ROBERT (1821-1872, b. Cincinnati)
Painter

DUNBAR, PAUL LAURENCE (1872-1906, Dayton)
Poet

GARVIN, CHARLES H. (1890-1968, Cleveland)
Medical doctor and professor of medicine

HOLLAND, JUSTIN MINER (1819-1887, Cleveland)
Musician, teacher and composer

HUNTER, JANE EDNA (1882-1971, Cleveland)
Founder and director of Phyllis Wheatley Association

LANGSTON, JOHN MERCER (1829-1897, Oberlin and Elyria)
First black elected to political office in U.S.

LEACH, ROBERT BOYD (1822-1863, Cleveland)
First black physician in Cleveland

MALVIN, JOHN (1795-1880, Cleveland)
Abolitionist and civil rights leader

MORGAN, GARRETT A. (1875-1963, Cleveland)
Inventor of traffic light and gas mask

OWENS, JESSE (1913-1980, Cleveland)
Olympic track and field star

PARKER, JOHN P. (?-?, Ripley)
Inventor

PARHAN, WILLIAM (?-?, Cincinnati)
First black graduate of Cincinnati Law School

POINDEXTER, JAMES PRESTON (?-?, Columbus)
Elected to Columbus City Council, 1881

SCARBOROUGH, WILLIAM SANDERS (1852-1926, Wilberforce)
Lecturer, scholar, linguist, and college president

SMITH, HARRY C. (1863-1941, Cleveland)
Newspaper editor, political leader and state legislator

TILLEY, MADISON (1809-1887, Cleveland)
Excavating contractor and political leader

TRUTH, SOJOURNER (1797-1883, Salem)
Orator, abolitionist, and reformer

TURNER, RACHEL WALKER (1868-1943, Cleveland)
Nationally-known soprano singer

WILCOX, SAMUEL T. (?-?, Cincinnati)
Operated first fancy grocery store in Cincinnati

WILLIAMS, GEORGE WASHINGTON (1849-1891, Cincinnati)
Attorney and historian; elected to Ohio General Assembly (1879)

WOODS, GRANVILLE T. (1856-1910, b. Columbus)
Inventor of steam boiler and automatic air brake

OHIO TEEN AGE HALL OF FAME

The Ohio Teen Age Hall of Fame, established in 1958 by James A. Rhodes, then state auditor, has a two-fold purpose:

1. To honor those whose achievements are already recognized.
2. To encourage today's youth in the development of talents necessary for the achievements of tomorrow.

Persons named to the Teen Age Hall of Fame made outstanding contributions to society before their twentieth birthdays.

Name	Achievement	Age
ERNEST R. BALL	Musician-Composer	15
JOE E. BROWN	Entertainer	14
WILSON BROWN	Soldier	19
CHARLES F. BRUSH	Scientist-Inventor	18
MILTON CANIFF	Cartoonist	18
ALICE CARY	Poet	17
PHOEBE CARY	Poet	13
HOWARD CHANDLER CHRISTY	Painter	16
JOHN CLEM	Soldier	9
ARTHUR COMPTON	Scientist	17
CROMWELL DIXON	Aviator	18
PAUL L. DUNBAR	Poet	16
THOMAS A. EDISON	Inventor	17
DANIEL D. EMMETT	Composer	18
DOROTHY GISH	Actress	14
LILLIAN GISH	Actress	17
WILLIAM GREEN	Labor Leader	18
ZANE GREY	Author	14
WILLIAM DEAN HOWELLS	Author	19
CHARLES F. KETTERING	Inventor-Scientist	19
TED LEWIS	Entertainer	13
MILLS BROTHERS	Singers	
HERBERT, HENRY, DONALD, JOHN Jr.		under 20
ANNIE OAKLEY	Markswoman	15
JESSE OWENS	Athlete	17
JACOB PARROTT	Soldier	18
EDDIE RICKENBACKER	World War I Hero and Auto Racing Pioneer	19
ROY ROGERS	Motion Picture Actor	17
PAUL A. SIPLE	Arctic Explorer	19
JOHN Q.A. WARD	Sculptor	19
ORVILLE WRIGHT	Aviator	17
WILBUR WRIGHT	Aviator	19

OHIO NOBEL PRIZE WINNERS

Awarded annually to individuals who have made the most outstanding contributions to their field during previous years.

CHARLES GATES DAWES	Nobel Prize for Peace, 1925
ARTHUR COMPTON	Nobel Prize for Physics, 1927

OHIO PULITZER PRIZE WINNERS

JAMES F. RHODES	History, 1918
LOUIS BROMFIELD	Literature, 1927
CANTON DAILY NEWS	Meritorious Public Service, 1927
DAVID DIETZ	Journalism, 1935
ANNE O'HARE McCORMICK	Journalism, 1937
PAUL H. BUCK	History, 1938
RUSSELL CROUSE	Drama, 1946
ARTHUR M. SCHLESINGER, Jr.	History, 1946
EDWARD D. KUEKES, Jr.	Newspaper Cartoons, 1953
BRUCE CATTON	History, 1954
LYNN HEINZERLING	Journalism, 1961
ARTHUR M. SCHLESINGER, Jr.	Biography, 1966
KNIGHT NEWSPAPERS	Journalism, 1968
AKRON BEACON JOURNAL	Journalism, 1971
XENIA DAILY GAZETTE	Journalism, 1975

OHIOANS IN HALL OF FAME FOR GREAT AMERICANS

Located on the campus of New York University, the Hall of Fame for Great Americans honors Americans of the past whose lives embody the highest ideals of American life. Members are admitted every five years. Ohio members and their dates of admission are:

ULYSSES S. GRANT, 1900
WILLIAM TECUMSEH SHERMAN, 1905
GEORGE BANCROFT, 1910
WILBUR WRIGHT, 1955
THOMAS ALVA EDISON, 1960
ORVILLE WRIGHT, 1965

CONSTITUTION OF THE STATE OF OHIO

Adopted March 10, 1851 with amendments to 1979 as supplied by the Office of the Secretary of State.
* This symbol denotes portions left out of this printing of the Ohio Constitution for lack of space.

[Preamble]

We, the people of the State of Ohio, grateful to Almighty God for our freedom, to secure its blessings and promote our common welfare, do establish this Constitution.

ARTICLE I: Bill of Rights
§1 Right to freedom and protection of property.

All men are, by nature, free and independent, and have certain inalienable rights, among which are those of enjoying and defending life and liberty, acquiring, possessing, and protecting property, and seeking and obtaining happiness and safety.

§2 Right to alter, reform, or abolish government, and repeal special privileges.

All political power is inherent in the people. Government is instituted for their equal protection and benefit, and they have the right to alter, reform, or abolish the same, whenever they may deem it necessary; and no special privileges or immunities shall ever be granted, that may not be altered, revoked, or repealed by the general assembly.

§3 [Right to assemble together.]

The people have the right to assemble together, in a peaceable manner, to consult for their common good; to instruct their representatives; and to petition the general assembly for the redress of grievances.

§4 [Bearing arms; standing armies; subordination of military power.]

The people have the right to bear arms for their defense and security; but standing armies, in time of peace, are dangerous to liberty, and shall not be kept up; and the military shall be in strict subordination to the civil power.

§5 Trial by jury; reform in civil jury system.

The right of trial by jury shall be inviolate, except that, in civil cases, laws may be passed to authorize the rendering of a verdict by the concurrence of not less than three-fourths of the jury.

§6 [Slavery and involuntary servitude.]

There shall be no slavery in this state; nor involuntary servitude, unless for the punishment of crime.

§7 [Rights of conscience; education; necessity of religion and knowledge.]

All men have a natural and indefeasible right to worship Almighty God according to the dictates of their own conscience. No person shall be compelled to attend, erect, or support any place of worship, or maintain any form of worship, against his consent; and no preference shall be given, by law, to any religious society; nor shall any interference with the rights of conscience be permitted. No religious test shall be required, as a qualification for office, nor shall any person be incompetent to be a witness on account of his religious belief; but nothing herein shall be construed to dispense with oaths and affirmations. Religion, morality, and knowledge, however, being essential to good government, it shall be the duty of the general assembly to pass suitable laws to protect every religious denomination in the peaceable enjoyment of its own mode of public worship, and to encourage schools and the means of instruction.

§8 [Writ of habeas corpus.]

The privilege of the writ of habeas corpus shall not be suspended, unless, in cases of rebellion or invasion, the public safety require it.

§9 Bailable offenses; of bail, fine, and punishment.

All persons shall be bailable by sufficient sureties, except for capital offenses where the proof is evident or the presumption great. Excessive bail shall not be required; nor excessive fines imposed; nor cruel and unusual punishments inflicted.

§10 [Trial of accused persons and their rights; depositions by state and comment on failure of accused to testify in criminal cases.]

Except in cases of impeachment, cases arising in the army and navy, or in the militia when in actual service in time of war or public danger, and cases involving offenses for which the penalty provided is less than imprisonment in the penitentiary, no person shall be held to answer for a capital, or otherwise infamous, crime, unless on presentment or indictment of a grand jury; and the number of persons necessary to constitute such grand jury and the number thereof necessary to concur in finding such indictment shall be determined by law. In any trial, in any court, the party accused shall be allowed to appear and defend in person and with counsel; to demand the nature and cause of the accusation against him, and to have a copy thereof; to meet the witnesses face to face, and to have compulsory process to procure the attendance of witnesses in his behalf, and a speedy public trial by an impartial jury of the county in which the offense is alleged to have been committed; but provision may be made by law for the taking of the deposition by the accused or by the state, to be used for or against the accused, of any trial, always securing to the accused means and the opportunity to be present in person and with counsel at the taking of such deposition, and to examine the witness face to face as fully and in the same manner as if in court. No person shall be compelled, in any criminal case, to be a witness against himself; but his failure to testify may be considered by the court and jury and may be made the subject of comment by counsel. No person shall be twice put in jeopardy for the same offense.

§11 [Freedom of speech and of the press; libel.]

Every citizen may freely speak, write, and publish his sentiments on all subjects, being responsible for the abuse of the right; and no law shall be passed to restrain or abridge the liberty of speech, or of the press. In all criminal prosecutions for libel, the truth may be given in evidence to the jury, and if it shall appear to the jury, that the matter charged as libelous is true, and was published with good motives, and for justifiable ends, the party shall be acquitted.

§12 Transportation, etc., for crime.

No person shall be transported out of the state, for any offense committed within the same; and no conviction shall work corruption of blood, or forfeiture of estate.

§13 [Quartering of troops.]

No soldier shall, in time of peace, be quartered in any house, without the consent of the owner; nor, in time of war, except in the manner prescribed by law.

§14 Search warrants and general warrants.

The right of the people to be secure in their persons, houses, papers, and possessions, against unreasonable searches and seizures shall not be violated; and no warrant shall issue, but upon probable cause, supported by oath or affirmation, particularly describing the place to be searched and the person and things to be seized.

§15 No imprisonment for debt.

No person shall be imprisoned for debt in any civil action, on mesne or final process, unless in cases of fraud.

§16 [Redress in courts.]

All courts shall be open, and every person, for an injury done him in his land, goods, person, or reputation, shall have remedy by due course of law, and shall have justice administered without denial or delay.

[Suits against the state.] Suits may be brought against the state, in such courts and in such manner, as may be provided by law.

§17 Hereditary privileges, etc.

No hereditary emoluments, honors, or privileges, shall ever be granted or conferred by this state.

§18 Suspension of laws.

No power of suspending laws shall ever be exercised, except by the general assembly.

§19 [Inviolability of private property.]

Private property shall ever be held inviolate, but subservient to the public welfare. When taken in time of war or other public exigency, imperatively requiring its immediate seizure or for the purpose of making or repairing roads, which shall be open to the public, without charge, a compensation shall be made to the owner, in money, and in all other cases, where private property shall be taken for public use, a compensation therefor shall first be made in money, or first secured by a deposit of money; and such compensation shall be assessed by a jury, without deduction for benefits to any property of the owner.

§19a Damage for wrongful death.

The amount of damages recoverable by civil action in the courts for death caused by the wrongful act, neglect, or default of another, shall not be limited by law.

§20 Powers reserved to the people.

This enumeration of rights shall not be construed to impair or deny others retained by the people; and all powers, not herein delegated, remain with the people.

ARTICLE II: Legislative
§1 [In whom legislative power is vested.]

The legislative power of the state shall be vested in a general assembly consisting of a senate and house of representatives but the people reserve to themselves the power to propose to the general assembly laws and amendments to the constitution, and to adopt or reject the same at the polls on a referendum vote as hereinafter provided. They also reserve the power to adopt or reject any law, section of any law or any item in any law appropriating money passed by the general assembly, except as hereinafter provided; and independent of the general assembly to propose amendments to the constitution and to adopt or reject the same at the polls. The limitations expressed in the constitution, on the power of the general assembly to enact laws, shall be deemed limitations on the power of the people to enact laws.

§1a [Initiative petition; text filed with secretary of state; submission.]

The first aforestated power reserved by the people is designated the initiative, and the signatures of ten per centum of the electors shall be required upon a petition to propose an amendment to the constitution. When a petition signed by the aforesaid required number of electors, shall have been filed with the secretary of state, and verified as herein provided, proposing an amendment to the constitution, the full text of which shall have been set forth in such petition, the secretary of state shall submit for the approval or rejection of the electors, the proposed amendment, in the manner hereinafter provided, at the next succeeding regular or general election in any year occurring subsequent to ninety days after the filing of such petition. The initiative petitions, above described, shall have printed across the top thereof; "Amendment to the Constitution Proposed by Initiative Petition to be Submitted Directly to the Electors."

§1b [Transmission to legislature; referendum; constitutional amendments.]

When at any time, not less than ten days prior to the commencement of any session of the general assembly, there shall have been filed with the secretary of state a petition signed by three per centum of the electors and verified as herein provided, proposing a law, the full text of which shall have been set forth in such petition, the secretary of state shall transmit the same to the general assembly as soon as it convenes. If said proposed law shall be passed by the general assembly, either as petitioned for or in an amended form, it shall be subject to the referendum. If it shall not be passed, or if it shall be passed on an amended form, or if no action shall be taken thereon within four months from the time it is received by the general assembly, it shall be submitted by the secretary of state to the electors for their approval or rejection at the next regular or general election, if such submission shall be demanded by supplementary petition verified as herein provided and signed by not less than three per centum of the electors in addition to those signing the original petition, which supplementary petition must be signed and filed with the secretary of state within ninety days after the proposed laws shall have been rejected by the general assembly or after the expiration of such term of four months, if no action has been taken thereon, or after the law as passed by the general assembly shall have been filed by the governor in the office of the secretary of state. The proposed law shall be submitted in the form demanded by such supplementary petition, which form shall be either as first petitioned for or with any amendment or amendments which may have been incorporated therein by either branch or by both branches, of the general assembly. If a proposed law so submitted is approved by a majority of the electors voting thereon, it shall be the law and shall go into effect as herein provided in lieu of any amended form of said law which may have been passed by the general assembly, and such amended law passed by the general assembly shall not go into effect until and unless the law proposed by supplementary petition shall have been rejected by the electors. All such initiative petitions, last above described, shall have printed across the top thereof, in case of proposed laws: "Law Proposed by Initiative Petition First to be Submitted to the General Assembly." Ballots shall be so printed as to permit an affirmative or negative vote upon each measure submitted to the electors. Any proposed law or amendment to the constitution submitted to the electors as provided in section 1a and section 1b, if approved by a majority of the electors voting thereon, shall take effect thirty days after the election at which it was approved and shall be published by the secretary of state. If conflicting proposed laws or conflicting proposed amendments to the constitution shall be approved at the same election by a majority of the total number of votes cast for and against the same, the one receiving the highest number of affirmative votes shall be the law, or in the case of amendments to the constitution shall be the amendment to the constitution. No law proposed by initiative petition and approved by the electors shall be subject to the veto of the governor.

§1c [Referendum petition; effective date of laws; item of law submitted.]

The second aforestated power reserved by the people is designated the referendum, and the signatures of six per centum of the electors shall be required upon a petition to order the submission to the electors of this state for their approval or rejection, of any law, section of any law or any item in any law appropriating money passed by the general assembly. No law passed by the general assembly shall go into effect until ninety days after it shall have been filed by the governor in the office of the secretary of state, except as herein provided. When a petition, signed by six per centum of the electors of the state and verified as herein provided, shall have been filed with the secretary of state within ninety days after any law shall have been filed by the governor in the office of the secretary of state, ordering that such law, section of such law or any item in such law appropriating money be submitted to the electors of the state for their approval or rejection, the secretary of state shall submit to the electors of the state for their approval or rejection such law, section or item, in the manner herein provided, at the next succeeding regular or general election in any year occuring subsequent to sixty days after the filing of such petition, and no such law, section or item shall go into effect until and unless approved by a majority of those voting upon the same. If, however, a referendum petition is filed against any such section or item, the remainder of the law shall not thereby be prevented or delayed from going into effect.

§1d [Effective date of laws not subject to referendum; emergency laws.]

Laws providing for tax levies, appropriations for the current expenses of the state government and state institutions, and emergency laws necessary for the immediate preservation of the public peace, health or safety, shall go into immediate effect. Such emergency laws upon a yea and nay vote must receive the vote of two-thirds of all the members elected to each branch of the general assembly, and the reasons for such necessity shall be set forth in one section of the law, which section shall be passed only upon a yea and nay vote, upon a separate roll call thereon. The laws mentioned in this section shall not be subject to the referendum.

§1e [When powers not to be used.]

The powers defined herein as the "initiative" and "referendum" shall not be used to pass a law authorizing any classification of property for the purpose of levying different rates of taxation thereon or of authorizing the levy of any single tax on land or land values or land sites at a higher rate or by a different rule than is or may be applied to improvements thereon or to personal property.

§1f [Power of municipalities.]

The initiative and referendum powers are hereby reserved to the people of each municipality on all questions which such municipalities may now or hereafter be authorized by law to control by legislative action; such powers shall be exercised in the manner now or hereafter provided by law.

*§1g [Initiative, supplementary, referendum petition; notice required; ballots.]

§2 [Election and term of legislators.]

Representatives shall be elected biennially by the electors of the respective house of representatives districts; their term of office shall commence on the first day of January next thereafter and continue two years.

Senators shall be elected by the electors of the respective senate districts; their terms of office shall commence on the first day of January next after their election. All terms of senators which commence on the first day of January, 1969 shall be four years, and all terms which commence on the first day of January, 1971 shall be four years. Thereafter, except for the filling of vacancies for unexpired terms, senators shall be elected to and hold offices for terms of four years.

§3 [Residence.]

Senators and representatives shall have resided in their respective districts one year next preceding their election, unless they shall have been absent on the public business of the United States, or of this State.

§4 Eligibility.

No member of the general assembly shall, during the term for which he was elected, unless during such term he resigns therefrom, hold any public office under the United States, or this state, or a political subdivision thereof; but this provision does not extend to officers of a political party, notaries public, or officers of the militia or of the United States armed forces.

No member of the general assembly shall, during the term for which he was elected, or for one year thereafter, be appointed to any public office under this state, which office was created or the compensation of which increased, during the term for which he was elected.

§5 Who shall not hold office.

No person hereafter convicted of an embezzlement of the public funds, shall hold any office in this state; nor shall any person holding public money for disbursement, or otherwise, have a seat in the general assembly, until he shall have accounted for, and paid such money into the treasury.

§6 Powers of each house.

Each House shall be judge of the election, returns, and qualifications of its own members. A majority of all the members elected to each House shall be a quorum to do business; but, a less number may adjourn from day to day, and compel the attendance of absent members, in such manner, and under such penalties, as shall be prescribed by law.

Each House may punish its members for disorderly conduct and, with the concurrence of two-thirds of the members elected thereto, expel a member, but not the second time for the same cause.

Each House has all powers necessary to provide for its safety and the undisturbed transaction of its business, and to obtain, through committees or otherwise, information affecting legislative action under consideration or in contemplation, or with reference to any alleged breach of its privileges or misconduct of its members, and to that end to enforce the attendance and testimony of witnesses, and the production of books and papers.

§7 Organization of House of Representatives.

The mode of organizing each House of the general assembly shall be prescribed by law.

Each House, except as otherwise provided in this Constitution, shall choose its own officers. The presiding officer in the Senate shall be designated as president of the Senate and in the House of Representatives as speaker of the House of Representatives.

Each House shall determine its own rules of proceeding.

§8 [Sessions of the general assembly.]

Each general assembly shall convene in first regular session on the first Monday of January in the odd-numbered year, or on the succeeding day if the first Monday of January is a legal holiday, and in second regular session on the same date of the following year. Either the governor, or the presiding officers of the general assembly chosen by the members thereof, acting jointly, may convene the general assembly in special session by a proclamation which may limit the purpose of the session. If the presiding officer of the Senate is not chosen by the members thereof, the President pro tempore of the Senate may act with the speaker of the House of Representatives in the calling of a special session.

§9 Journal, and yeas and nays.

Each House shall keep a correct journal of its proceedings, which shall be published. At the desire of any two members, the yeas and nays shall be entered upon the journal; and, on the passage of every bill, in either house, the vote shall be taken by yeas and nays, and entered upon the journal.

*§10 Right of members to protest.

*§11 Vacancies in either house, how filled.

§12 Privilege of members from arrest, and of speech.

Senators and representatives, during the session of the general assembly, and in going to, and returning from the same, shall be privileged from arrest, in all cases, except treason, felony, or breach of the peace; and for any speech, or debate, in either house, they shall not be questioned elsewhere.

§13 When session to be public.

The proceedings of both houses shall be public, except in cases which, in the opinion of two-thirds of those present, require secrecy.

§14 Power of adjournment.

Neither House shall, without the consent of the other, adjourn for more than five days, Sundays excluded; nor to any other place than that, in which the two Houses are in session.

§15 [How bills shall be passed.]

(A) The general assembly shall enact no law except by bill, and no bill shall be passed without the concurrence of a majority of the members elected to each house. Bills may originate in either house, but may be altered, amended, or rejected in the other.

(B) The style of the laws of this state shall be, "be it enacted by the general assembly of the state of Ohio."

(C) Every bill shall be considered by each house on three different days, unless two-thirds of the members elected to the house in which it is pending suspend this requirement, and every individual consideration of a bill or action suspending the requirement shall be recorded in the journal of the respective house. No bill may be passed until the bill has been reproduced and distributed to members of the house in which it is pending and every amendment been made available upon a member's request.

(D) No bill shall contain more than one subject, which shall be clearly expressed in its title. No law shall be revived or amended unless the new act contains the entire act revived, or the section or sections amended, and the section or sections amended shall be repealed.

(E) Every bill which has passed both houses of the general assembly shall be signed by the presiding officer of each house to certify that the procedural requirements for passage have been met and shall be presented forthwith to the governor for his approval.

(F) Every joint resolution which has been adopted in both houses of the general assembly shall be signed by the presiding officer of each house to certify that the procedural requirements for adoption have been met and shall forthwith be filed with the secretary of state.

§16 [Bills to be signed by governor; veto.]

If the governor approves an act, he shall sign it, it becomes law and he shall file it with the secretary of state.

If he does not approve it, he shall return it with his objections in writing, to the house in which it originated, which shall enter the objections at large upon its journal, and may then reconsider the vote on its passage. If three-fifths of the members elected to the house of origin vote to repass the bill, it shall be sent, with the objections of the governor, to the other house, which may also reconsider the vote on its passage. If three-fifths of the members elected to the second house vote to repass it, it becomes law notwithstanding the objections of the governor, and the presiding officer of the second house shall file it with the secretary of state. In no case shall a bill be repassed by a smaller vote than is required by the constitution on its original passage. In all cases of reconsideration the vote of each house shall be determined by yeas and nays, and the names of the members voting for and against the bill shall be entered upon the journal.

If a bill is not returned by the governor within ten days, Sundays excepted, after being presented to him, it becomes law in like manner as if he had signed it, unless the general assembly by adjournment prevents its return; in which case, it becomes law unless, within ten days after such adjournment, it is filed by him, with his objections in writing, in the office of the secretary of state. The governor shall file with the secretary of state every bill not returned by him to the house of origin that becomes law with his signature.

The governor may disapprove any item or items in any bill making an appropriation of money and the item or items, so disapproved, shall be void, unless repassed in the manner prescribed by this section for the repassage of a bill.

§17-19 Repealed.

*§20 Term of office, and compensation of officers in certain cases.

*§21 Contested elections.

§22 Appropriations.

No money shall be drawn from the treasury, except in pursuance of a specific appropriation, made by law; and no appropriation shall be made for a longer period than two years.

§23 Impeachments; how instituted and conducted.

The house of representatives shall have the sole power of impeachment, but a majority of the members elected must concur therein. Impeachments shall be tried by the senate; and the senators, when sitting for that purpose, shall be upon oath or affirmation to do justice according to law and evidence. No person shall be convicted without the concurrence of two-thirds of the senators.

§24 Who liable to impeachment, and punishment.

The governor, judges, and all state officers, may be impeached for any misdemeanor in office; but judgment shall not extend further than removal from office, and disqualification to hold any office under the authority of this state. The party impeached, whether convicted or not, shall be liable to indictment, trial, and judgment, according to law.

§25 Repealed.

§26 What laws to have a uniform operation.

All laws, of a general nature, shall have a uniform operation throughout the state; nor, shall any act, except such as relates to public schools, be passed, to take effect upon the approval of any other authority than the general assembly, except, as otherwise provided in this constitution.

*§27 [Election and appointment of officers; filling vacancies.]

§28 Retroactive laws.

The general assembly shall have no power to pass retroactive laws, or laws impairing the obligation of contracts; but may, by general laws, authorize courts to carry into effect, upon such terms as shall be just and equitable, the manifest intention of parties, and officers, by curing omissions, defects, and errors, in instruments and proceedings, arising out of their want of conformity with the laws of this state.

§29 No extra compensation.

No extra compensation shall be made to any officer, public agent, or contractor, after the service shall have been rendered, or the contract entered into; nor shall any money be paid, on any claim, the subject matter of which shall not have been provided for by pre-existing law, unless such compensation, or claim, be allowed by two-thirds of the members elected to each branch of the general assembly.

§30 New counties.

No new county shall contain less than four hundred square miles of territory, nor shall any county be reduced below that amount; and all laws creating new counties, changing county lines, or removing county seats, shall, before taking effect, be submitted to the electors of the several counties to be affected thereby, at the next general election after the passage thereof, and be adopted by a majority of all the electors voting at such election, in each of said counties; but any county now or hereafter containing one hundred thousand in-

habitants, may be divided, whenever a majority of the voters residing in each of the proposed divisions shall approve of the law passed for that purpose; but no town or city within the same shall be divided, nor shall either of the divisions contain less than twenty thousand inhabitants.

§31 Compensation of members and officers of the general assembly.

The members and officers of the general assembly shall receive a fixed compensation, to be prescribed by law, and no other allowance or perquisites, either in the payment of postage or otherwise; and no change in their compensation shall take effect during their term of office.

*§32 Divorces and judicial power.

§33 Mechanics' and builders' liens.

Laws may be passed to secure to mechanics, artisans, laborers, sub-contractors and material men, their just dues by direct lien upon the property, upon which they have bestowed labor or for which they have furnished material. No other provision of the constitution shall impair or limit this power.

§34 Welfare of employes.

Laws may be passed fixing and regulating the hours of labor, establishing a minimum wage, and providing for the comfort, health, safety and general welfare of all employes; and no other provision of the constitution shall impair or limit this power.

§35 Workmen's compensation.

For the purpose of providing compensation to workmen and their dependents, for death, injuries or occupational disease, occasioned in the course of such workmen's employment, laws may be passed establishing a state fund to be created by compulsory contribution thereto by employers, and administered by the state, determining the terms and conditions upon which payment shall be made therefrom. Such compensation shall be in lieu of all other rights to compensation, or damages, for such death, injuries, or occupational disease, and any employer who pays the premium or compensation provided by law, passed in accordance herewith, shall not be liable to respond in damages at common law or by statute for such death, injuries or occupational disease. Laws may be passed establishing a board which may be empowered to classify all occupations, according to their degree of hazard, to fix rates of contribution to such fund according to such classification, and to collect, administer and distribute such fund, and to determine all right of claimants thereto. Such board shall set aside as a separate fund such proportion of the contributions paid by employers as in its judgment may be necessary, not to exceed one per centum thereof in any year, and so as to equalize, insofar as possible, the burden thereof, to be expended by such board in such manner as may be provided by law for the investigation and prevention of industrial accidents and diseases. Such board shall have full power and authority to hear and determine whether or not an injury, disease or death resulted because of the failure of the employer to comply with any specific requirement for the protection of the lives, health or safety of employes, enacted by the General Assembly or in the form of an order adopted by such board, and its decision shall be final; and for the purpose of such investigations and inquiries it may appoint referees. When it is found, upon hearing, that an injury, disease or death resulted because of such failure by the employer, such amount as shall be found to be just, not greater than fifty nor less than fifteen per centum of the maximum award established by law, shall be added by the board, to the amount of the compensation that may be awarded on account of such injury, disease, or death, and paid in like manner as other awards; and, if such compensation is paid from the state fund, the premium of such employer shall be increased in such amount, covering such period of time as may be fixed, as will recoup the state fund in the amount of such additional award, notwithstanding any and all other provisions in this constitution.

§36 Conservation of natural resources.

Laws may be passed to encourage forestry and agriculture, and to that end areas devoted exclusively to forestry may be exempted, in whole or in part, from taxation. Notwithstanding the provisions of section 2 of Article XII, laws may be passed to provide that land devoted exclusively to agricultural use be valued for real property tax purposes at the current value such land has for such agricultural use. Laws may also be passed to provide for the deferral or recoupment of any part of the difference in the dollar amount of real property tax levied in any year on land valued in accordance with its agricultural use and the dollar amount of real property tax which would have been levied upon such land had it been valued for such year in accordance with section 2 of Article XII. Laws may also be passed to provide for converting into forest reserves such lands or parts of lands as have been or may be forfeited to the state, and to authorize the acquiring of other lands for that purpose; also, to provide for the conservation of the natural resources of the state, including streams lakes, submerged and swamp lands and the development and regulation of water power and the formation of drainage and conservation districts; and to provide for the regulation of methods of mining, weighing, measuring and marketing coal, oil, gas and all other minerals.

§37 Eight hour day on public work.

Except in cases of extraordinary emergency, not to exceed eight hours shall constitute a day's work, and not to exceed forty-eight hours a week's work, for workmen engaged on any public work carried on or aided by the state, or any political subdivision thereof, whether done by contract, or otherwise.

§38 Removal of officials.

Laws shall be passed providing for the prompt removal from office, upon complaint and hearing, of all officers, including state officers, judges and members of the general assembly, for any misconduct involving moral turpitude or for other cause provided by law; and this method of removal shall be in addition to impeachment or other method of removal authorized by the constitution.

§39 Regulating expert testimony in criminal trials.

Laws may be passed for the regulation of the use of expert witnesses and expert testimony in criminal trials and proceedings.

§40 Registering and warranting land titles.

Laws may be passed providing for a system of registering, transferring, insuring and guaranteeing land titles by the state or by the counties thereof, and for settling and determining adverse or other claims to and interests in, lands the titles to which are so registered, insured or guaranteed, and for the creation and collection of guaranty funds by fees to be assessed against lands, the titles to which are registered; and judicial powers with right of appeal may by law be conferred upon county recorders or other officers in matters arising under the operation of such system.

§41 [Prison labor.]

Laws may be passed providing for and regulating the occupation and employment of prisoners sentenced to the several penal institutions and reformatories in the state.

§42 [Continuity of government operations in emergencies caused by enemy attack.]

The General Assembly shall have the power and the immediate duty to pass laws to provide for prompt and temporary succession to the powers and duties of public offices, of whatever nature and whether filled by election or appointment, the incumbents of which may become unavailable for carrying on the powers and duties of such offices and to pass such other laws as may be necessary and proper for insuring the continuity of governmental operations in periods of emergency resulting from disaster caused by enemy attack.

ARTICLE III: Executive
§1 Executive department.

The executive department shall consist of a governor, lieutenant governor, secretary of state, auditor of state, treasurer of state, and an attorney general, who shall be elected on the first Tuesday after the first Monday in November, by the electors of the state, and at the places of voting for members of the general assembly.

*§1a [Joint vote cast for governor and lieutenant.]

§1b [Lieutenant governor duties assigned by governor.]

The lieutenant governor shall perform such duties in the executive department as are assigned to him by the governor and as are prescribed by law.

§2 Term of office.

The governor, lieutenant governor, secretary of state, treasurer of state, and attorney general shall hold their offices for four years commencing on the second Monday of January, l959. Their terms of office shall continue until their succesors are elected and qualified. The auditor of state shall hold his office for a term of two years from the second

Monday of January, 1961 to the second Monday of January, 1963 and thereafter shall hold his office for a four year term. No person shall hold the office of governor for a period longer than two successive terms of four years.

§3 Election returns.

The returns of every election for the officers, named in the foregoing section, shall be sealed and transmitted to the seat of government, by the returning officers, directed to the President of the Senate, who, during the first week of the next regular session, shall open and publish them, and declare the result, in the presence of a majority of the members of each House of the General Assembly. The joint candidates having the highest number of votes cast for governor and lieutenant governor and the person having the highest number of votes for any other office shall be declared duly elected; but if any two or more have an equal and the highest number of votes for the same office or officers, one of them or any two for whom joint votes were cast for governor and lieutenant governor, shall be chosen by joint vote of both houses.

§4 Repealed.

§5 Executive power vested in governor.

The supreme executive power of this state shall be vested in the governor.

§6 He may require written information, etc.

He may require information, in writing from the officers in the executive department, upon any subject relating to the duties of their respective offices; and shall see that the laws are faithfully executed.

§7 He shall recommend measures, etc.

He shall communicate at every session, by message, to the general assembly, the condition of the state, and recommend such measures as he shall deem expedient.

§8 Limiting power of general assembly in extra session.

The governor on extraordinary occasions may convene the general assembly by proclamation and shall state in the proclamation the purpose for which such special session is called, and no other business shall be transacted at such special session except that named in the proclamation, or in a subsequent public proclamation or message to the general assembly issued by the governor during said special session, but the general assembly may provide for the expenses of the session and other matters incidental thereto.

§9 When he may adjourn the general assembly.

In case of disagreement between the two houses, in respect to the time of adjournment, he shall have power to adjourn the general assembly to such time as he may think proper, but not beyond the regular meetings thereof.

§10 Commander-in-chief of militia.

He shall be commander-in-chief of the military and naval forces of the state, except when they shall be called in to the service of the United States.

§11 May grant reprieves, commutations, and pardons.

He shall have power, after conviction, to grant reprieves, commutations, and pardons, for all crimes and offenses, except treason and cases of impeachment, upon such conditions as he may think proper; subject, however, to such regulations as to the manner of applying for pardons, as may be prescribed by law. Upon conviction for treason, he may suspend the execution of the sentence, and report the case to the general assembly, at its next meeting, when the general assembly shall either pardon, commute the sentence, direct its execution, or grant a further reprieve. He shall communicate to the general assembly, at every regular session, each case of reprieve, commutation, or pardon granted, stating the name and crime of the convict, the sentence, its date, and the date of the commutation, pardon, or reprieve, with his reasons therefor.

§12 Seal of state, and by whom kept.

All grants and commissions shall be issued in the name, and by the authority, of the state of Ohio; sealed with the great seal; signed by the governor, and countersigned by the secretary of state.

*§13 How grants and commissions used.

§14 Who ineligible for governor.

No member of congress, or other person holding office under the authority of this state, or of the United States, shall execute the office of governor, except as herein provided.

§15 Who shall fill his place when vacancy occurs.

(A) In the case of the death, conviction on impeachment, resignation, or removal, of the Governor, the Lieutenant Governor shall succeed to the office of Governor.

(B) When the Governor is unable to discharge the duties of office by reason of disability, the Lieutenant Governor shall serve as governor until the Governor's disability terminates.

(C) In the event of a vacancy in the office of governor or when the Governor is unable to discharge the duties of office, the line of succession to the office of governor or to the position of serving as governor for the duration of the Governor's disability shall proceed from the Lieutenant Governor to the President of the senate and then to the Speaker of the House of Representatives.

(D) Any person serving as governor for the duration of the Governor's disability shall have the powers, duties, and compensation of the office of governor. Any person who succeeds to the office of governor shall have the powers, duties, title, and compensation of the office of governor.

(E) No person shall simultaneously serve as Governor and Lieutenant Governor, President of the senate, or Speaker of the House of Representatives, nor shall any person simultaneously receive the compensation of the office of governor and that of lieutenant governor, president of the senate, or speaker of the house of representatives.

§16 Repealed.

*§17 If vacancy shall occur while executing the office of governor, who shall act.

§18 What vacancies governor to fill.

Should the office of Auditor of State, Treasurer of State, Secretary of State, or Attorney General become vacant, for any of the causes specified in the fifteenth section of the article, the Governor shall fill the vacancy until the disability is removed, or a successor elected and qualified. Such successor shall be elected for the unexpired term of the vacant office at the first general election in an even numbered year that occurs more than forty days after the vacancy has occurred; provided, that when the unexpired term ends within one year immediately following the date of such general election, an election to fill such unexpired term shall not be held and the appointment shall be for such unexpired term.

§19 Compensation.

The officers mentioned in this article shall, at stated times, receive for their services, a compensation to be established by law, which shall neither be increased nor diminished during the period for which they shall have been elected.

§20 Officers to report to governor, and when.

The officers of the executive department, and of the public state institutions shall, at least five days preceding each regular session of the general assembly, severally report to the governor, who shall transmit such reports, with his message to the general assembly.

§21 [Appointments subject to advice and consent of Senate.]

When required by law, appointments to state offices shall be subject to the advice and consent of the Senate. All statutory provisions requiring advice and consent of the Senate to appointments to state office heretofore enacted by the General Assembly are hereby validated, ratified and confirmed as to all appointments made hereafter, but any such provision may be altered or repealed by law.

No appointment shall be consented to without concurrence of a majority of the total number of Senators provided for by this Constitution, except as hereinafter provided for in the case of failure of the Senate to act. If the Senate has acted upon any appointment to which its consent is required and has refused to consent, and appointment of another person shall be made to fill the vacancy.

If an appointment is submitted during a session of the General Assembly, it shall be acted upon by the Senate during such session of the General Assembly, except that if such session of the General Assembly adjourns sine die within ten days after such submission without acting upon such appointment, it may be acted upon at the next session of the General Assembly.

If an appointment is made after the Senate has adjourned sine die, it shall be submitted to the Senate during the next session of the General Assembly.

In acting upon an appointment a vote shall be taken by a yea and nay vote of the members of the Senate and shall be entered upon its journal. Failure of the Senate to act by a roll call vote on an appointment by the governor within the time provided for herein shall constitute consent to such appointment.

*§22 [Jurisdiction to determine disability; succession.]

ARTICLE IV: Judicial
§1 In whom judicial power vested.

The judicial power of the state is vested in a supreme court, courts of appeals, courts of common pleas and divisions thereof, and such other courts inferior to the supreme court as may from time to time be established by law.

§2 The supreme court.

(A) The supreme court shall, until otherwise provided by law, consist of seven judges, who shall be known as the chief justice and justices. In case of the absence or disability of the chief justice, the judge having the period of longest total service upon the court shall be the acting chief justice. If any member of the court shall be unable, by reason of illness, disability or disqualification, to hear, consider and decide a cause or causes, the chief justice or the acting chief justice may direct any judge of any court of appeals to sit with the judges of the supreme court in the place and stead of the absent judge. A majority of the supreme court shall be necessary to constitute a quorum or to render a judgment.

(B)(1) The supreme court shall have original jurisdiction in the following:

(a) Quo warranto;

(b) Mandamus;

(c) Habeas corpus;

(d) Prohibition;

(e) Procedendo;

(f) In any cause on review as may be necessary to its complete determination;

(g) Admission to the practice of law, the discipline of persons so admitted, and all other matters relating to the practice of law.

(2) The supreme court shall have appellate jurisdiction as follows:

(a) In appeals from the courts of appeals as a matter of right in the following:

(i) Cases originating in the courts of appeals;

(ii) Cases in which the death penalty has been affirmed;

(iii) Cases involving questions arising under the constitution of the United States or of this state.

(b) In appeals from the courts of appeals in cases of felony on leave first obtained.

(c) Such revisory jurisdiction of the proceedings of administrative officers or agencies as may be conferred by law;

(d) In cases of public or great general interest, the supreme court may direct any court of appeals to certify its record to the supreme court, and may review and affirm, modify, or reverse the judgment of the court of appeals;

(e) The supreme court shall review and affirm, modify, or reverse the judgment in any case certified by any court of appeals pursuant to section 3(B)(4) of this article.

(3) No law shall be passed or rule made whereby any person shall be prevented from invoking the original jurisdiction of the supreme court.

(C) The decisions in all cases in the supreme court shall be reported, together with the reasons therefor.

§3 Court of appeals.

(A) The state shall be divided by law into compact appellate districts in each of which there shall be a court of appeals consisting of three judges. Laws may be passed increasing the number of judges in any district wherein the volume of business may require such additional judge or judges. In districts having additional judges, three judges shall participate in the hearing and disposition of each case. The court shall hold sessions in each county of the district as the necessity arises. The county commissioners of each county shall provide a proper and convenient place for the court of appeals to hold court.

(B)(1) The courts of appeals shall have original jurisdiction in the following:

(a) Quo warranto;

(b) Mandamus;

(c) Habeas corpus;

(d) Prohibition;

(e) Procedendo;

(f) In any cause on review as may be necessary to its complete determination.

(2) Courts of appeals shall have such jurisdiction as may be provided by law to review and affirm, modify, or reverse judgments or final orders of the courts of record inferior to the court of appeals within the district and shall have such appellate jurisdiction as may be provided by law to review and affirm, modify, or reverse final orders or actions of administrative officers or agencies.

(3) A majority of the judges hearing the cause shall be necessary to render a judgment. Judgments of the courts of appeals are final except as provided in section 2(B)(2) of this article. No judgment resulting from a trial by jury shall be reversed on the weight of the evidence except by the concurrence of all three judges hearing the cause.

(4) Whenever the judges of a court of appeals find that a judgment upon which they have agreed is in conflict with a judgment pronounced upon the same question by any other court of appeals of the state, the judges shall certify the record of the case to the supreme court for review and final determination.

(C) Laws may be passed providing for the reporting of cases in the courts of appeals.

§4 Common pleas court.

(A) There shall be a court of common pleas and such divisions thereof as may be established by law serving each county of the state. Any judge of a court of common pleas or a division thereof may temporarily hold court in any county. In the interests of the fair, impartial, speedy, and sure administration of justice, each county shall have one or more resident judges, or two or more counties may be combined into districts having one or more judges resident in the district and serving the common pleas courts of all counties in the district, as may be provided by law. Judges serving a district shall sit in each county in the district as the business of the court requires. In counties or districts having more than one judge of the court of common pleas, the judges shall select one of their number to act as presiding judge, to serve at their pleasure. If the judges are unable because of equal division of the vote to make such selection, the judge having the longest total service on the court of common pleas shall serve as presiding judge until selection is made by vote. The presiding judge shall have such duties and exercise such powers as are prescribed by rule of the supreme court.

(B) The courts of common pleas and divisions thereof shall have such original jurisdiction over all justiciable matters and such powers of review of proceedings of administrative officers and agencies as may be provided by law.

(C) Unless otherwise provided by law, there shall be a probate division and such other divisions of the courts of common pleas as may be provided by law. Judges shall be elected specifically to such probate division and to such other divisions. The judges of the probate division shall be empowered to employ and control the clerks, employees, deputies, and referees of such probate division of the common pleas courts.

§5 [Additional powers of supreme court; supervision; rule making.]

(A)(1) In addition to all other powers vested by this article in the supreme court, the supreme court shall have general superintendence over all courts in the state. Such general superintending power shall be exercised by the chief justice in accordance with rules promulgated by the supreme court. . . . *

§6 [Election of judges; compensation.]

(A)(1) The chief justice and the justices of the supreme court shall be elected by the electors of the state at large, for terms of not less than six years.

(2) The judges of the courts of appeals shall be elected by the electors of their respective appellate districts, for terms of not less than six years.

(3) The judges of the courts of common pleas and the divisions thereof shall be elected by the electors of the counties, districts, or, as may be provided by law, other subdivisions, in which their respective courts are located, for terms of not less than six years, and each judge of a court of common pleas or division thereof shall reside during his term of office in the county, district, or subdivision in which his court is located.

(4) Terms of office of all judges shall begin on the days fixed by law, and laws shall be enacted to prescribe the times and mode of their election.

(B) The judges of the supreme court, courts of appeals, courts of common pleas, and divisions thereof, and of all courts of record established by law, shall, at stated times, receive, for their services such compensation as may be provided by law, which shall not be diminished during their term of office. The compensation of all judges of the supreme court, except that of the chief justice, shall be the same. The compensation of all judges of the courts of appeals shall be the same. Common pleas judges and judges of divisions thereof, and judges of all courts of record established by law shall receive such compensation as may be provided by law. Judges shall receive no fees or perquisites, nor hold any other office of profit or trust, under the authority of this state, or of the United States. All votes for any judge, for any elective office, except a judicial office, under the authority of this state, given by the general assembly, or the people shall be void.

(C) No person shall be elected or appointed to any judicial office if on or before the day when he shall assume the office and enter upon the discharge of its duties he shall have attained the age of seventy years. Any voluntarily retired judge, or any judge who is retired under this section, may be assigned with his consent by the chief justice or acting chief justice of the supreme court to active duty as a judge and while so serving shall receive the established compensation for such office, computed upon a per diem basis, in addition to any retirement benefits to which he may be entitled. Laws may be passed providing retirement benefits for judges.

§7-12 Repealed.

*§13 Vacancy in office of judge, how filled.

§14 Repealed.

§15 Number of judges may be increased or diminished, districts altered, and other courts estabished.

Laws may be passed to increase or diminish the number of judges of the supreme court, to increase beyond one or diminish to one the number of judges of the court of common pleas in any county, and to establish other courts, whenever two-thirds of the members elected to each house shall concur therein; but no such change, addition or diminution shall vacate the office of any judge; and any existing court heretofore created by law shall continue in existence until otherwise provided.

§16 Repealed.

§17 Judges removable.

Judges may be removed from office, by concurrent resolution of both houses of the general assembly, if two-thirds of the members, elected to each house, concur therein; but, no such removal shall be made, except upon complaint, the substance of which shall be entered on the journal, nor, until the party charged shall have had notice thereof, and an opportunity to be heard.

§18 Powers and jurisdiction.

The several judges of the supreme court, of the common pleas, and of such other courts as may be created, shall, respectively, have and exercise such power and jurisdiction, at chambers, or otherwise, as may be directed by law.

§19 Courts of conciliation.

The general assembly may establish courts of conciliation, and prescribe their powers and duties; but such courts shall not render final judgment in any case, except upon submission, by the parties, of the matter in dispute, and their agreement to abide such judgment.

§20 Style of process, prosecution, and indictment.

The style of all process shall be, "The State of Ohio;" all prosecutions shall be carried on, in the name, and by the authority, of the state of Ohio; and all indictments shall conclude, "against the peace and dignity of the state of Ohio."

§[21] 22 Supreme court commission.

A commission, which shall consist of five members, shall be appointed by the governor, with the advice and consent of the senate, the members of which shall hold office for term of three years from and after the first day for February, 1876, to dispose of such part of the business then on the dockets of the supreme court, as shall, by arrangement between said commission and said court, be transferred to such commission; and said commission shall have like jurisdiction and power in respect to such business as are or may be vested in said court; and the members of said commission shall receive a like compensation for the time being, with the judges of said court. A majority of the members of said commission shall be necessary to form a quorum or pronounce a decision, and its decision shall be certified, entered, and enforced as the judgments of the supreme court, and at the expiration of the term of said commission, all business undisposed of shall by it be certified to the supreme court and disposed of as if said commission had never existed. . . . *

*§23 [Judges may serve on more than one court in less populous counties.]

ARTICLE V: Elective Franchise
§1 [Who may vote.]

Every citizen of the United States, of the age of eighteen years, who has been a resident of the state, county, township, or ward, such time as may be provided by law, and has been registered to vote for thirty days, has the qualifications of an elector, and is entitled to vote at all elections. Any elector who fails to vote in at least one election during any period of four consecutive years shall cease to be an elector unless he again registers to vote.

§2 By ballot.

All elections shall be by ballot.

§2a [Names of candidates on ballot.]

The names of all candidates for an office at any election shall be arranged in a group under the title of that office. The general assembly shall provide by law the means by which ballots shall give each candidate's name reasonably equal position by rotation or other comparable methods to the extent practical and appropriate to the voting procedure used. At any election in which a candidate's party designation appears on the ballot, the name or designation of each candidate's party, if any, shall be printed under or after each candidate's name in less prominent type face than that in which the candidate's name is printed. An elector may vote for candidates (other than candidates for electors of President and Vice-President of the United States, and other than candidates for governor and lieutenant governor) only and in no other way than by indicating his vote for each candidate separately from the indication of his vote for any other candidate.

§3 Repealed.

§4 Forfeiture of elective franchise.

The General Assembly shall have power to exclude from the privilege of voting, or of being eligible to office, any person convicted of a felony.

§5 Repealed.

§6 Idiots or insane persons.

No idiot, or insane person, shall be entitled to the privileges of an elector.

§7 Primary elections

All nominations for elective state, district, county and municipal offices shall be made at direct primary elections or by petition as provided by law, and provision shall be made by law for a preferential vote for United States senator; but direct primaries shall not be held for the nomination of township officers or for the officers of municipalities of less than two thousand population, unless petitioned for by a majority of the electors of such township or municipality. All delegates from this state to the national conventions of political parties shall be chosen by direct vote of the electors in a manner provided by law. Each candidate for such delegate shall state his first and second choices for the presidency, but the name of no candidate for the presidency shall be so used without his written authority.

ARTICLE VI: Education
§1 Funds for religious and educational purposes.

The principal of all funds, arising from the sale, or other disposition of lands, or other property, granted or entrusted to this State for educational and religious purposes, shall be used or disposed of in such manner as the General Assembly shall prescribe by law.

§2 School funds.

The general assembly shall make such provisions, by taxation, or otherwise, as, with the income arising from the school trust fund, will secure a thorough and efficient system of common schools throughout the state; but no religious or other sect, or sects, shall ever have any exclusive right to, or control of, any part of the school funds of this state.

§3 Public school system; boards of education.

Provision shall be made by law for the organization, administration and control of the public school system of the state supported by public funds: provided, that each school district embraced wholly or in part within any city shall have the power by referendum vote to determine for itself the number of members and the organization of the district board of education, and provision shall be made by law for the exercise of this power by such school districts.

§4 State board of education.

There shall be a state board of education which shall be selected in such manner and for such terms as shall be provided by law. There shall be a superintendent of public instruction, who shall be appointed by the state board of education. The respective powers and duties of the board and of the superintendent shall be prescribed by law.

§5 [Guaranteed loans to residents attending colleges and universities.]

To increase opportunities to the residents of this state for higher education, it is hereby determined to be in the public interest and a proper public purpose for the state to guarantee the repayment of loans made to residents of this state to assist them in meeting the expenses of attending an institution of higher education. Laws may be passed to carry into effect such purpose including the payment, when required, of any such guarantee from money available for such payment after first providing the money necessary to meet the requirements of any bonds or other obligations heretofore or hereafter authorized by any section of the Constitution. . . . *

ARTICLE VII: Public Institutions
§1 Insane, blind, and deaf and dumb.

Institutions for the benefit of the insane, blind, and deaf and dumb, shall always be fostered and supported by the state; and be subject to such regulations as may be prescribed by the general assembly.

§2 Directors of penitentiary, trustees of benevolent and other state institutions; how appointed.

The directors of the penitentiary shall be appointed or elected in such manner as the general assembly may direct; and the trustees of the benevolent, and other state institutions, now elected by the general assembly, and of such other state institutions, as may be hereafter created, shall be appointed by the governor, by and with the advice and consent of the senate; and upon all nominations made by the governor, the question shall be taken by yeas and nays, and entered upon the journals of the state.

*§3 Vacancies, how filled.

ARTICLE VIII: Public Debt and Public Works
§1 Public debt.

The state may contract debts to supply casual deficits or failures in revenues, or to meet expenses not otherwise provided for; but the aggregate amount of such debts, direct and contingent, whether contracted by virtue of one or more acts of the general assembly, or at different periods of time, shall never exceed seven hundred and fifty thousand dollars; and the money, arising from the creation of such debts, shall be applied to the purpose for which it was obtained, or to repay the debts so contracted, and to no other purpose whatever.

§2 Additional, and for what purposes.

In addition to the above limited power, the state may contract debts to repel invasion, suppress insurrection, defend the state in war, or to redeem the present outstanding indebtedness of the state; but the money, arising from the contracting of such debts, shall be applied to the purpose for which it was raised, or to repay such debts, and to no other purpose whatever; and all debts, incurred to redeem the present outstanding indebtedness of the state, shall be so contracted as to be payable by the sinking fund, hereinafter provided for, as the same shall accumulate.

§2a Repealed.

*§2b [Adjusted compensation for service in World War II.]

§2c [Construction of state highway system.]

The state may contract debts not exceeding five hundred million dollars for the purpose of pro-

viding moneys for acquisition of rights-of-way and for construction and reconstruction of highways on the state highway system. Not more than one hundred twenty-five million dollars of the debt authorized by this section shall be contracted within any calendar year, and no part of such debt shall be contracted after the thirty-first day of March, 1962. The principal amount of any part of such debt at any time contracted shall be paid in substantially equal semi-annual or annual installments, beginning not later than eighteen months after such debt is contracted, and in such number of installments, beginning not later than eighteen months after such debt is contracted, and in such number of installments that the entire debt shall be discharged not later than the year 1972. . . . *

*§2d [Korean War bonus.]

*§2e [Providing means for securing funds for highway and public building construction.]

§2f [Authorizing bond issue to provide school classrooms, support for universities, for recreation and conservation and for state buildings.]

In addition to the authorization in Article VIII, Section 2e, the state may borrow not to exceed two hundred fifty million dollars and issue bonds or other obligations therefor, for the purpose of acquiring lands and interests in lands for sites for such buildings and structures; and, for the purpose of assisting in the development of the State, to acquire lands and interests in lands and to develop such lands and interests or other state land for water impoundment sites, park and recreational uses, and conservation of natural resources; and for use in conjunction with federal grants or loans for any of such purposes. Of said amount, for the purpose of acquiring, constructing, reconstructing, and otherwise improving and equipping buildings and structures, excluding highways, and for the purpose of acquiring lands and interests in lands for sites for such buildings and structures, one hundred seventy-five million dollars shall be issued for providing classroom facilities for the public schools to be leased or sold by the State to public school districts unable, within the limitations provided by law, to provide adequate facilities without assistance from the state, and fifteen million dollars shall be issued for state functions, activities, offices, institutions, including penal, correctional, mental, and welfare, and research and development; and for the purpose of assisting in the development of the state by acquiring lands and interests of other state lands for water impoundment sites, park and recreational uses, and conservation of natural resources twenty-five million dollars shall be issued. Not more than one hundred million dollars of such borrowing shall be contracted within any calendar year. No part of such borrowing shall be contracted after the thiry-first day of December, 1972. All bonds or other obligations issued pursuant to this section shall mature at such time or times not exceeding thirty years from date of issue and in such amounts as shall be fixed by the commissioners of the sinking fund, and shall bear interest and be sold as shall be authorized by law. Both the principal of such debt and the interest thereon shall be exempt from taxation within this state.

The faith and credit of the state are hereby pledged for the payment of such bonds or other obligations, and the interest thereon. They shall be payable from all excises and taxes of the state except ad valorem taxes on real and personal property, income taxes, and fees, excises or license taxes relating to registration, operation, or use of vehicles on public highways or to fuels used for propelling such vehicles. The excises and taxes of the state from which such bonds and other obligations shall be paid shall include an excise tax on sales of cigarettes at the rate of one-half cent on each ten cigarettes or fractional part thereof, and an excise tax on the use, consumption, or storage for consumption of cigarettes by consumers in this

state, at the rate of one-half cent on each ten cigarettes or fractional part thereof, which shall be levied during the period beginning with January 1, 1965, and continuing until December 31, 1972, and thereafter as long as any of such bonds and other obligations are outstanding and moneys in the separate and distinct bond retirement fund hereinafter created are insufficient to pay all interest, principal, and charges for the issuance and retirement of such bonds and other obligations. Such tax on the use, consumption, or storage for consumption of cigarettes by consumers in this state shall not be levied upon cigarettes upon which the tax on sales has been paid. The General Assembly of the State of Ohio shall enact laws providing for the collection of such taxes. The moneys received into the state treasury from such one-half cent excise tax on sales of cigarettes and from such one-half cent excise tax on the use, consumption, or storage for consumption of cigarettes by consumers in this state shall be paid into a separate and distinct bond retirement fund hereby created. . . . *

*§2g [Authorizing bond issue or other obligations for highway construction.]

*§2h [Bond issue for development.]

*§2i [Capital improvement bonds.]

*§2j [Vietnam conflict compensation fund.]

§3 The state to create no other debt.

Except the debts above specified in sections one and two of this article, no debt whatever shall hereafter be created by or on behalf of the state.

§4 Credit of state; the state shall not become joint owner or stockholder.

The credit of the state shall not, in any manner, be given or loaned to, or in aid of, any individual association or corporation whatever; nor shall the state ever hereafter become a joint owner, or stockholder, in any company or association in this state, or elsewhere, formed for any purpose whatever.

§5 No assumption of debts by the state.

The state shall never assume the debts of any county, city, town, or township, or of any corporation whatever, unless such debt shall have been created to repel invasion, suppress insurrection, or defend the state in war.

*§6 Counties, cities, towns, or townships, not authorized to become stockholders, etc.; insurance, etc.

§7 Sinking fund.

The faith of the state being pledged for the payment of its public debt, in order to provide therefor, there shall be created a sinking fund, which shall be sufficient to pay the accruing interest on such debt, and, annually, to reduce the principal thereof, by a sum not less than one hundred thousand dollars, increased yearly, and each and every year, by compounding, at the rate of six per cent. per annum. The said sinking fund shall consist, of the net annual income of the public works and stocks owned by the state, of any other funds or resources that are, or may be, provided by law, and of such further use, to be raised by taxation, as may be required for the purposes aforesaid.

*§8 The commissioners of the sinking fund.

*§9 Their biennial report.

*§10 Application of sinking fund.

*§11 Semi-annual report.

§12 Repealed.

§13 [Guaranteed loans for industrial development.]

To create or preserve jobs and employment opportunities, to improve the economic welfare of the people of the state, to control air, water, and thermal pollution, or to dispose of solid waste, it is hereby determined to be in the public interest and a proper public purpose for the state or its political subdivisions, taxing districts, or public authorities, its or their agencies or instrumentalities, or corporations not for profit designated by any of them as such agencies or instrumentalities, to acquire, construct, enlarge, improve, or equip, and to sell, lease, exchange, or otherwise dispose of property, structures, equipment, and facilities within the State of Ohio or industry, commerce, distribution, and research, to make or guarantee loans and to borrow money and issue bonds or other obligations to provide moneys for the acquisition, construction, enlargement, improvement, or equipment, of such property, structures, equipment and facilities. Laws may be passed to carry into effect such purposes and to authorize for such purposes the borrowing of money by, and the issuance of bonds or other obligations of, the state, or its political subdivisions, taxing districts, or public authorities, its or their agencies or instrumentalities, or corporations not for profit designated by any of them as such agencies or instrumentalities, and to authorize the making of guarantees and loans and the lending of aid and credit, which laws, bonds, obligations, loans, guarantees, and lending of aid and credit shall not be subject to the requirements, limitations, or prohibitions of any other section of Article VIII, or of Article XII, Section 6 and 11, of the Constitution provided that moneys raised by taxation shall not be obligated or pledged for the payment of bonds or other obligations issued or guarantees made pursuant to laws enacted under this section.

Except for facilities for pollution control or solid waste disposal, as determined by law, no guarantees or loans and no lending of aid or credit shall be made under the laws enacted pursuant to this section of the constitution for facilities to be constructed for the purpose of providing electric or gas utility service to the public.

The powers herein granted shall be in addition to and not in derogation of existing powers of the state or its political subdivisions, taxing districts, or public authorities, or their agencies or instrumentalities or corporations not for profit designated by any of them as such agencies or instrumentalities.

Any corporation organized under the laws of Ohio is hereby authorized to lend or contribute moneys to the state or its political subdivisions or agencies or instrumentalities thereof on such terms as may be agreed upon in furtherance of laws enacted pursuant to this section.

ARTICLE IX: Militia
§1 Who shall perform military duty.

All citizens, residents of this state, being seventeen years of age, and under the age of sixty-seven years, shall be subject to enrollment in the militia and the performance of military duty, in such manner, not incompatible with the Constitution and laws of the United States, as may be prescribed by law.

§2 Repealed.

§3 [Officers to be appointed by governor.]

The governor shall appoint the adjutant general, and such other officers and warrant officers, as may be provided for by law.

§4 [Power of governor to call forth militia.]

The governor shall have power to call forth the militia, to execute the laws of the state, to suppress insurrection, to repel invasion, and to act in the event of a disaster within the state.

§5 Public arms.

The general assembly shall provide, by law, for the protection and safe keeping of the public arms.

ARTICLE X: County and Township Organizations
§1 [Organization and government of counties; county home rule; submission.]

The general assembly shall provide by general law for the organization and government of counties, and may provide by general law alternative forms of county government. No alternative form shall become operative in any county until submitted to the electors thereof and approved by a majority of those voting thereon under regulations provided by law. Municipalities and townships shall have authority, with the consent of the county, to transfer to the county any of their powers or to revoke the transfer of any such power, under regulations provided by general law, but the rights of initiative and referendum shall be secured to the people of such municipalities or townships in respect of every measure making or revoking such transfer, and to the people of such county in respect of every measure giving or withdrawing such consent.

§2 [Township officers; election; powers.]

The general assembly shall provide by general law for the election of such township officers as may be necessary. The trustees of townships shall have such powers of local taxation as may be prescribed by law. No money shall be drawn from any township treasury except by authority of law.

*§3 [County charters; approval by voters.]

*§4 [County charter commission; election, etc.]

§5-7 Repealed.

ARTICLE XI: Apportionment

*§1 [Persons responsible for apportionment of state for members of general assembly.]

§2 [Method of apportionment of state for members of general assembly.]

The apportionment of this state for members of the general assembly shall be made in the following manner: The whole population of the state, as determined by the federal decennial census or, if such is unavailable, such other basis as the general assembly may direct, shall be divided by the number "ninety-nine" and the quotient shall be the ratio of representation in house of representatives for ten years next succeeding such apportionment. The whole population of the state as determined by the federal decennial census or, if such is unavailable, such other basis as the general assembly may direct, shall be divided by the number "thirty-three" and the quotient shall be the ratio of representation in the senate for ten years next succeeding such apportionment.

§3 [Population of each house of representatives district.]

The population of each house of representatives district shall be substantially equal to the ratio of representation in the house of representatives, as provided in section 2 of this Article, and in no event shall any house of representatives district contain a population of less than ninety-five per cent nor more than one hundred five per cent of the ratio of representation in the house of representatives, except in those instances where reasonable effort is made to avoid dividing a county in accordance with section 9 of this Article.

§4 [Population of each senate district.]

The population of each senate district shall be substantially equal to the ratio of representation in the senate, as provided in section 2 of this Arti-cle, and in no event shall any senate district contain a populaton of less than ninety-five per cent nor more than one hundred five per cent of the ratio or representation in the senate as determined pursuant to the Article.

§5 [Representation.]

Each house of representatives district shall be entitled to a single representative in each General Assembly. Every senate district shall be entitled to a single senator in each General Assembly.

*§6 [Creation of district boundaries; change at end of decennial period.]

*§6a Repealed.

§7 [Boundary lines of house of representatives districts.]

(A) Every house of representatives district shall be compact and composed of contiguous territory, and the boundary of each district shall be a single non-intersecting continuous line. To the extent consistent with the requirements of section 3 of this Article, the boundary lines of districts shall be so drawn as to delineate an area containing one or more whole counties.

(B) Where the requirements of section 3 of this Article cannot feasibly be attained by forming a district from a whole county or counties, such district shall be formed by combining the area of governmental units giving preference in the order named to counties, townships, municipalities, and city wards. . . . *

*§8 [Determination of number of house of representatives districts within each county.]

*§9 [When population of county is fraction of ratio of representation.]

*§10 [Creation and numbering of house of representatives districts.]

§11 [Senate districts.]

Senate districts shall be composed of three contiguous house of representatives districts. A county having at least one whole senate ratio of representation shall have as many senate districts wholly within the boundaries of the county as it has whole senate ratios of representation. Any fraction of the population in excess of a whole ratio shall be a part of only one adjoining senate district. Counties having less than one senate ratio of representation, but at least one house of representatives ratio of representation shall be part of only one senate district.

The number of whole ratios of representation for a county shall be determined by dividing the population of the county by the ratio of representation in the senate determined under section 2 of this Article.

Senate districts shall be numbered from one through thirty-three and as provided in section 12 of this Article.

*§12 Change in boundaries of senate districts.

*§13 Jurisdiction of supreme court, effect of determination of unconstitutionality; apportionment.

ARTICLE XII: Finance and Taxation
§1 Poll tax.

No poll tax shall ever be levied in this state, or service required, which may be commuted in money or other thing of value.

§2 [Limitation on tax rate; exemption.]

No property, taxed according to value, shall be so taxed in excess of one per cent of its true value in money for all state and local purposes, but laws may be passed authorizing additional taxes to be levied outside of such limitation, either when approved by at least a majority of the electors of the taxing district voting on such proposition, or when provided for by the charter of a municipal corporation. Land and improvements thereon shall be taxed by uniform rule according to value, except that laws may be passed to reduce taxes by providing for a reduction in value of the homestead of permanently and totally disabled residents and residents sixty-five years of age and older, and providing for income and other qualifications to obtain such reduction. . . . *

§3 [Imposition of taxes.]

Laws may be passed providing for:

(A) The taxation of decedents' estates or of the right to receive or succeed to such estates, and the rates of such taxation may be uniform or may be graduated based on the value of the estate, inheritance, or succession. Such tax may also be levied at different rates upon collateral and direct inheritances, and a portion of each estate may be exempt from such taxation as provided by law.

(B) The taxation of incomes, and the rates of such taxation may be either uniform or graduated, and may be applied to such incomes and with such exemptions as may be provided by law.

(C) Excise and franchise taxes and for the imposition of taxes upon the production of coal, oil, gas, and other minerals; except that no excise tax shall be levied or collected upon the sale or purchase of food for human consumption off the premises where sold.

§4 Revenue.

The General Assembly shall provide for raising revenue, sufficient to defray the expenses of the state, for each year, and also a sufficient sum to pay principal and interest as they become due on the state debt.

§5 Levying of taxes.

No tax shall be levied, except in pursuance of law; and every law imposing a tax shall state, distinctly, the object of the same, to which only, it shall be applied.

§5a [Use of motor vehicle license and fuel taxes restricted.]

No moneys derived from fees, excises, or license taxes relating to registration, operation, or use of vehicles on public highways, or to fuels used for propelling such vehicles, shall be expended for other than costs of administering such laws, statutory refunds and adjustments provided therein, payment of highway obligations, costs for construction, reconstruction, maintenance and repair of public highways and bridges and other statutory highways and bridges and other statutory highway purposes, expense of state enforcement of traffic laws, and expenditures authorized for hospitalization of indigent persons injured in motor vehicle accidents on the public highways.

§6 Debt for internal improvement.

Except as otherwise provided in this constitution the state shall never contract any debt for purposes of internal improvement.

§7-8 Repealed.

§9 [Apportionment of income, estate, and inheritance taxes.]

Not less than fifty per cent of the income, estate, and inheritance taxes that may be collected by the state shall be returned to the county, school district, city, village, or township in which said income, estate, or inheritance tax originates, or to any of the same, as may be provided by law.

§10 Repealed.

*§11 Sinking fund.

ARTICLE XIII: Corporations

§1 Corporate powers.

The general assembly shall pass no special act conferring corporate powers.

§2 Corporations, how formed.

Corporations may be formed under general laws; but all such laws may, from time to time, be altered or repealed. Corporations may be classified and there may be conferred upon proper boards, commissions or officers, such supervisory and regulatory powers over their organization, business and issue and sale of stocks and securities, and over the business and sale of stocks and securities of foreign corporations and joint stock companies in their state, as may be prescribed by law. Laws may be passed regulating the sale and conveyance of other personal property, whether owned by a corporation, joint stock company or individual.

*§3 [Dues from corporations; how secured; inspection of private banks.]

§4 Corporate property subject to taxation.

The property of corporations, now existing or hereafter created, shall forever be subject to taxation, the same as the property of individuals.

§5 Right of way.

No right of way shall be appropriated to the use of any corporation, until full compensation therefor be first made in money or first secured by a deposit of money, to the owner, irrespective of any benefit from any improvement proposed by such corporation; which compensation shall be ascertained by a jury of twelve men, in a court of record, as shall be prescribed by law.

§6 Organization of cities, etc.

The general assembly shall provide for the organization of cities, and incorporated villages, by general laws, and restrict their power of taxation, assessment, borrowing money, contracting debts and loaning their credit, so as to prevent the abuse of such power.

*§7 Associations with banking powers.

ARTICLE XV: Miscellaneous
§1 Seat of government.

Columbus shall be the seat of government, until otherwise directed by law.

§2 Repealed.

§3 [Receipts and expenditures.]

An accurate and detailed statement of the receipts and expenditures of the public money, the several amounts paid, to whom, and on what account, shall, from time to time, be published, as shall be prescribed by law.

§4 Who eligible to office.

No person shall be elected or appointed to any office in this state unless possessed of the qualifications of an elector.

§5 Repealed.

§6 Lotteries.

Lotteries, and the sale of lottery tickets, for any purpose whatever, shall forever be prohibited in this State, except that the General Assembly may authorize an agency of the state to conduct lotteries, to sell rights to participate therein, and to award prizes by chance to participants, provided the entire net proceeds of any such lottery are paid into the general revenue fund of the state and the General Assembly may authorize and regulate the operation of bingo to be conducted by charitable organizations for charitable purposes.

§7 [Oath of officers.]

Every person chosen or appointed to any office under this state, before entering upon the discharge of its duties, shall take an oath or affirmation, to support the Constitution of the United States, and of this state, and also an oath of office.

§8-9 Repealed.

§10 Civil service.

Appointments and promotions in the civil service of the state, the several counties, and cities, shall be made according to merit and fitness, to be ascertained, as far as practicable, by competitive examinations. Laws shall be passed providing for the enforcement of this provision.

ARTICLE XVI: Amendments
§1 How constitution to be amended; ballot; supreme court to hear challenges.

Either branch of the general assembly may propose amendments to this constitution; and, if the same shall be agreed to by three-fifths of the members elected to each house, such proposed amendments shall be entered on the journals, with the yeas and nays, and shall be filed with the secretary of state at least ninety days before the date of the election at which they are to be submitted to the electors, for their approval or rejection. They shall be submitted on a separate ballot without party designation of any kind, at either a special or general election as the general assembly may prescribe.

The ballot language for such proposed amendments shall be prescribed by a majority of the Ohio ballot board, consisting of the secretary of state and four other members, who shall be designated in a manner prescribed by law and not more than two of whom shall be members of the same political party. The ballot language shall properly identify the substance of the proposal to be voted upon. The ballot need not contain the full text nor a condensed text of the proposal. The board shall also prepare an explanation of the proposal, which may include its purpose and effects, and shall certify the ballot language and the explanation to the secretary of state not later than seventy-five days before the election. The ballot language and the explanation shall be available for public inspection in the office of the secretary of state.

The supreme court shall have exclusive, original jurisdiction in all cases challenging the adoption or submission of a proposed constitutional amendment to the electors. No such case challenging the ballot language, the explanation, or the actions or procedures of the general assembly in adopting and submitting a constitutional amendment shall be filed later than sixty-four days before the election. The ballot language shall not be held invalid unless it is such as to mislead, deceive, or defraud the voters.

Unless the general assembly otherwise provides by law for the preparation of arguments for and, if any, against a proposed amendment, the board may prepare such arguments.

Such proposed amendments, the ballot language, the explanations, and the arguments, if any, shall be published once a week for three consecutive weeks preceding such election, in at least one newspaper of general circulation in each county of the state, where a newspaper is published. The general assembly shall provide by law for other dissemination of information in order to inform the electors concerning proposed amendments. An election on a proposed constitutional amendment submitted by the general assembly shall not be enjoined nor invalidated because the explanation, arguments, or other information is faulty in any way. If the majority of the electors voting on the same shall adopt such amendments the same shall become a part of the constitution. When more than one amendment shall be sub-

mitted at the same time, they shall be so submitted as to enable the electors to vote on each amendment, separately.

*§2 [Conventions.]

*§3 [Question of constitutional convention to be submitted periodically.]

ARTICLE XVII: Elections
§1 Time for holding.

Elections for state and county officers shall be held on the first Tuesday after the first Monday in November in even numbered years; and all elections for all other elective officers shall be held on the first Tuesday after the first Monday in November in the odd numbered years.

The term of office of all elective county, township, municipal, and school officers shall be such even number of years not exceeding four as may be prescribed by law of such even number of years as may be provided in municipal or county charters.

The term of office of all judges shall be as provided in Article IV of this constitution or, if not so provided, an even number of years not exceeding six as provided by law.

The general assembly may extend existing terms of office as to effect the purpose of this section.

*§2 [Terms of officers, vacancies, etc.]

§3 Repealed.

ARTICLE XVIII: Municipal Corporations
§1 [Classification.]

Municipal corporations are hereby classified into cities and villages. All such corporations having a population of five thousand or over shall be cities; all others shall be villages. The method of transition from one class to the other shall be regulated by law.

*§2 [General and additional laws.]

§3 [Powers.]

Municipalities shall have authority to exercise all powers of local self-government and to adopt and enforce within their limits such local police, sanitary and other similar regualtions, as are not in conflict with general laws.

§4 [Acquisition of public utility; contract for service; condemnation.]

Any municipality may acquire, construct, own, lease and operate within or without its corporate limits, any public utility the product or service of which is or is to be supplied to the municipality or its inhabitants, and may contract with others for any such product or service. The acquisition of any such public utility may be by condemnation or otherwise, and a municipality may acquire thereby the use of, or full title to, the property and franchise of any company or person supplying to the municipality or its inhabitants the service or product of any such utility.

*§5 [Acquisition by ordinance; procedure; referendum; submission.]

*§6 [Sale of surplus.]

§7 [Home rule.]

Any municipality may frame and adopt or amend a charter for its government and may, subject to the provisions of section 3 of this article, exercise thereunder all powers of local self-government.

*§8 [Submission of question of election of charter commission; approval.]

*§9 [Amendments to charter; submission; approval.]

*§10 [Appropriation in excess of public use.]

*§11 [Assessments for cost of appropriating property.]

§12 [Bonds for public utilities.]

Any municipality which acquires, constructs or extends any public utility and desires to raise money for such purposes may issue mortgage bonds therefor beyond the general limit of bonded indebtedness prescribed by law; provided that such mortgage bonds issued beyond the general limit of bonded indebtedness prescribed by law shall not impose any liability upon such municipality but shall be secured only upon the property and revenues of such public utility, including a franchise stating the terms upon which, in case of foreclosure, the purchaser may operate the same, which franchise shall in no case extend for a longer period than twenty years from the date of the sale of such utility and franchise on foreclosure.

§13 [Taxation, debts, reports and accounts.]

Laws may be passed to limit the power of municipalities to levy taxes and incur debts for local purposes, and may require reports from municipalities as to their financial condition and transactions, in such form as may be provided by law, and may provide for the examination of the vouchers, books, and accounts of all municipal authorities, or of public undertakings conducted by such authorities.

§14 [Elections.]

All elections and submissions of questions provided for in this article shall be conducted by the election authorities prescribed by general law. The percentage of electors required to sign any petition provided for herein shall be based upon the total vote cast at the last preceding general municipal election.

ACKNOWLEDGEMENTS AND CREDITS

We wish to express appreciation to the following individuals who read portions of the manuscript and made valuable suggestions:

Randall Buchman, Defiance College;
Jane L. Forsyth, Bowling Green State University;
John Grabowski, Western Reserve Historical Society, Cleveland;
Willie E. Green, Toledo Public Schools;
George W. Knepper, University of Akron;
Roy M. Kottman, Ohio State University, professor emeritus;
Lora V. Murphy, Cleveland Public Schools;
Alma B. Payne, Bowling Green State University, professor emerita;
G. Michael Pratt, Heidelberg College, Tiffin;
Philip R. Shriver, Miami University, Oxford;
George M. Waller, Butler University, Indianapolis.

Special thanks to Joseph Tucker, Ohio University, Athens, for his work in preparation of Chapter 15 on government.

Madge Baird, our editor at Peregrine Smith Books, shaped our material for publication with skill and patience, and guided the project to completion. We are grateful for her help.

J.L.B.   K.E.D.

The specific pictures used in this book are credited below. The authors and the publisher also wish to thank the people who offered pictures that could not be used for lack of space.

Letters beside the numbers designate position on the page: L (left side), R (right side), T (top), M (middle), and B (bottom).

INDEX